YAKUZA DIARY

YAKUZA DIARY

Doing Time in the Japanese Underworld

BY CHRISTOPHER SEYMOUR

The Atlantic Monthly Press
New York

FIRST EDITION
Published simultaneously in Canada
Printed in the United States of America

Library of Congress Cataloging-in-Publication Data
Seymour, Christopher.
Yakuza diary: doing time in the Japanese underworld / by Christopher Seymour.
p.   cm.
ISBN 0-87113-604-X
1. Yakuza—Japan—History. 2. Organized crime—Japan—History.
3. Crime—Japan—History. 4. Gangs—Japan—History. I. Title.
HV6453.J33Y357   1996
364.1'06'0952—dc20   95-51263

DESIGN BY LAURA HAMMOND HOUGH

Atlantic Monthly Press
841 Broadway
New York, NY 10003

10 9 8 7 6 5 4 3 2 1

To my parents, with love and gratitude

TABLE OF CONTENTS

TABLE OF CONTENTS

The following events took place in Japan during the middle four months of 1993. The personal journals on which this book is based were begun as a private accounting of my adventures in meeting underworld types. When both Japanese names are given, they have been Americanized in that the given name is first and family name second. Often I have just used nicknames in my casual translations of gangster speech. Many Japanese words are the same whether singular or plural, as in *yakuza, sumo,* and *geisha*.

Yakuza Diary is not intended to represent an objective or exhaustive treatise on the huge and tangled web of organized crime in Japan. It is personal, subjective, and episodic; glimpses into real lives of real yakuza.

DANGEROUS GAIJIN!

"DANGEROUS GAIJIN!" screamed the headlines. "TERRIFYING NEW THREAT TO SOCIETY!"; "GAIJIN, GUNS, AND MONEY!"; "WILD GAIJIN IN THE STREETS!" and "SEND DANGEROUS GAIJIN HOME!"

Gaijin is the casual, some say derogatory, form of *gaikokujin*, Japanese for "foreigner." Before June of 1993 I had never heard "gaijin" used by a television anchorman but, suddenly, on all the nightly news it was "Gaijin this," "Gaijin that," and "Gaijin out!"

This semantical switch debuted after two Middle Easterners were questioned for the robbery of a Sapporo convenience store. The reports explained that dangerous gaijin originally were "nice" gaijin who had come to Japan for work. And while the economy was good these foreign men, womanless men, worked diligently at their jobs, with many (imagine!) learning to speak Japanese. In the pall of the recent recession, however, redundant gaijin workers were turning to crime—often using their language skills as a weapon to threaten cashiers and shop owners.

Although the Sapporo men were found innocent of the holdup, they were guilty of overstaying their visas. The antigaijin media onslaught continued with dubious reports about how visa-abusing, bad-driving, Japanese-speaking, Middle Eastern gaijin were wreaking havoc throughout the archipelago.

I had heard that the National Police Agency and immigration officials were turning back hundreds of potentially "dangerous" gaijin as quickly as planes could be refueled and pointed back to Tehran. It was an "international outrage," said the Iranian official who invited me to a news conference where the world would learn of Japan's clandestine and racist policies. Vaguely alarmed, I showed up at the consulate at the appointed time; I was alone.

For us First World gaijin the ramifications of spring '93's DANGEROUS GAIJIN! alarm had been an increased police presence on the streets of the Roppongi nightlife district and other expatriate haunts. For most of us it was an irritation that forced us to carry our passports everywhere; and if you were going to take a bicycle anywhere, you'd better have something to prove you owned that bike—preferably something in Japanese. Gaijin with transportation are a singular obsession of the Tokyo Metropolitan Police.

On the evening of June 22, 1993, the air rife with antigaijin aggression, I was taking no chances. Like a good, quasi-legal, foreign resident, I was obeying the superfluous stop sign at a deserted backstreet intersection. There I was, sitting at the end of the narrow road on my Honda scooter with a bulging bag of dirty clothes between my knees, harmlessly dreaming about the Mos Burger (a domestic chain that has improved on the fast-food concept the way other Japanese companies have done with other products and services of Americana). For no other reason than the whiteness of the backs of my hands, I was ambushed by the police. Although I could produce a legal Japanese drivers' license (with photo), my passport, alas, was back home.

My laundry and I were shoved roughly into the back of a Tokyo Metropolitan Police black and white, then driven a few blocks to the Roppongi Police Station. Inside I was shooed upstairs, where I was benched with a good view of the evening's activities.

During my long wait I observed a parade of drunken salarymen questioned—berated, really—by a paunchy plainclothes cop whose tough-love technique for forcing confessions repeatedly worked without a hitch. It was a thing of psycho-beauty: With disgust the cop would take the drunk's business card from his wallet (each had plenty of cards), then the cop would read out loud the entire card—name, position, and the company's name and address. All the while the drunk executive Osamu Tanaka (or whoever) hung his head, eyes downcast and chin mushed against the knot of his tie.

"Are you indeed Osamu Tanaka?!" the cop screamed at the drunk, who would initially answer with a mild *"hai."* Then again Osamu Tanaka was asked if he was Osamu Tanaka . . . and again and again until he barked out his "HAI!" bringing all work in the room to a silent halt.

With Osamu Tanaka sobered and shaking, the cop would wistfully but loudly hypothesize about what would happen when Tanaka's coworkers found out about his arrest. This tale of workplace shame, demotion, and the inevitable giggles of office ladies crushed Tanaka (and a string of others like him) into sobbing apologies augmented by fits of deep bowing. This final display of contrition and naked remorse brought immediate freedom (and even a loan for cab or subway fare).

As disconcerting as it was to watch grown men cry, I came to understand the power of the Japanese apology. Indeed, in a Japanese station house, the truth will set you free. It was a lesson that would serve me well a week later when I was eventually released with the stern warning that I should "forever keep passport in your trousers!"

"Go home! Go back to your country!" boomed the fat immigration official in well-honed English. "You have taken advantage of the rules for tourism. You must go home now!"

From the mouth of a Japanese, these harsh declarative statements, unadorned with a "please" or a "thank you," made my situation seem hopeless. To illustrate the depths of my crime, the fat official began counting the consecutive ninety-day tourist visas I had procured in the recent past. With his pudgy index finger he poked at the pages of my splayed passport. Each poke was followed by a hesitation and then a number in English. Poke . . . "One!" Poke

. . . "Two!" He plodded on until "Five!" Then came "Eight!" Then again "Five," before resorting to Japanese to bring the count to thirteen. This tally included the many fifteen-day extensions I had tacked on to drag out each of my supposedly final departures.

"Extensions are for serious emergency only!" he growled as he placed the passport in a drawer. "Serious emergency only . . . Now you must go home!"

Had I finally lost? For the last two years I had been playing visa roulette, and now a loaded chamber had come up. I had a routine: Every three months or so I would leave Japan and touch down on foreign tarmacs just long enough to qualify for another ninety-day stay. By adhering to the letter of the law I had managed to live legally in Japan while building a career as a freelance writer. But after this July 1993 foray, a thirty-one-hour holiday in Seoul, I was detained by a suspicious junior immigration official—taken aside and escorted through the maze of glass-wall partitions that constitutes Narita Airport's mini–immigration office. The place's ambience of hopelessness and hostility made Tokyo's main immigration center seem as accommodating as the American Express office.

I was seated in front of the worst kind of Japanese bureaucrat, a fat one. He was fat because he never stands up to bow. Unlike the thinner-model bureaucrat, often downright obsequious, the fatsos don't mind delivering bad news. They don't break sweats by digging through regulation books searching for loopholes, nor do they burn calories whimsically stamping visa extensions. They are fat because they are immovable, or at least that's what you are supposed to think. But I knew better.

In Japan, rule enforcers—police, teachers, and low-level immigration officials—have tremendous latitude in the interpretation and enforcement of rules. Essentially, any man in uniform is a policy maker. This quirk in the system has important ramifications for everyone from big-time rule breakers like gangsters and politicians all the way down to foreigners facing immediate deportation. Thus, I still had a slim chance to get in the country. But much to my horror, I had no idea how to play him.

Dangerous Gaijin!

I was suffering the con man's equivalent of writer's block. It wasn't that I lacked experience. A youthful propensity for minor police run-ins had followed me from the American suburbs to the cities of Europe and Asia. Experience told me that I should say anything the official might want to hear, even lie if necessary. But to be caught in some kind of fabrication might bar me from Japan for good. Anyway, what the hell would this angry Japanese bureaucrat want to hear from me? Could I repeat the phrase I had memorized, "I truly believe your profession is an important facet of Japanese culture with a fascinating but maligned history"? It worked well with yakuza . . . but might not be quite right for a civil servant banished to life in a flimsy office in a dismal airport.

"Please, sir! Let me slide past for a final journalistic foray into the underbelly of the beast that is modern Japan." But, I didn't say that or anything else. I just looked at the official's magnified eyes floating behind thick glass. Eyes that told his prosaic brain what was obvious: *Here is one of those dangerous gaijin who must be filtered out!*

In a country where judging a book by its cover is good common sense, where photographs must be attached to job applications, where career counselors will suggest cosmetic surgery—I was as good as airborne. If I wasn't a dead ringer for a police sketch and description of a typical gaijin drug smuggler—long haired, scruffy, and speaking suspiciously coherent Japanese—it was only because I wasn't wearing a tie-dyed shirt. I knew his assessment: Even if my luggage and colon were drug-free, I was still up to no good.

I had resigned myself to the forced trip to America. The untold expenses of a return voyage would effectively burn the money I had set aside for this final investigative offensive. Sitting in that immigration office in the bowels of Narita Airport, I almost cried recalling the complex arrangements I had made to meet assorted yakuza-beat writers, high-ranking police, and old yakuza contacts on whom I was depending for new leads and favors. To cancel now and try to reorganize these delicate plans months later would be impossible. This impending personal disaster was enough to make me try the truth.

"Sir," I pleaded. "I am a journalist. I need to be in Tokyo for my job!"

"Oh, you too?" The big man frowned, as I knew he would. Every other hippie traveler in the Far East had taken to carrying a fake photo ID proclaiming "JOURNALIST" status. The first time I discovered these things for sale in Bangkok, I was dumbfounded. Considering the shabby treatment I had received as the genuine article, how would such a ruse ever help a besandaled backpacker? (Although, standing there in the Narita Airport immigration office, I was living proof that a journalist *could* look like a hashish mule.) I cursed those imposters whose dubious scams were ruining it for me, a freelance journalist getting by on my wits without the corporate association that means so much in Far East countries.

Without any journalistic credentials—real or fake—I produced my bilingual *meishi*, my business card, which in conventional Japanese wisdom is the measure of the man. A man's meishi lists his title and his company's name and logo. It sanctions his life. My plain, logoless meishi did nothing beyond spell out my name in English on one side and Japanese on the other. The official turned my meishi over and over until he slid it in his shirt pocket.

Desperate, I dug through my knapsack looking for anything that might legitimize my claim. At the very bottom I discovered a torn piece of a newspaper story I had written about sumo. I smoothed out the picture of the interlocked behemoths and pointed to my name in black and white. The fat man leaned his girth forward to match the name on the meishi with the name on the byline. I saw my opening and, recalling the sobbing salaryman in the Roppongi Police Station, I spewed and spewed apologies. "Sir! I will never again misuse an emergency extension!"

The man snorted before producing an ink pad, a stamp, and my passport. In five minutes I was out of there, with ninety more days in a country where, even beyond the airport, I was hardly welcome. At home in my Tokyo apartment were letters telling me I had been excommunicated by two of Japan's three long-distance services for nonpayment. I was a million yen in arrears with the third, Nippon Telephone & Telegraph's "Zero Zero wONEderful"

long-distance systems, which, when cut, would effectively termi-
nate my working life in Japan. Besides NTT, other unpaid entities
like Tokyo Gas and Tokyo Power & Light didn't care if their threatened legal actions and shutoffs also put a damper on my career.

If the Tokyo utilities seemed to want me gone, my Japanese
girlfriend, Kie, came right out and said it. Her patience with my
deviant career path had evaporated. As my once-objective interest
in organized crime evolved into something closer to an apprenticeship, she found my activities embarrassing. Although her night job
as a Ginza bar hostess brought her into daily contact with gangsters, she hated them. They scared her. Two years earlier, however,
when I needed a gangster to serve as a subject for a magazine story,
she had found me a good one. The owner of her club had been a
grammar school friend of an intelligent yakuza boss called Z.-san.

I would tag along with Z.-san as he went about his daily routine.
Although he declared each of the two days uneventful, I was enthralled. We spent one particular morning at an elaborate funeral
service for a minor yakuza, a lowlife ticket scalper about whom
no one really gave a damn. Even his chubby widow in her black
kimono was laughing and flirting with the younger men. The funeral
was more about passing money around than about mourning the
departed.

The concrete temple grounds normally served as a workaday
parking lot. But on that morning, a large, black-and-white striped
tent had been set up in the center. Traditional lanterns and funeral
banners with calligraphy were hanging both inside the tent and
round the perimeter of the lot.

This temple was in the heart of a neighborhood that I considered my own backyard. We were down the street from the Azabu
National Supermarket, the hub of Tokyo's expatriate shopping and
social life. But on that day the place and these proceedings seemed
so, well, Japanese.

The sunlight was sharp and bright outside the reception tent.
I dropped back as Z.-san entered the tent and received the respect-

ful bows and grunts from his soldiers and members of other gangs. Soon Z.-san was swallowed up in a sea of wide-bodied gangsters.

I hesitated to push through the imposing crowd. This was my first encounter with Japanese men who, aside from sumo wrestlers, were *physically* intimidating. The broad backs of the gangsters blocked my view of the Shinto ceremony and the "grieving" women. I could watch only the smoke of ceremonial joss sticks twist to the tent roof. That was enough to satisfy me that it was a great "scene" for my piece.

But then the two men separated, allowing Z.-san to emerge from the shadow of the tent. With a nod, he called me inside, guiding me past the bruisers into a tiny temple office. We drank green tea while his men counted out the semiextorted widow's bounty, one using a calculator, the other an abacus. Sitting there in close quarters with these thugs, I was strangely at ease.

Later that afternoon we drove out to a prison to pick up one of Z.-san's soldiers who had just completed a three-year stint. When this lowly ranked gangster recognized his superior, he dropped his belongings. Right there on the cement sidewalk, the young man knelt down on the ground and executed a formal bow at Z.-san's feet!

The experience of watching the yakuza prostrate himself near my Doc Martens spoiled me. In fact, the whole time I had spent seeing the Tokyo gangland from Z.-san's perspective ruined me for the more detached, totally objective school of reporting.

After Z.-san, there was no way I was going to approach Japanese organized crime in the manner conventional American journalists cover the U.S. mob.

First, although I would find some fine speakers, I didn't expect to come across any Japanese Joe Valachis or Henry Hills. I would need to be involved.

Second, descriptions of yakuza control of cargo trucking routes between Osaka and Niigata City would not mean a thing to non-Japanese readers. To uncover and explain the details of mob-run Japanese businesses, I would need more visceral information.

Finally, if any Westerners have an image of the so-called Japanese mafia, they likely picture some pale imitation of the "real thing," kind of like Japanese professional baseball. If I wanted to get the feel of Japanese baseball, I could go to the park and after a few games tell whether it's double A, triple A, or major league ball. But one needs Cecil Fielder or Jesse Barfield to tell you what it's like to play.

This is how I felt: To really know the Japanese mob, I would need to get on the field. If I wasn't exactly going to be on the team, I had to be in the dugout, on the bus, in the locker room—maybe even take some batting practice. If I didn't understand all the signs or the language subtleties, I would just have to ask and ask again. On-the-spot communication would cause me some problems, but I was willing to risk embarrassment and confusion—or even an ass kicking over a major faux pas.

Fortunately, beginning in February I received a de facto submersion course in advanced Japanese conversation from my native girlfriend. As she began to feel displaced by my work Japanese replaced English as the lingua franca of our apartment. After I had removed etchings from the wall to put up photos of Japanese crime bosses and charts of their associations and territories life became 100 percent Japanese. I stared at these newspaper portraits like a pensive DA trying to head off a gang war.

But I was doing my homework. I was learning the gang players and their stats. The stars and the teams, even the geography, of the yakuza world changed with the seasons. I learned yakuza lore and knew its clichés. I screened endless yards of microfilm documenting the travails of the postwar yakuza and rented every yakuza B movie available!

Beneath our bed lurked my own private trove of yakuza memorabilia including transcripts, clippings, notebooks, and even a homemade dictionary of yakuza slang. Most of the stuff, however, related to my first yakuza contacts and now seemed like ancient news. By the summer of 1993, I was tired of learning the history and rules of the yakuza game; I wanted a gang war!

At least, I wanted to replicate with other yakuza the kind of experience I had shared with Z.-san. But beside hotshots like Z.-san, I wanted to observe also an older boss, a young enforcer, a grunt, a loser, a newcomer, a star and a godfather.

Rather than just repeat the duties of a young yakuza as they had been explained to me, I would hang with such a character and see for myself. I took a cue from the cinema verité TV programs where cameras follow cops into the fray. I would follow my leads, letting the yakuza men—and women—show me their world.

The killer heat of the summer still felt a long way off. I was comfortable strolling about my Tokyo neighborhood looking for possible subjects. It didn't take a trained eye to pick the gangsters out from the straight citizens. Yakuza call them *katagi*, short for *katagi no shu*, "people who walk in the sun." The yakuza, on the other hand, are the men of the shade who avoid attention. But in my Tokyo neighborhood they didn't hide very well: the guy waiting on line at the post office in a banana yellow sweat suit; behind the wheel of a white gold-trimmed BMW, the kid with the big coif sleeping with his mouth open; the pocked-face smoker monopolizing the corner ATM for two dozen transactions. Yakuza were ubiquitous. And I still hadn't gone looking in the pachinko halls or mah-jongg parlors.

If I were to just walk up to a tough-looking man on the street and ask whether he'd like to be profiled in an American book, the outcome didn't seem promising. In my years in Tokyo, however, I had made connections and I was about to begin using them.

BAD ADVICE

Brit Scott C. was a fixer, a Tokyo hustler—the rare kind of foreign resident who got by purely on his wits and linguistic ability. He earned his big yen supplying drugs to jonesing American rock bands, supplying apartments to needy Europeans, and supplying blond Scandinavians to hostess bars specializing in the genre. Scott could get you hash from Pakistan or condoms from England, and, above all, he could get you out of any Tokyo jam. Not only did Scott speak Japanese without an English twang, he could imitate six or seven regional Japanese accents to perfection. The guy was so plugged in, so aware of Japanese culture and current events, that when I joked about the emergence of the "dangerous gaijin," Scott flashed me the back of his denim jacket. In white he had painted a police-taunting "DANGEROUS GAIJIN!" in Japanese! "'Dangerous gaijin'? Christ!" spat an incredulous Scott. "You can't read Japanese. It says, 'BAD BARBARIAN!'"

"Okay," Scott C. said. "You want yakuza, well, I have a friend with a yakuza situation. . . . Go help him."

The cramped old neighborhood of Okobu squats in the shadows of Tokyo's newest skyscrapers. Near Shin-Okobu Station a narrow road runs below the tracks of the Yamanote circle line. On one side of this road is a sheer retaining wall, on the other is a row of old ferroconcrete "love" hotels with façades so quaint and demure, they could pass for traditional inns. Their rates are posted outside: four thousand yen for a two-hour "rest" or ten thousand yen for a full-night stay. Another sign, in Japanese and English, warns "DO NOT BRING THE FOREIGN LADIES FROM STREET HERE." It seems a pretty haughty policy for businesses that rely on local prostitutes.

"I think the police made them put up the signs against the gaijin," says a shriveled palm reader set up on the sidewalk. "There are many Brazilian and Peruvian ladies working the streets around here. I've been on this spot for the last five years, so I see things. The Filipino and Thai ladies came first, but now there are these white ladies from South America. At first, it was quite a shock to see white prostitutes working for Japanese yakuza, but now I'm used to it."

I'm waiting to meet the Brit named Jeremy. It was through the self-proclaimed "dangerous gaijin" Scott that I had once briefly met Jeremy and later heard of his intriguing crusade to help foreign prostitutes escape the grips of their yakuza pimps. Most of the girls had been brought to Japan on the promise of their becoming "entertainers" or, at worst, bar hostesses. Now, by force or circumstance, they are virtual prisoners in a strange land.

"Cheers!" I turn to see the smiling Jeremy dismounting his bicycle and wearing just a tank-top, shorts, and Birkenstock sandals. He had come to Japan four years earlier and had even married a Japanese girl, but it lasted only a year. Like many young Westerners before him, Jeremy had an obsession with Asian women. It's a common British syndrome likely rooted in their colonial past. As the days of the empire are long gone, a contemporary pattern has emerged: Toil in a Tokyo English-language school, save enough money to stay in Thailand for a few months, fall in love with a Thai bar girl, return to Japan, save money . . .

"Yes," admits the blond-haired and fair-skinned Jeremy. "I do think it's a national character trait. We go mad for these lovely brown girls who seem so exotic compared to the pale drabness of the women back home." Despite his weakness for fleshpots like Bangkok and Manila, in Tokyo Jeremy is a highly moral man with a dangerous mission. He has transformed his Tokyo flat into a safe house for foreign prostitutes who are desperate to escape their brutal and isolated existence.

Jeremy locks his bicycle on the fence at the front of his ground-floor apartment. With a quick glance up and down the street, he ushers me through a weathered teakwood door. The front room is cluttered with stacked suitcases and laundry piled high on the hardwood floor. Six suddenly silent young women look up with tentative smiles. After Jeremy introduces me as a friend, they relax and resume their chatter. Four of them are Filipino and two are Thai, but they find a common tongue in basic English and act quite jolly, given the circumstances. A Hong Kong action film with English subtitles blares on the television while hands from a round of gin rummy are spread out in front of each girl.

Jeremy supports the lot while plans are made to escort the girls back to their countries. There are a myriad of problems to overcome. All have overstayed their tourist visas; some actually came over using fake passports supplied by their yakuza recruiters in Bangkok and Manila.

"I was successful repatriating the first group," Jeremy says, as we sit cross-legged on the tatami-mat floor. Across the room, two Filipina are now watching a John Woo action movie with Tagalog subtitles. "The pimps don't know yet where their girls have gone. It's not that hard to hide out in a big place like Tokyo, but recently a situation has developed that Scott thought you might assist me with."

I shrug my shoulders and tilt my head to indicate something like a noncommittal interest. Apparently it is enough encouragement to let him press his case.

"A Filipina here named Cory broke my cardinal rule." Jeremy pauses for effect and sips his green tea. "She rang up one of her girlfriends back at her old flat. Then she stupidly told the friend where she was staying and god knows what else. The next time Cory calls, she gets a sobbing friend who confesses that her yakuza pimp has beaten the shit out of her to get her to tell him where Cory is hiding. She insists that she remembered only the name of the neighborhood, but not the address. Still, I think it's only a matter of time before this sick bastard and his buddies discover this place . . . "

"I'm not worried about myself," Jeremy boasts. "I reckon the cops would help a European, but I'm concerned about the word getting around the Okobu pimp circles. I mean, I walk through the Shin-Okobu Station every day. I'd be easy to find."

I ask him what he wants from me.

"Scott says you know a lot of these yakuza." Jeremy hands me a Japanese business card. "Maybe you know this guy's godfather or something. I wasn't quite sure . . . "

I recognize the gang logo on the business card, but I don't let on. I recall a yakuza once saying that katagi prefer difficult solutions to problems rather than simple ones, so I suggest that Jeremy just confront the pimp and offer him payment. Unless the guy is in love with Cory, I figure he'll take the money and run.

"Yeah?" Jeremy brightens. "Just like that?"

"Why not?" I assure him. "You took money out of his pocket, just put it back."

"How much?"

"Not too much," I say. "Two hundred thousand yen should do it."

"That's all?" Jeremy seems dubious.

"I think this guy will be utterly confused when confronted with you, a gaijin speaking perfect Japanese."

"Will you come?" Jeremy asks. "You know how to deal with these creeps."

"You don't need me," I assure him. Making not just a bad decision but an absolutely chickenshit one. Then I continue with more bull. "It will work better just one-on-one. Make sure you meet him in a public place, like the railroad station during rush hour."

A week later, on the Hiro-o shopping street, I run into Scott. He's in a pay Laundromat rolling a Drum cigarette on top of a washing machine. He's not his usual smiling self and ignores my greeting.

"Did you hear about Jeremy?" Scott asks rather curtly.

Bad Advice

"No," I admit. "But I was wondering how things worked out."

"You're joking," says Scott, as he lights his handmade cigarette. "He got his jaw busted by that creep."

"What?" I'm shocked and sick.

"He took your goddamn advice to buy the yakuza off for that girl," Scott says incredulously. "The pimp took the money all right. But then, in broad daylight, he proceeded to beat the crap out of poor Jeremy."

"Is he okay?" I ask hopefully.

"He'll live . . . but his mouth is bandaged shut, so he can't teach, can he?" Scott chides. "He's losing wages. I can't believe you advised him to confront this yakuza alone—without you!"

Guiltily I avert my eyes, only to discover the accusing stares of a half-dozen Japanese grannies at their machines.

But Scott isn't done with me: "Don't you understand the most basic thing about yakuza is that they love to fight? I thought you knew all about these maniacs! I thought that was your territory; you were supposed to hold Jeremy's hand. I thought your knowledge went deeper than copping black-market telephone cards!"

It's a wake-up call. If I am going to deal with yakuza outside of formal interviews, if I am going to be engaged, I must not forget a most important rule. As conformist and civil as Japan society may be, a member of its criminal underground, a yakuza, can be dangerously unpredictable. What separates the yakuza from katagi is the same thing that separates gangsters from the common man in Marseilles, Palermo, and New York: Violence is never the option of last resort. Hell, in the two-dimensional gangster mind, violence is always an alternative—an eternal plan B.

What I will come to realize is that violence can even be the *preferred* course of action. For both the yakuza and the American Mob, the pure pleasure of hitting a man with a fist or a baseball bat is hard to resist.

Alas, for Jeremy, I am still learning *yakuza no michi*, the way of the yakuza.

YAKUZA NO MICHI

"Yakuza are not criminals," a Tokyo boss explained. "Criminals are antisocial, unpatriotic, and undisciplined, like animals. Yakuza are not wild animals. We have tradition and obey the law. It's our own law but it's law just the same."

Thus, in 1992, when police and media reports replaced all references to yakuza with the name *Boryokudan*, it made the gangsters absolutely irate and indignant. Literally it means "organized violent gangs," whereas yakuza, loosely, means "loser." "Losers" is how yakuza like to describe themselves, but not quite how they want to be perceived.

Yakuza drive big cars in a small car country. They used to drive Cadillacs and Lincolns but, like the rest of their newly affluent countrymen many have taken to Mercedes-Benz and BMW. And then there are many yakuza in the congested inner city who choose to have no car at all. With cigarettes clenched between their lips, many of these gangsters make their rounds on bicycles looking hard driven even while ringing their little bells to clear the sidewalk.

To me, the yakuza on a bicycle is a familiar gangland image. Surely, to many Japanese too, the mobster on the bike is commonplace. But when it comes to popular entertainment, the yakuza is usually an over-the-top Asian interpretation of Nathan Detroit sporting a pinstriped zoot suit, chauffeured in a Bentley with a

Japanese flag painted on the trunk. It's pointless to go over the hackneyed yakuza clichés perpetuated in the media when my ambition is to negate them.

Real or fictional, there's no denying that yakuza carry lots of cash and curse the Bank of Japan for not issuing a bill larger than a pissant ten thousand yen, worth about one hundred bucks. They've got to carry a brick of the beige bills for a night in the bars, clubs, and streets where they operate. Like the fishmonger and pharmacist, local yakuza are accepted as staple characters in the neighborhood scene. One might be a man of respect whose presence is weighty. Another might be an outright buffoon. But even the goofballs are treated well at the local *izakaya,* the pub, where they drink Bushmills and Johnnie Walker Black.

Yakuza are uniformly tough (another accurate stereotype). While the bulkier men (who in America would only be average-sized) seem huge and brutish, even the slight, positively tiny, yakuza possess the aura of brawlers. In my preyakuza days as a general-interest journalist, I met captains of Japanese industry and big-shot politicians, but they impressed me only because I knew beforehand of their power and wealth. Yakuza, on the other hand, always strike me as larger than life.

In the postwar years societal forces fed many young men into the yakuza. Blue-collar fathers, just like white-collar salarymen, were obliged to work long days that made them nonfactors in the raising of their children. The lack of a controlling influence and the discipline of a strong father figure often led to wild uncontrolled boys. Most yakuza have nothing good to say about their fathers.

A disproportionately large percentage of yakuza are the products of divorced or separated parents (some stats says as many as 30 percent versus the national average of 2.1 percent). Lacking a father or mentor, many yakuza describe feeling alienated and antisocial as children. Sensing the distress of these potential yakuza, the teachers and administrators of the school system tend to channel these troublemakers into dead-end high schools, some of which have *never* sent a single student on to college. Bad boys they may be, but they're still Japanese who want to belong. Invariably they're drawn to the groups of fellow futureless teens who make up Japan's vast network of motorcycle gangs called *bosozoku;* these are Japan's criminal minor leagues, whose standouts are called upon to become yakuza.

Yakuza dwarf the American Mafia in sheer numbers. With less than half the population of the United States, Japan has one hundred thousand organized gangsters (compared with, perhaps, two thousand recruited American mafiosi). Yakuza ventures generate an estimated yearly income of $50 billion, an amount that would easily place them atop the *Fortune* 500. Yet whatever business they're in—from extortion to prostitution, drugs to real estate, stock market manipulation to computer hacking—the yakuza maintain many traditions adapted from their roots in feudal Japan.

The "true" origins of the yakuza depend on whose "truth" you're buying. Some scholars say that the yakuza descend from the marauding gangs that terrorized the old, agrarian Japan. The yakuza like to see themselves as unlucky but chivalrous Robin Hoods, forced to "live in the shadows." It's really a mixed tradition, inherited from both the outlaw and the samurai who met in the brothels, gambling dens, and inns of the old Tokaido Highway. (This legendary road once connected the seat of shogun political power, Edo—now Tokyo—with the old capital of Kyoto and the ports of Osaka and Kobe.) The yakuza try to emphasize the more heroic side of the myth, the macho samurai. Like samurai warriors, yakuza prove their *otokoiki* (their balls) through stoic endurance of pain, hunger, and imprisonment.

A notable gangster-turned-writer, Goro Fujita, has written over fifty books about the yakuza and is a contributor to the largest gang's own monthly magazine. One of his works, a sentimental poem called "A Man's Grief," depicts grim jail conditions and the yakuza practice of letting a lesser gang member "confess" to the crime of an arrested superior:

> It's the middle of March, almost cherry blossom season.
> But the cold wind feels like it's going back to winter. . . .

The jail feels like an icehouse and the food tastes like an icicle.
That thing they call "The Confession" gets stuck in the throat. . . .
Why do they go there even though they'll face grief?
They call it "giri," a yakuza's obligation.
Sometimes it's just false courage.
This is a man's life, a man's grief.
Yakuza life was created in this spirit.
Be patient!

Literally, the word *ya-ku-za* means "eight-nine-three," a losing hand in an old card game. It's no longer an apt title. Though they romanticize their humble roots as *bakuto* (petty gamblers), today's state-of-the-art yakuza operations bear little resemblance to the hardscrabble lives of their ancestors.

Since the 1950s, the yakuza have become so wealthy, so diversified and omnipresent in Japanese society that their agenda is virtually indistinguishable from that of the national government. There is a strong symbiotic relationship between the two sectors that fosters the notion of Japan as a harmonious, crime-free society. It is, however, very much an illusion. Even disregarding the many well-publicized (and often yakuza-related) government and business scandals, the urban Japanese are experiencing their share of unreported rapes, shootings, and drug-related problems. But if there are fewer creeps and random killers on the streets of Japan than in the United States, the reason is that the yakuza make it their civic duty to absorb dangerous types into their gangs, thus preventing the evolution of lone-wolf criminals.

The Japanese yakuza constitute a parallel universe running beneath virtually every institution and industry in the nation. It's a mind-numbing thought, considering the already Byzantine nature of Japan's "legitimate" corporate and "democratic" political institutions. The structure of yakuza organizations are, however, fairly straightforward and basically unchanging. Though recent years have seen small independent gangs absorbed into massive supergangs, the feudal *oyabun-kobun* (father-child) relationship between boss and soldier is still the fundamental building block of all *gumis* (groups) and *kais* (associations). Allegiance to one's oyabun is total, unquestioning and unwavering. "IF YOUR BOSS SAYS A PASSING CROW IS WHITE," goes an old yakuza adage, "IT'S WHITE."

The gangs are formed by elaborate networks of personal relationships forged by Shinto-based sake-sharing ceremonies called *sakazuki* that bind men for life. Many gangs can indeed trace their roots back to the nineteenth and even eighteenth centuries, while some of the most powerful gangs were founded in recent decades. Today, as in the past, the yakuza exist to satisfy the public's need for vice. And no Japanese needs vice like the salaryman.

Japan's salarymen, the white-collar executives and staff employees of the nation's corporate infrastructure, make up about 15 percent of the population. They have been the subject of much study and praise as the workaholic cadre that has been the key to the nation's "economic miracle." Some observers have noted, however, that much of the vaunted ten-to-twelve-hour workday is given to activities that serve little function except to make the salaryman look good to his superior and his peers. Even when salarymen do finish their long work day, they don't leave it behind. Most nights they take it with them to the countless bars, clubs, massage parlors, and restaurants that cluster in the city centers. After a few rounds of overpriced scotch they tend to relax their guard, turning into fraternity brothers on the loose. Free spending, if awkward conviviality, prevails until the time arrives to get the last train home to a tiny flat in a distant suburb.

Much of the money left behind in the pubs and restaurants goes to the yakuza. It's all part of Japan's vast world of the *mizu shobai*, the so-called water trades, which also include many geisha inns, massage parlors, and outright houses of prostitution. Little wonder that the yakuza draw whispered admiration from the Japanese business mainstream, while at the same time evoking fear and loathing.

My daily perusal of the news reveals that no scheme is beneath them. Recently, an Osaka gang set up an "antidrug help center." They rented an office, printed pamphlets, and then used fake documents to secure huge government loans. The "help center" disappeared the day after the loans came through. Another gang bought land beside a well-heeled country club and threatened to construct pigsties beside the fairways. The payoff was $6.4 million. A Tokyo gang threatened to publish a consumer "watchdog" newsletter that, instead of protecting the consumer, was used to extort cash from targeted companies. A hefty payment, $12.5 million, ensured the suppression of the newsletter with its damaging assessments and invented gossip.

Indeed, the yakuza have made blackmail a true art form. Their practice of *sokaiya* plays on the Establishment's fear of "losing face." A yakuza will buy a single share of stock and then threaten the corporation with "disrupting" the shareholder's meeting by asking awkward questions. The company usually will preempt the problem by paying big hush money. Recently, the president of the Ito-Yokada, the corporation that owns 7-Eleven, resigned in disgrace after it was revealed that he paid out $1 million in past years to stop sokaiya threats. Many big companies have formed special divisions in yakuza relations and bury these payoffs under "social expenses."

While the yakuza maintain their traditional stranglehold on prostitution, gambling, and loan-sharking, they continue to expand and diversify into "legitimate" businesses. Recent decades have shown that nothing is beyond them, including the buttoned-down world of real estate speculation and corporate takeovers. Even the American media, which normally accept Japan's sanitized public image, covered the downfall of the political power broker Shin Kanemaru, who received a $4-million bribe from a yakuza-tainted parcel delivery company. The company, comparable to FedEx, was duped into providing $2.5 billion in loans to the Inagawa-kai Tokyo gang and their paper companies. The extorted money was then used to buy controlling shares in some of Japan's biggest corporations via the Nikko and Nomura Securities companies.

Making money from money is a concept the yakuza have grown to love. Indeed, they have been deeply involved in stock manipulation in recent years and are, in fact, a significant reason for the Tokyo Stock Exchange's fall and the demise of the superheated "bubble economy." In the two and a half years following its 1989 peak, the Tokyo Stock Exchange's Nikkei Index plummeted by 60 percent, with trading volume down 80 percent and real estate value cut in half. By the end of 1995, the Nikkei had barely regained 10 percent of its old value, with no end to the Japanese recession in sight.

"I've been calling this the yakuza recession," Raisuke Miyazawa, former head of the National Police Agency's organized crime division, told James Sterngold of the *New York Times* in an October 1994 interview. "During the bubble years, companies became very nonchalant about organized-crime contacts, from top to bottom. All sorts of relationships were built up."

The story is told of a small credit association called Gifu Shogin that had gone belly-up in the wake of the four-year collapse of real estate prices. Government officials moved in to force a lifesaving merger of Gifu Shogin with another financial institution. Then there was a fantastic revelation: Of Gifu Shogin's $110 million in bad loans, about $70 million were to organized crime gangs or their front companies!

That this provincial bank, located 180 miles west of Tokyo, was in bed with gangsters shocked the Japanese. It finally brought home the true extent of yakuza power in corporate Japan. A series of murders of high-level bankers was a somewhat darker hint of the depth of the yakuza involvement in the banking world. The National Police Agency offered broad clemency to corrupt bank officials who would come clean about their yakuza contacts. The police have also created special units (in addition to their already extensive antiyakuza programs) to fight yakuza attacks on businessmen.

Imagine if the American Mafia helped cause a financial calamity bigger than the savings and loan crisis. That's exactly what the yakuza have done with a $350 billion disaster that destroyed lifetime savings and sent shock waves through financial markets around the globe. The well-documented connections between yakuza and politicians as well as the tales of multimillion-dollar extortion scams all pale beside the yakuza's hand in the inflation and crash of the most awesome economy in the world.

On March 1, 1992, the strong new antigang laws went into effect. The laws designated Japan's "Big Seven" yakuza groups—including the giant Kobe/Osaka–based Yamaguchi-gumi, Kyoto's Aizu Kotetsu, and Tokyo's Inagawa-kai and Sumiyoshi-kai as Boryo-kudan. Suddenly, around fifty thousand yakuza found themselves accountable to a separate set of legal criteria and rules that allow them to be prosecuted and jailed without the full constitutional protections afforded the average Joe-san. The guilt-by-association essence of the new law rubs against many tenets of Japan's American-written constitution, just as, it could be argued, the RICO laws do in the States.

Intense heat has been felt at the lowest levels of the yakuza world, where money is made on the streets via petty extortion and gambling. Even the lowly pushcart businesses of yakuza-associated food vendors have been routinely hassled by the newly empow-ered police. Lesser bosses have scrambled to diversify their group's activities in order to appear more legit. Top yakuza bosses like the Yamaguchi-gumi's Yoshinori Watanabe and the Aizu Kotetsu's Tokutaro Takayama have separately pursued legal actions and staged demonstrations to fight the new law's constitutionality. Imagine the Mafia picketing city hall: That's the scene that's been televised in many Japanese cities.

During one of my early excursions to western Japan, to the area known as Kansai, I had an audience with Tokutaro Takayama. Tall, white-haired, and imposing, the revered boss had his own ideas about the new laws.

"The police are the 'violent gang,'" insists the boss of Aizu Kotetsu. His organization maintains control over most of the Kyoto and Nara underworld despite the ever-growing Yamaguchi-gumi. "We're patriots! I can give you names of politicians who take money and support from me, then go to Tokyo and stab me in the back! The yakuza fought the Communists, and the yakuza give jobs and discipline to dropouts who would have nothing to do but make trouble. Now the police are bothering everyone associated with me—even my son, who's not a yakuza!

"This law is a smoke screen to distract everyone from the bad economy," explains Takayama. "It's a show. The law is part of a government publicity campaign. Remember, in the old days, Japanese were divided in castes: warriors, farmers, merchants, 'polluted' trades, and outcasts. The old shogun government invented this system, to help rule the people. This is a country fully capable of creating discrimination when it wants to." He pauses and looks pleased with his wry observation of official hypocrisy. I am pleased as well. A journalist could spend a lifetime waiting for a Japanese official to make such a bold statement.

"Okay, so they outlawed the old system on the premise of ensuring equality for all. But this new law is also discriminatory, creating new castes and new forms of prejudice. Arbitrarily labeling people like us as 'violent gangs' is a wholesale violation of the basic human rights of the youth and men who make up our organization. These labels and definitions are decided entirely by the police, internally and secretly. Neither the process nor the evidence is open to public review or appeal; it's insane. This could never happen in America—only in Japan!"

In accordance with the new laws, the Osaka police have set up an antiyakuza task force, which has worked the literal eight-nine-three of the word *yakuza* into their PR campaign: "HASSLED BY ORGANIZED CRIME? DIAL 946-YA-KU-ZA-ZERO!" In the summer of 1992 I visited Osaka.

"My dream is to eliminate the yakuza," confided the wide-eyed Mr. Minoda, a retired cop who heads up the new Osaka antiyakuza center. In the modern office several men and women sit poised to pick up the phone should anyone call the hot line. The center's dramatic posters, posted all over the city, show screaming people being devoured by hellish red flames. "I was a policeman for thirty-seven years, I watched these yakuza, these lazy dogs pushing drugs on housewives and kids! They drive around in Mercedeses; it's a disgrace! And those silly movies glorifying these jerks. Don't get me started . . .

"We have a massive publicity effort going on right now, post-

ers, TV, radio and newspaper ads. People can call us and we'll step
in," Minoda explained excitedly. "We'll counsel the victims while
hitting the yakuza with a legal body blow!

"So far we haven't received a lot of calls, but the publicity will
help," he said hopefully. "Mostly we get calls from old ladies com-
plaining about kids blowing off fireworks near their homes. But
things will pick up."

One would like to believe Mr. Minoda, but I have come to feel
that corruption is rampant in Japan. Certainly a tacit, usually petty,
criminality is ingrained in the daily business and social transactions
of all strata of society. There is institutionalized payola that flows
from parent to teacher, patient to doctor, contractors to officials,
distributors to suppliers, and within just about any important relationship imaginable. All these cash "gifts"—sliding under, over, and
around the proverbial table—softens up the populace for real
yakuza exploitation and corruption.

In a society where "lite" bribes (in the forms of cash "gifts"
and favors) are the coin of the realm, gangsters have taken on the
roles of facilitator, lobbyist, and troubleshooters. In a real, though
distorted way, yakuza are to Japan what corporate lawyers are to
America. Of course, law firms draw from the elite young minds of
the nation. The yakuza make do with Japan's rejects and rebels.

The yakuza subculture may be the most compelling aspect
of modern Japanese society. It is an extraordinary mix of traditional
Japan insularity and social openness. As an example of the latter,
yakuza are at the forefront in providing employment opportuni-
ties for ostracized Japanese citizens of Korean and Chinese descent;
indeed, these third- and fourth-generation "foreigners" are some
of the yakuza's biggest guns. In this respect, the yakuza seems thoroughly progressive, almost politically correct compared to their
ethnocentric countrymen.

On the other hand (or shoulder), the gangs are quite retro-
grade in their observance of the ancient practice of body tattooing. This elaborate art, often covering the complete torso and

thighs, is traditionally executed with wooden needles and is an excruciatingly slow and painful process. Even with an electric needle, a full body tattoo can take a year to complete. But the tattoos are considered an important rite of passage and symbol of commitment for a yakuza. Those who do without these "in-for-life" markings are viewed somewhat suspiciously.

The *hari-maki*, an old-fashioned money belt formed by wrapping a wide cloth strip around the midsection, is a key item of yakuza casual wear. Newer yakuza trademarks such as dark suits, punch-permed hair, and tinted glasses have evolved to become part of the tradition. Some yakuza have had pearls surgically inserted into their penile foreskin, supposedly to enhance their sexual prowess and appeal.

The Yamaguchi-gumi, the General Motors of the yakuza, and other gangs publish glossy magazines and hardcover books and have even produced feature films glorifying their history. In a Japan of obsequious salarymen, squeamish teenagers who avoid touching public handrails, and *otaku* computer freaks who fear all human contact, the brazen gangsters sometimes become public heroes.

A few dissidents aside, the Japanese public tolerates yakuza power with the same passivity it accords its often corrupt oligarchy of politicians. Mobsters benefit from popular movie and TV lore that paints them as heroic, dignified rebels in a nation of Westernized wimps. A case in point is Japan's biggest movie star, Ken Takakura. This sullen, talented actor made his mark by playing the archetypal yakuza hero who maintains tradition in a changing Japan. Takakura's stock character is the brutal yet honorable Japanese man who finds strength and solace in yakuza discipline. He also loves a simple (but pretty) Japanese woman who helps him to shoulder his unique Japanese angst (and wash his socks). His yakuza persona is the polar opposite of (and even an affront to) his country's other, more mundane hero, the salaryman.

One of Japan's most popular soap operas depicts the romanticized adventures of legendary nineteenth-century outlaws, epecially Jinrocho of Shimizu. This most famous yakuza chief of the past has his counterpart today in the person of Yoshinori Watanabe, the top boss of the thirty-three-thousand-strong Yamaguchi-gumi. He stands at the apex of Japan's largest, fastest-growing, and most-feared organized crime syndicate.

Like most of the powerful men in Japan, Watanabe loves golf, and he happens to play the game well. Unlike corporate VIPs, Watanabe is chauffeured to the first tee via helicopter and plays alone—with the exception of a few kobun for protection and, perhaps, for hunting down the occasional shanked ball.

Watanabe, fifty-five, is a big man with a strong jaw and a serious disposition who, even when dressed in tasteful golfing attire, looks 100 percent yakuza. He is known for his passions for classic Chinese literature and the works of the Confucian philosopher Mencius. He and his family live in the sprawling Yamaguchi-gumi complex beside the Australian consulate in an exclusive district of Kobe, which was left untouched by the earthquake.

The tabloids, as well as Watanabe's official police dossier, describe him as handsome. But, in person, the man just looks scary, towering over his own bodyguards as he ducks into his black Benz. This burly traditionalist wears his black hair in the old yakuza crew cut, yet his European suits give him a hip look—like he's the movie star playing a yakuza boss. But the elaborate tattoos beneath his tailored suit don't wash off after a day on location. Incised on his right shoulder is a serpentine dragon (signifying power and objectivity), and on his left is a roaring tiger (signifying strength).

In order to maintain the organization's delicate network of personal loyalties, the man at the Yamaguchi-gumi helm must possess those animal traits and more. It takes enormous personal charisma on Watanabe's part to secure the allegiance of men he has never met and will never meet. If not for his emergence in 1990, the chain of Yamaguchi-gumi relationships (reaching north to Sapporo, south to Fukuoka, and even into restricted Tokyo) would have disintegrated.

With Watanabe, the Yamaguchi-gumi organization has not just survived, but thrived. Estimates for the year 1994 put its revenue in the range of twenty-five to thirty-eight billion dollars. But the Yamaguchi-gumi membership, like all of the big gangs, believes itself to be about more than just money. When the earthquakes of 1995 brought tragic destruction to the Yamaguchi-gumi hometown of Kobe, the true altruism of yakuza found instant expression. While the ill-prepared government rescue squads took precious days to mobilize, the men of the Yamaguchi-gumi swung into action. The gangsters were the first on many scenes of destruction. Men with missing fingers and prison records were soon pulling victims from collasped buildings. Without official assistance or approval, yakuza also brought needed water and food to the homeless. Meanwhile, the inept government was trying to save face by haughtily rejecting help from the United States.

Not since the chaos right after the Second World War, when the yakuza—including the Yamaguchi-gumi boss at the time and the present boss of the Aizu Kotetsu—helped keep the peace, have the yakuza shone so dramatically. Assisting the earthquake victims is of course a public relations coup, one that should move Yamaguchi-gumi companies to the front of the line for millions of dollars in rebuilding contracts.

On July 17, 1993, a single murder in Sapporo (by samurai sword, no less) sent lead flying between affiliates of the Yamaguchi-gumi and members of the Far East Brotherhood (Kyokuto-kai). This triggered a violent reshuffling of complex gang alliances, with repercussions sending lead flying in plenty of other directions. At first the hits and misses were going down far from the capital. But, by the nineteenth, bullets were blasting into torsos and through office doors in the Tokyo Überhoods of Shinjuku and Shibuya—my own backyard. I was thrilled.

It is nearly midnight on Ginza's Namiki Dori. I am leaning on a curvaceous Lexus and nursing a beer while waiting for my girlfriend to finish her shift at the Champagne Club. It's one of the hundreds of expensive, mob-run hostess bars stacked floor upon floor, on the most expensive real estate in the world. I focus on the crew-cut yakuza soldiers milling around on the sidewalk as they wait for their bosses to emerge from the hostess bars.

Things have cooled down a bit since the superheated eighties when the price of a square foot of Ginza land approached the GNP of a Central American nation. My girlfriend is still taking home (with tips) eight hundred dollars a night as a hostess—and that's for only three hours of moronic smiling, small talk, and whiskey pouring. But her customers, mostly gray-haired Liberal

Democratic Party honchos, just aren't tossing back hundred dollar highballs like they used to.

Out on the streets, however, the grand panorama of the Ginza is unchanged—and I love it all: the avuncular cabbies who cruise the streets in spotless sedans; the drunken businessmen lurching towards the subway stations; the chirping hostesses (some in kimonos) bidding their clients farewell; and, of course, the signs.

In their daily interaction, the Japanese can be the most reserved, polite, and self-effacing of people. The reverse is true of their advertising signs. The Ginza, the huge shopping and entertainment district, is the apotheosis of the sign maker's craft. Incandescent, fluorescent, neon, electronic, computerized—a mêlée of large and small signs shoulder, jostle, and piggyback each other in a near-hopeless attempt to be recognized by the passing throngs. The eyes glaze over.

I am finishing my beer when a white Excalibur glides up to the corner where two yakuza are lounging under the streetlight. Simultaneously, the wise guys drop their cigarettes, reach into their blazers, and, with a certain grace, pull out their revolvers. They blast shots into the hood of the fiberglass "classic," as if the car itself had offended them. With a frantic screeching of its whitewall tires, the car roars off. The guys jog after it as they casually empty their guns into its elegant backside. Before I can register my own panic, the yakuza have disappeared into a side alley, and the street is empty.

It is just another night of anonymous Tokyo gunshots that wouldn't be reported anywhere except, perhaps, over a few cellular phones. There isn't supposed to be gunplay in Japan. Both the police and civilians seem oblivious to it—or forgetful—even when they see it.

In the days preceding this minor Ginza skirmish, the whole nation was let in on the bloodiest gang war since the RICO-type antiyakuza laws were ramrodded through the Diet (the Japanese Parliament) back in 1992. Officials were even describing the latest carnage as worse than the notorious Osaka yakuza shoot-outs of 1985. That battle between the Yamaguchi-gumi and a splinter gang lingers in the popular imagination like a Japanese Saint Valentine's Day Massacre.

After the "new laws" went into effect in 1992, I tracked the shifting allegiances on a chart tacked to my apartment wall. Because they avoid the press, the twenty-three-hundred-man Far East Brotherhood didn't figure prominently. But in Tokyo underworld lore, the sixty-six-year-old gang is reputed to have stocked its ranks with the best street fighters in Japan. Unaffiliated with any of the Tokyo mega-organizations, the Far East Brotherhood is based in a blue-collar corner of northeastern Tokyo called Akebane.

The Yamaguchi-gumi used the Sapporo incident as an honorable excuse to probe the brotherhood turf. The Yamaguchi men attacked the brotherhood not in its Akebane home, but in the crowded Shinjuku district, where nearly 250 yakuza gangs maintain branch offices.

During the week it was difficult to read behind the faux outrage (they are shocked, simply shocked) and the muddled accounts. I half-expected the mainstream press to be confused, but I was frustrated because unlike most Japanese journalists I wanted the truth.

Fortunately for me, the one man who wasn't confused called me out of the blue. Sumiya-san is the chief yakuza reporter of Asahi Geino, a popular weekly men's magazine that regularly covers, besides sex and sports, yakuza activities. The Asahi Geino (along with some other tabloid publications) has better mob connections than any of the big national newspapers. Hell, Sumiya has better yakuza connections than a lot of mob bosses. When there's no legitimate yakuza news, the tabloids will run puff features about how various yakuza bosses passed their summer vacations. Of course when real news, such as a scandalous "gift" to a politician, is exposed about the gangs, the tabloids not only report it, they revel in it. With Japan's bland self-serving, party-line newspapers and TV stations against them, the tawdry tabloid press are the only media friends the yakuza have.

I first contacted Sumiya a while back because I found in the Asahi

Geino the most compelling gangland reporting—between the photos of top-less teens and ads for massage parlors. A tall man in his mid-fifties, Sumiya has a hard, angular face and the unique disposition of a free spirit who has lived life on his own terms and timetable. By the eighth day, the nationwide confrontation between Yamaguchi-gumi and the brotherhood's network of goons had reached a war-zone intensity with five dead. Sumiya called me up and instructed me to meet him in Akebane outside a place called Club Hollywood, where we would meet the boss of the Far East Brotherhood. Maybe he was just doing me a favor because he knew it was an exciting time, a fortuitous time, to be on the yakuza beat.

The air is cool on the honky-tonk strip of sake bars and inexpensive hostess clubs, a world away from the rarefied (and violent) Ginza scene.

Young, bow-tied barkers stand outside the clubs clapping and yakking up the virtues (or lack thereof) of their hostesses and the cheapness of their booze. These low-end hostess bars, still pricier than four-star New York restaurants, are the haunts of second-level salarymen who punch clocks at low-status companies and commute to middle-class communities (that look, by the way, exactly like the high-status communities a few train stops beyond). I find the Akebane red-light district immensely appealing; even the name Club Hollywood rings less pretentious than the marbleized monikers of its snooty Ginza counterparts, like Lalique and Louis Vuitton's.

There are about a dozen hostess bars on the narrow pedestrian zone but Club Hollywood is the most enticing because its entrance is at street level. The neighboring joints feature dark, foreboding, descending stairways to dens where indentured Thai and Filipino "hostesses" could frequently be discovered working off their fifty-thousand-dollar debts—one ten-dollar-screw at a time. Club Hollywood is cheery, though it seems an odd place to hold a discreet meeting with a top Far East Brotherhood boss in the middle of the biggest gang war in a decade.

* * *

On the Yakuza Beat

Akebane doesn't get many gaijin. After checking out the Polaroids of smiling hostesses posted on the outside wall, I'm psyched to get inside. I get a frosty once-over by the doorman; when he hears who I'm waiting for, he treats me to a full, ninety-degree bow. Then, ridiculously, this grinning *chimpira* (a punk, a "little prick" in yakuza slang) offers to have a chair brought outside for my comfort. I casually decline.

To my relief, he hustles back to perform some further bows and door opening for a stream of short, darkly serious men in off-brand golfwear and sandals. Some of the guys sport smokey glasses and hair shorn in severe brush cuts, the latest yakuza fashion. This short hairstyle is fast replacing the Afroish punch-perm that has defined yakuza style to most Japanese for decades. (Actually, the brush-cut fad is a revival of the predominate yakuza hairdo of the sixties.) I believe the brush-cut craze was ignited a few months ago when Yamaguchi-gumi boss Yoshinori Watanabe, a man whose rough-hewn handsomeness is the embodiment of the perfect yakuza, deserted the perm for the brush cut. Whether a punch-permed traditionalist or a trendy brush cutter, each yak is carrying a clutch-type purse. Along with a wafer-thin portable phone, this oddly feminine purse seems to be a *must* accessory for all yakuza.

Each of the gangsters glances at me before ducking into the club. Looking aside, I see Sumiya-san turning the corner with cigarette in hand, his double-breasted jacket rakishly unbuttoned. He walks in the slow, distinctly yakuza stride of a man who has never and will never rush for a commuter train. I've seen this semiswagger affected by teenage bosozoku as they dismount from their motorcycles and other yakuza wanna-bes, but of all the slo-mo, cool-strutting dudes I've seen in Japan, Sumiya really pulls it off. Ignoring the line of barkers who seem to freeze as he passes their establishments, Sumiya looks more like a gunslinger at high noon. Without warning, the bicycle handlebars of a passing ramen-delivery man brush against Sumiya's elbow. Sumiya roars at the guy in the manner of an angry oyabun at his underling. Upon glancing back to see whom he's nicked, the delivery guy jumps off his bike, turns, and apologizes with a series of backbreaking bows. He lets his bike and its contents crash to the ground. Sumiya just grunts a dismissal and continues toward me.

After a formal nod and a handshake, Sumiya allows a smug smile to break across his face: "Seymour-san, the little war is over," he confides sotto voce. "You are the first to know, the mass media won't know for three days." I am flattered—and honored. A few days ago I was excited by the war; its timing seemed a godsend. But then I wondered what to do. How the hell do I access this gang war? I couldn't participate, I couldn't watch it from some bleachers. But here I am.

It turns out that I have been invited to the fête celebrating Yamaguchi-gumi's "defeat" at the hands of the Far East Brotherhood! I will be drinking with K., the boss who engineered the yakuza upset of the decade! Head of a gang that I hadn't even included on my wall chart! Now that I am sharing in this underworld history, I am tempted to put myself up on the chart.

Club Hollywood's interior is bigger, more brightly lit, and flaunts more decorative Plexiglas than any other hostess bar I have ever seen. And it is unusually lively: There's a decent rock band, drunken salarymen comically hopping around on the dance floor, and the advertised hostesses wearing numbered badges, like dancers in a Bangkok girlie bar.

An entire corner of the place is reserved for the Far East Brotherhood plus two. I am ushered to a seat beside hostess number forty-nine on the big boss K.'s left; Sumiya sits across, next to number twenty-nine. K. is smiling and with his open silk shirt and gold medallion looks like an Oriental Caligula. The various kobun, yakuza subordinates, at nearby tables don't allow themselves to get as gregarious as their boss.

While K. is quietly conferring with Sumiya, I talk to K.'s soldier. S. is missing two joints from his left pinky and the tip of his left ring finger (three strikes and he's still in, I think to myself). After years of meeting yakuza, I barely notice such details anymore, but I can't help staring at the bluish edge of a lotus petal tattoo peeking above S.'s open shirt collar. Like most Japanese, he wants to talk about America. S. seems obsessed with the well-documented dangers of American cities. This wiry, forty-five-year-old gangster, who admits to shooting maybe ten men, is afraid to visit Florida.

Like most yakuza, S. isn't exactly sure how many men he's killed because, "unlike the heartless American Mafia" (a favorite yakuza refrain), yakuza have traditionally preferred to shoot (or slash) and run. If the victim recovers from the wounds, then he is supposedly indebted to his would-be murderer. Though I have read and heard all this stuff before, S.'s slow, thoughtful explanation of the yakuza's classic self-conflict about killing is fascinating. His stoic talk of obligation, burden, and honor transcends the tacky surroundings. "If I kill another yakuza from any faction," says S. finally, "it's still like killing a brother, like I'm killing myself."

At S.'s urging I finish off four whiskey-and-oolong-teas. Sumiya is still engaged with K., who possesses tremendous girth for an Asian. The spread collar of his pink silk shirt reveals beads of sweat that don't move. Also unmoved are numbers twenty-nine and forty-nine, who look glum, not nearly as grateful as I to be included in this party of the elite of the Far East Brotherhood.

K. is about sixty, which is not old for a man in a leadership position in any Japanese organization. His full, dark hair is gray on the sides and slicked straight back from his pudgy face. He wears yellow-tinted wire-frames, and his constant laughing exposes lots of gold dental work.

"OK," the mouth now booms at me. "Fire away! Ask me anything!" Though I am into my fifth (sixth?) drink, I sober up at the idea of asking K. "anything." Nervously I clear my throat and in my best professional manner begin:

"This war, as I understand it, was basically a bid by Yamaguchi-gumi to take over some of the Far East Brotherhood's Shinjuku territory. Since you, the Far East Brotherhood, aren't in the Kanto-kai alliance with Inagawa-kai and other Tokyo gangs, nor do you have any pact that I'm aware of with Sumiyoshi-kai . . . " The mention of these other groups wipes the grin off K.'s mug. Sumiya cuts me off, saying that all the details about the war will be laid out in his piece in the next *Asahi Geino*. "Don't ask him about the war," Sumiya repeats.

"What does K.-san want to talk about?" I ask the big guy directly.

"Sex!" he pronounces. I laugh while hostesses twenty-nine and forty-nine grimace. Sex is too idiosyncratic in Japan for me to really discuss it with confidence, so I get K. rolling about his wealth, his many girlfriends, his country house with its built-in pool, his custom-made golf clubs, and his car. "It's American!" he shouts. "A GMC Jimmy four-by-four."

Suddenly, the jocularity drains from the big boss's face. It's as though he has reassessed the absurdity of my presence at his celebration, deciding I am evil. "I want to know why you're interested in my company! Why are you honoring me with your presence at my humble party?"

The man's sudden sarcasm is frightening. There's no reason for K.'s hostility, but dictators and crime bosses don't need reasons to instill fear. That's their talent, that's what they do. His sudden brutality reverberates to the far end of the table, where S. is noticeably cowering. For the first time I taste the fear that's instrumental in maintaining an underground organization and I feel nauseous. I taste bile rising into my dry throat. Sumiya and the hostesses avert their eyes, looking down at their hands. A few of the kobun at the next table turn around to sneer. Everyone's attitude is suddenly charged with contempt—or is it pity? I shut the small notebook I have in my lap and mumble an obsequious apology. Suddenly, Sumiya explodes into a hearty laugh. K. finally breaks into a silly grin. He says something to the effect that he is only joking with me—and that I better have some whiskey to get some color back in my face. It turns out to be one of the great evenings of my life.

A few days later, Sumiya's gangland truce story appears in *Asahi Geino*. Next to the text, they run two stock photographs of the Far East Brotherhood and the Yamaguchi-gumi leadership striding across the grounds of some temple. This type of photo is a standard pose that presents gangland leaders, with their lapel pins glistening, as forward-moving, unstoppable, and proud. I instantly recognize K. in the triumvirate of Far East Brotherhood top bosses. Ruefully I have to admit that K., in the photo at least, looks as awesome as the Yamaguchi-gumi's Watanabe.

Though I skim the entire story three times, I can't find the rather simple Japanese characters identifying K., even though Watanabe's name appears over and over. I later learn that K.'s name has been intentionally omitted as a favor to the gang boss, in the typically Japanese spirit of mutual benefit. Not being identified in a hugely popular magazine affords K. a degree of safety from any Yamaguchi-gumi wanna-be who might try to make a name for himself by shooting K. He earned this measure of anonymity by giving Sumiya exclusive information and putting up with his gaijin friend.

The details of the secret pact ending the "BLOODY ECONOMIC WAR" (as the papers had dubbed it) is just the type of juicy news I expect from Sumiya. I find the story great and call Sumiya to congratulate him. He cuts me off with a growl, telling me to hang on. He picks up another phone but I continue to hear his barking. I hear him say distinctly: "You told me the war was over, K.! You assured me it was finished four days ago!"

It takes me a moment to figure out what has happened. In his arrangement with K., Sumiya thought he was given rock-solid information. Now that his "scoop" about the gang cease-fire is proving to be premature, he goes ballistic at his informant-buddy! He has balls! Sumiya is a tabloid journalist I can respect. I've heard of protecting a source, but berating one, especially of this magnitude, is a new and brazen twist.

The latest victim of the war was discovered in a field by police in Shizuoka prefecture last night. They suspect members of the Yamaguchi-gumi affiliate, Goto-gumi. Inspired by Sumiya's brashness, I plan a trip down to Shizuoka to check things out for myself.

Goto-gumi has intrigued me since a well-publicized affair at the end of March that got the yakuza into the international news. Five Goto-gumi soldiers were arrested for the stabbing of the celebrated movie director Juzo Itami, whose Tampopo *and* A Taxing Woman *were international hits. His latest release was* Mimbo no Onna *(or, as it was called in America,* The Sweet Science of Japanese Extortion).*

To me it seemed to be another one of Itami's clever send-ups of Japanese society. But the film was released in a flurry of righteous public relations pushing the idea that Mimbo no Onna's *protagonist should inspire and instruct real people to fight against the real yakuza.*

"In the old days," Itami's press release stated, "the yakuza didn't terrorize katagi. *But now working stiffs are seen as just another resource for moneymaking. The idea of the chivalrous yakuza has disappeared. Nowadays everybody is afraid of the yakuza. People drop their eyes to avoid confronting a yakuza. Those forced to deal with yakuza have their pride trampled. I cannot forgive the yakuza for the way they threaten and humiliate society. Through* Mimbo no Onna, *I want people to see that they can fight the yakuza and win."*

Itami was jumped outside his Tokyo home. Television news crews captured live footage of the renowned and bloodied artist being wheeled into the hospital. After he was patched up, Itami, with his face dramatically bandaged, made another public plea to stop yakuza terror.

In Search of Mount Fuji

By positioning Mimbo no Onna *as a message film, Itami asked for trouble. In my eyes, his brilliantly cartoonish portrayals of yakuza made them such bumbling characters that it nullified any legitimate fight-the-mob theme. At that time, however, the antiyakuza laws and the police PR machine had already put the gangsters on the defensive. The movie ballyhoo had simply pushed the five Goto-gumi guys over the edge.*

When I call down to the Goto-gumi *honbun* (head office) in Shizuoka prefecture, I'm told that their boss, Goto-san, is out playing golf. I rent a car anyway and head south, naïvely confident that I can just drop in on the criminal shogun in one of the Yamaguchi-gumi's most lucrative territories. The yakuza have an old tradition called *isshuku ippan*, a kind of mutual aid agreement. A yakuza on the run from the law or even his own clan can present himself at the doorstep of any gang's headquarters for food, cash, and a place to crash.

One of the rules is that he is to show up only in daylight. At the entrance, the supplicant performs a highly stylized, formal greeting adapted from the samurai. He announces his name, his gang, and his boss's name. The greeting is executed with a wide stance and a half-squat as you open your jacket to show that you are unarmed. In yakuza flicks, this is a standard touch of exoticism. I've been told that this exaggerated ceremonial greeting has been replaced by the presentation of business cards. It is in this hopeful spirit that I drive down to Shizuoka with my notebook, my tape recorder, and my business cards.

The fact that heavy police surveillance is focused on the Goto-gumi and I have absolutely no connection to arrange a meeting with their reclusive boss doesn't deter me a bit. It's a pretty good indication of my mind-set at this time: Rent a car and stop in on the local yakuza warlord. My only firm rule of conduct is to never use names of past yakuza contacts to cajole or impress other gangsters.

A low haze blots out any chance to see Mount Fuji. I rarely get out of Tokyo and am dying to see some sights before Shizuoka. I stop for refreshments at a 7-Eleven in Yamato. Some teenagers are leaning against their cars in the parking lot. Out here in Kanagawa prefecture, on the south side of Yokohama, the kids can be rough around the edges. In a surprisingly harsh tone, two girls ask me for some of the Budweiser I'm loading into the back of my rented Mazda. Both the girls have blond streaks in their shoulder-length hair. They thank me for the beers with sweet smiles that display amazingly crooked teeth.

One of their boyfriends is sprawled on some carpet scraps in the bed of a lime green Toyoto pickup. He is looking pretty zoned out for 10 A.M. The girls hand the guy a beer and say something that makes him sit up and run his fingers through his thick black hair. He nods and raises a bandaged paw to thank me. On a whim, I cut off my engine and walk over to the kid. His hand is wrapped with white gauze and taped like a boxer's, with all his fingertips exposed except the last. Given my recent experience, I rashly presume that he has cut off his own pinky.

I ask if he is in the yakuza.

"No, no, no," he denies, with a slightly sheepish grin. One of the girls lights a joint and passes it to the other, who immediately draws hard on the weed, then bursts into uncontrollable giggles.

"He was trying to be a yakuza." She leans forward to maul the guy and spills beer in his lap. "Look!" The other girl joins in on the mock attack, reaching over his back, pulling up his T-shirt. They both squeal with glee as they expose his bruised and hairless torso, which is covered with dark blue striations.

Obviously this isn't the guy's first joint of the day. He starts jerking in a laughing fit as he twists compliantly to show me his boney back. The design is just an outline, the initial step of a full-body yakuza tattoo. It features an apparent portrait of Buddha and doesn't look half bad. I can visualize it filled in with the luscious reds and blues that make yakuza tattoos wonderfully distinct from anything you would ever see in the West. Mocking the dry responsible tone an adult might use to advise a dropout to finish school, I tell him to go ahead and have his body completely defiled.

My ironic tone escapes the tipsy girls, who berate me for try-ing to push the young wretch over the line. I smile and say that I think yakuza are cool.

"No! Yakuza bad, bad, bad!" one of the girls barks at me in English, like I must be confused. They don't figure me as the kind of idiot who finds the yakuza interesting. Only marginally employed social rejects buy into that bullshit. Apparently, that's exactly what the guy is. He takes a big hit from the joint as the more-coherent girl proceeds to tell me how he almost lost his pinky.

This guy, Toru, was in a bosozoku motorcycle gang that acted (as they normally do) as a minor league for the local yakuza pow-ers. He's no macho man, the girl insists, and he just smiles dopily as if to confirm the assessment. The girl explains that two weeks into his yakuza apprenticeship, Toru knew he wasn't up to its rig-ors. When he told his oyabun that he wanted to quit, the boss suggested he get tattooed "to feel more a part of the life." The boss even paid the tattoo master to begin the forty-week process. But the painful tattooing made Toru feel worse.

The girl steps down from the truck bed and pulls me away from Toru, who is now laid flat out with his head propped on a beige throw rug. He slides dark glasses over his bloodshot eyes and seems to be staring into the sun, which is beginning to burn through the overcast morning.

"Toru's mother kicked him out of the house," the girl contin-ues. "He stayed with me for a while. Then, about a week ago some yakuza soldiers kicked in the door of my apartment.

"They pulled Toru out of bed." The girl is almost in tears. "One of the men kept repeating, 'You can't quit yet!' They laid Toru flat on his stomach. Two men put their knees into his back as a third stood on his wrist and crushed Toru's pinky with the heel of his shoe. I heard the bones breaking. One man said, 'You're lucky we don't cut off your balls!' The other kept singing, 'You can't quit now! You can't quit now!' Finally they left saying 'Now you've quit!' . . . What a mess!"

The girl nods towards the pickup. "So, please, don't tell him to finish the tattoo." I apologize and give them a couple more beers from my trunk. "Bye, bye," they sing out as I belt up and merge onto the highway.

My first stop in Shizuoka prefecture is at a strip mall in regally named Fujinomiya. Again, I look for majestic Mount Fuji. I survey the sky over the parking lot but see nothing. Finally, I ask a passing cop for the specific direction where I might glimpse the great Fuji-san. He smiles and personally takes the blame for the low clouds hovering over the Kentucky Fried Chicken and blocking the more inspiring sight.

I seize the moment and casually ask the cop how to find the Goto-gumi headquarters. I only had a vague address gleaned from a tabloid newspaper story. He looks at me as if I couldn't be asking what I am asking, but then speaks slowly. I follow his explicit instructions, which take me a mile down the road, right to the front door of a store called something like Goto's Discount Outlet Store.

I decide to put another call through to Goto-san—the yakuza, not the clothier. This time the kobun who answers is less friendly. Before slamming down the phone, he grunts that his boss isn't in—and doesn't talk to the media, ever. Out of frustration more than hunger, I drive to a McDonald's. Two tables from me a man holds a local newspaper whose headline blares "YAKUZA WAR BATHES US IN BLOOD!"

I sip a soda and decide to wait awhile, then simply show up at the headquarters of this rather provincial gang. What is the worst that could happen? I might be turned away, but there won't be a scene. If nothing else, yakuza have good manners. I feel there's a good chance the boss will return and choose to meet me despite what his kobun said. Kobun are always thinking for their bosses, but they aren't always right.

After some prodding, the McDonald's manager reluctantly points me in the direction of the Goto-gumi complex. I drive away from the eyesore of the main drag and soon find myself in the verdant old Japan of my young dreams.

In Search of Mount Fuji

Rows of tea plants march across a terraced landscape. Elegant two-story Japanese-style homes big enough to hold a dozen Tokyo apartments sit on reclaimed farm land. I drive slowly across a series of small stone bridges over irrigation ditches, then—suddenly— jam on the brakes. I've stopped dead in the middle of a narrow country lane, utterly dumbfounded.

A vast white wall rises up, angling its way around the Goto-gumi compound. It looks twenty feet high and appears to completely enclose a good three acres of Fujinomiya real estate. Unlike the traditional Japanese walls built with rough stone and mortar, this wall is slickly high-tech. Peering up, I can discern sinister-looking electrified wires running along its top edge. There are four surveillance cameras pointing down at the garage door, which is, in fact, the entrance.

Looming over some sections of the wall, fancifully trimmed branches billow out like giant bonsai. These trees are dominated by the institutional bulk of a multistoried gray-beige building. A turretlike enclosure, rising above the flat roof, seems a good place to be holed up ready to repel any attack. How did the local officials abide this outrageous display of criminal wealth and power?

With its grandeur and arrogance, the Goto-gumi headquarters would make an appropriate hall of fame or shrine to the Japanese underworld. Its location in Shizuoka prefecture, at the foot of Mount Fuji near the city of Shimizu—of Jinrocho no Shimizu— makes it the ancestral home of all yakuza. A more reverential pilgrim-yakuza might genuflect at this underworld cathedral. I simply shiver. The fortress of Goto-gumi doesn't seem to share the mythic humility of old Jinrocho. Isshuku ippan seems unlikely. Two scowling men in golf jackets suddenly step from the shadows of the wall into the street where I'm leaning against my car dashboard, trying to fit the entire building into my camera viewfinder. I decide against the photograph and the free meal and the impromptu visit. I smile as I drive away, just in case, and wave back with a dumb tourist grin. Maybe I should have sent a letter of introduction.

FIREPOWER AND ICE

After bolting from the unhospitable Goto-gumi headquarters, I made another phone call to a friendlier contact in the area. At his suggestion I then went to the beach. Although the shoreline of Shizuoka prefecture is revered and the afternoon was hot, the Shimizu City beach was deserted. It was a Friday, a workday, when every good Japanese was busy looking busy, so the beach was empty.

Almost as empty were the pleasingly quaint beach pavilions, constructed of bamboo and palm fronds, which shaded straw mats and a cluster of low tables. At one table, three richly tanned surfer-girls-cum-waitresses were killing time gossiping and smoking, and waiting for the day's first customer. Unnoticed, I waited to be it. Only when the six-foot, high-cheekboned, ruddy skinned Taro Mura joined me did the girls stop their yakking and look at my table.

I had met Taro the year before when he was to be the star in a magazine story that fell through. Taro was then wrestling with the idea of committing his life to the yakuza.

"Yeah," Taro grunts. "I'm now an official yakuza, tattoos and all."

Yakuza talk in grunts. A grunt for yes, a grunt for no, a grunt for maybe, a grunt for fuck off, a grunt for anything. Taro grunts like a typical Japanese gangster, but he doesn't look like one. His

44

black hair is cut in a decidedly preppie mode, short on the sides with a big shock always falling in his eyes. In a nation where physical attractiveness usually decides your fate, Taro's looks could have given him unlimited marriage possibilities—if only he had finished college and wasn't "self-employed." Insurmountable *ifs* in the *Ozzie and Harriet* world of mainstream Japan. Another *if:* He's thinking of marrying Michiko—if he can resist the temptation of making her an AV (adult video) porn star.

"AV is such easy money," Taro wryly admits between swigs of Budweiser. "I recruit film school guys who do better work than the slobs other yakuza producers dig up. The college kids are lots cheaper. Paying the tuna, the main 'actress,' is the biggest cost, but if I used Michi . . . " Taro sighs. His long-legged girlfriend returns with three more beers balanced on her Louis Vuitton wallet. Then he laughs and whispers to me, "No, no, no! Guns and speed are my specialties."

Ironically, Taro met Michiko on the hotel-room set of a hardcore porno video where she was about to make her debut. But, before the camera rolled, Taro had fallen for her. It set him back around six thousand dollars to buy her way out of the production.

Although he was once a romantic, Taro is now pure yakuza. He makes you forget that this is a nation of early-rising, late-working hypercommuters. He's his own man—one who sleeps late, talks tough, and struts around in flashy warm-up suits. But, when his boss orders him to, say, beat the shit out of some poor slob who is six hours late with an eighty-dollar loan payment, he responds with merciless cruelty.

"I'm surprised you tried to meet Goto-san." Taro smiles, sipping a beer. "You must be insane. That's a really crazy gang. They even keep a pet grizzly bear on their property! The huge bear runs free inside those walls. I bet the animal does more for their security than that big wall and electric wire!" Taro laughs and orders another beer. He tells me he was going up to Tokyo that evening on business, and, if I cared to, I could follow his motorcycle in my rental car. "You can meet a lion instead of a bear!" he says cryptically.

There are many hours to kill before Taro's assault on Tokyo, so we go back to his apartment. Michiko steps out onto the studio's narrow terrace, to gather the laundry hanging from a circular plastic rack. Her long wet hair has left a dark patch on the back of her blue T-shirt. The studio has been thoroughly cleaned and the clothes washed; steam billows from the electronic rice cooker.

Since I first met him, Taro has followed through on his promise to officially join the local branch of the Yamaguchi-gumi. Although he has brought himself to tattoo part of his once-perfect body, he hasn't followed through on his promises to Michiko to stop dealing *shabu* (crystal methamphetamine, ice, also called just *shab*). And Taro doesn't want to marry until he has given up dealing; it is as high-risk an operation as there is in Japan. The penalties for drug dealing are insanely harsh. "I'd rather get busted for murder," Taro says with all seriousness.

Shabu has a notorious history in Japan. In the thirties, the government manufactured it to be pumped into the bloodstream of the frontline soldiers who were annexing Korea and Manchuria. And, during World War II, the manic warrior spirit encountered by American troops wasn't just for love of the emperor. A hearty dose of shabu was often dissolved in the sake stoically imbibed by kamikaze pilots before their one-way missions. After the war, shabu's invigorating powers were harnessed to help workers rebuild the destroyed infrastructure of the nation.

Today there is no sector of Japanese society that doesn't pull its weight in shabu consumption. Businessmen, politicians, housewives, laborers, students, entertainers, cabbies, pachinko players, and yakuza themselves love the stuff. Supplying the needs of those seven hundred thousand–plus shabu freaks accounts for half of all yakuza income.

Taro first encountered shabu in his college dorm. In Japan, even more than in the United States, college time is playtime. The constant rigors of cramming for the competitive tests to get into the right grade schools, the best high school, and the elite college are over. A corporate future is now a given. Living away from home in the big city with time on one's hands, there is nothing pressing to do but get high.

Most adult shabu heads cook the crystals in water and shoot it mainline. Taro has heard of housewives who skin-pop by inserting the syringe needle into their fingertips beneath their lacquered nails to hide the prick marks. For a more euphoric effect, most collegians smoke it off foil. For a speedier rush, they chop the shab and snort it like cocaine. A half-inch line can get a sluggish student through the most tedious morning lectures.

"It's too painful to sniff regularly," says Taro, who now abides by the don't-smoke-the-product policy of successful crack dealers. In his sophomore year, Taro was seriously into smoking shab but got tired of paying the dorm connection, a tough-talking girl who hung around giving everyone the hard sell and lousy prices. "Deciding to take over her territory at the university was the first idea I had ever initiated on my own . . . and I was pretty ruthless in its execution." He smiles, then flips some hair out of his eyes.

Taro started buying shabu in bulk from a young yakuza he knew who worked in a pachinko parlor near the campus. The yakuza had no connection with the enterprising girl on campus. In fact, when he got wind of this unconnected female dealer, he was happy to help Taro move in on the territory. Between the metallic cacophony of the pachinko machines and the constant wail of loudspeakers blasting tunes like the "Theme from Rocky" and "The Notre Dame Fight Song," the noise in these joints numbs the brain. A pachinko parlor will often feature additional floors stocked with one-armed bandits and electronic blackjack. Won tokens and accumulated pachinko balls are exchanged for cheap prizes like cigarettes or candy. These are again traded for cash at a nearby yakuza-protected shop, a drugstore, or even a sushi restaurant. Pachinko junkies include kimonoed grannies, tranquilized housewives, truant salarymen, and pachinko pros—shady zombies who make their living playing the game. The fuel for a pachinko pro's monotonous ten-hour day is often shabu. The source of this fuel is often a chimpira, a neophyte yakuza for whom working the pachinko floor is a common first job. Dressed in a bow tie, a tux-edo shirt, and polyblend slacks, this entry-level yakuza will greet customers, make change, unstick machines, and deal shabu. While many pachinko operations have no yakuza ties, all have regulars for whom shabu is the name of the game.

"From the initial ten grams I bought, I made around thirty small packets and gave them away," Taro recalls. "After that bit of advertising, everyone in the dorm came to me. It was so easy. As shabu can't really be cut, a dealer's profit is earned by simply break-ing the crystals up, repackaging, and reselling. "After the first time," Taro says, "I never needed any front money. I'd get the stuff on consignment and settle once a week."

One evening the boyfriend of the girl dealer confronted Taro in the dorm bathroom. The guy got tough, threatening to pummel Taro and then call the police. "It was strange," says Taro. "When he said 'police,' I exploded. I tossed the guy to the tile floor, straddled him, then punched him in the face three or four times, but that hurt my hand! So then I grabbed a can of shaving cream and jammed it into his mouth." Taro shot the foam down the boyfriend's throat until the stuff spurted out of his nose like white worms. The cream muffled the guy's cries for help. Then Taro dragged him to a toilet stall.

"I squatted on his chest and wedged his slippery head between my thighs." Taro laughs. "Then, with both my hands, I grabbed the bottom of the stall door and whacked his head. *Bang! Bang! Bang!* It was great! Then the guy went silent, but he was breathing, still blowing bits of shaving cream out of his nose and mouth.

"I got up to rinse my face," Taro continues. "Then I kicked him twice and ordered him to stand up—and he did! I was pretty surprised and disappointed." Taro claps his hands, laughing. "Oh, he would go on to get, like, nine stitches and spend three days in the hospital, but at the time, he looked too healthy to me. I was too fucking exhausted to fight anymore, so I ordered him to bow and beg my forgiveness. He fell to his knees and touched his head to the floor, resting it on the back of his bloody hands. I thought he might choke to death before he finished his apology. I recall stepping between bloody puddles as I left the bathroom.

Firepower and Ice

"I keep thinking that the jerk absorbed ten years of my personal frustration." Taro finished out the school year with passing grades and $85,000 in five different bank accounts under five different names. (Japanese banks make up for their minuscule interest rates on saving accounts by not asking depositors nosey questions; the country is a virtual Switzerland.) These days Taro keeps seven accounts that total over $170,000. And that's not all from shabu. Like the yakuza itself, Taro is diversified and looking for new sources of income.

Taro grew up in Kawasaki, a grungy industrial city wedged between big-town Tokyo and affluent Yokohama. He broke his mother's heart when he dropped out of Tokyo's Komazawa University. It may also have hastened the demise of his blue-collar dad, who dropped dead of cardiac arrest at fifty-seven. Not that Taro often crossed paths with his "poppa," who was always busy putting in his mandatory overtime while Taro ran from public school to cram school to his own little study desk stuck in the corner of their three-room, company-sponsored apartment.

"It was all so meaningless." Taro sighs, a lament many Japanese men surely feel but cannot articulate. "All the studying and the money my parents paid out to cram schools, paying off my instructors to use their connections to land me in a good high school, then trying to get me into college. I really wasn't any smarter than anyone else, but I was tall and my mom's friends always said good-looking, so I was pushed. To get me to study more, they wouldn't allow me to play baseball in high school. Baseball was the one place where I was actually superior! I had talent and an aggressive spirit, but I was forced to burn up my energy preparing for tests to enter a world where I could never really excel. Does that make sense?

"I gave up baseball for what? Luckily I managed to surf for two summers. I invented a story about studying at a friend's house in a rich part of Yokohama," Taro remembers. "I knew my mother was too uptight to ever call the house of my 'wealthy' friend. So, for two summers in high school, I got to spend three days a week surfing at Shonan Beach. I claimed my suntan was from studying on my friend's rooftop garden! My mom said, 'Oh, how nice.' I later heard her boasting about it to the ladies."

Five years ago Taro left the urban squalor of the capital for Shimizu City near Shizuoka prefecture's beaches with their reputation for excellent surfing. But Taro rarely has time to don his wet suit. Instead he's preoccupied with his job as a high-speed delivery boy who rides the roads and expressways of Greater Tokyo consumed with the desire to take care of business quickly and quietly.

At around 2 A.M. Michiko wakes me from a nap that I began in the middle of some Jean-Claude Van Damme video. Taro popped in the movie after an elaborate sashimi dinner that Michiko prepared and served with the efficient elegance of a professional hostess. In my eyes Taro's home life seems so nice and quiet, so thoroughly conventional, it seems ludicrous that this is Japan's antisocial element. "With rebels like Taro, who needs model citizens?" I scribble in my notebook just as Taro emerges shirtless from the bathroom. Like a black and blue fungus, his newly minted tattoos envelop his shoulders and chest as if to claim Taro's soul for the forces of evil. Well, at the very least, the markings do say "ANTISOCIAL ELEMENT."

At 2:30 A.M., light from a three-quarter moon illuminates the driveway down which Taro pushes his 500 cc black customized Suzuki GSX racing bike. Taro digs American styles (he's wearing a white Brooks Brothers button-down beneath a red letterman's jacket) but draws the line at the Harley-Davidsons in vogue on Japanese streets. "I love the looks, but Harleys make too much noise." With respect for his sleeping neighbors, Taro rolls his bike up the block before donning a black Arai helmet and mounting the machine. He then reaches behind to adjust a piece of black electrical tape that changes the first digit on his plate from a 6 to an 8.

Taro turns the key and pushes an ignition button that rips a throaty blast through the still night. He flips down the visor, taps the bike in gear, and launches himself down the empty streets. I start my rented Mazda and follow at high-beams' distance. We are soon speeding northeast on Route 1, the banal modern name of what was the old Tokaido Highway, the ancestral route where the original yakuza plied their trades.

Reaching the outskirts of Yokohama, I follow Taro into a dark corner of a closed Mobil station. Nearby looms a huge nightclub that is popular with American GIs from Yokosuka Naval Base—and the Japanese girls who love them.

Taro and I take the long way around the disco's parking lot, which is jammed with the jacked-up pickups and tricked Camaros of the off-duty NCOs. It seems like half of the American car population of Japan is arrayed before me. All these wide-bodied, pastel-colored American muscle cars make it easy for Taro to find his man in the somber gray Nissan sedan. Casually Taro opens the back door and ducks his head in. Then he calls me up to the car where I'm instructed to stand right outside the Nissan while he takes care of business inside. Luckily I can make out their conversational jumble of Japanese and English, which now feels like my mother tongue.

A guy with a scrawny mustache and an almost platinum crew cut turns from behind the steering wheel to nod at Taro. A weathered-looking American man, about fifty, is slumped in the backseat. He calls himself the "Greaseman" and claims to be a civilian mechanic on the base. Whether the guy means Yokosuka Naval Base, Atsugi Air Force Base, or some other base, Taro doesn't know. Taro does know that Greaseman is certainly no active soldier—the guy's too fat and speaks Japanese too well.

Through the windows I can hear Taro tell the two that I am his friend, that I am an English teacher and certainly not an MP. With everyone assured and relaxed, Greaseman lifts a Converse shoe box from the car floor and places it between himself and Taro. Lifting off the top, Greaseman coyly reveals six boxes of Federal .9 mm cartridges. Taro nods in appreciation. Selling ammo has become Taro's fastest growth industry. Sure, trafficking guns in the underworld means even sweeter profits, but the downside is fifteen to life. Although hustling the cartridges is a kinder, gentler business, the thought of even a couple of years in Japanese prison keeps Taro extra careful.

That's why Taro buys such things from these gaijin. Though cheap Chinese pistols and ammo have been flowing steadily into Japan for the last few years, Taro doesn't like the risk inherent in dealing with crooked Taiwanese nationals and their Chinese-Japanese yakuza cousins. Like most Japanese, Taro possesses a strong distrust and contempt for other Asians, but from where I'm standing the paunchy Greaseman and his redneck buddy don't look like models of trustworthiness. In fact, they look like screwups personified. "At least I know they're definitely not police," Taro explains later. "And that's enough. And if they do fuck me over, they'd be easy to find." I have to agree. Greaseman looks like a bloated Jack Nicholson while the shocking white of the other's crew cut makes him an easy man to spot in Japan.

I can hear Taro's halting English.

"Ninety thousand yen?" Taro asks.

"Hai," grunts the Greaseman. "Just like last time." Taro fans out the nine bills and hands them to Greaseman.

"What's that in real money?" asks the crew cut in a too-loud Appalachian twang.

"Just about a grand," drawls the mechanic with no small amount of satisfaction.

"Ho-lee shit!" squeals the geek while banging the dashboard like a monkey. "Ho-lee shit!" And more banging.

This psycho celebratory outburst pisses off Taro. It's not just the noise or the unprofessional gloating, it's the rudeness. Taro hesitates before shaking Greaseman's extended hand.

"Thank you very much," Greaseman says in sparkling Japanese while pumping Taro's hand. But then, in English, more rudeness: "Still got all ten fingers, Slim?" I can only assume Greaseman is drunk.

Taro grunts. He tucks the box under his arm and reaches for the door.

"You a Japanese mafia?" the crew cut blurts before Taro can exit. "Mafia" is a loaded word. Taro turns square to Greaseman. The young Japanese gangster stares into the pale eyes of the mechanic. Then, in the low brutal voice of a Japanese drill sergeant, Taro barks, "Greaseman-san, do not bring this idiot again, or our business together is finished." He might have said "you are finished." Whatever the exact words, the threat was heard.

"I understand," Greaseman mumbles in English, followed by a whispered Japanese apology. Taro and Greaseman get out of the car. Taro nods to me before tucking the shoe box of ammo under his arm. Without looking back he returns through the maze of American automobiles to the Mobil station. The floodlights of the parking lot make the slumping Greaseman appear even older. I can't imagine who he really is or how his life has brought him to this spot in his late fifties. I'm standing beside Greaseman as he folds up his bills and tucks them in his shirt pocket. He runs a sweaty palm over his balding pate and takes a deep breath. He asks me for a cigarette. I tell him that I can't help him.

"Well, son, will you do me a favor?" the man pleads.

"Sure, what?" I cough in his whiskey breath.

"Tell your buddy about the kid," he says earnestly. "I needed a ride. I had to bring the kid . . . just this once, for a ride. . . . I just needed a ride."

If I stay on to yak with Greaseman, I will never catch Taro. But with my rental hot on his knobby tires we roar through Kawasaki over the Tokyo city line. At the first red light in the capital Taro lifts his visor, revealing a grinning face.

"Look!" Taro yells, and points. I follow his finger to the concrete police box attached to the Shinagawa Station. Behind the large window, the sleeping policeman is backlit like a museum display. In his gray uniform and crooked cap, this snoozing member of the Tokyo Metropolitan Police appears no less ferocious than and just about as helpful as when he is awake. Sleeping cops are common. Tokyo cops work long shifts when they patrol the city's mean streets on three-speed bicycles making sure that all is well. (Invariably, they find that it is.) In a greater city of twelve million kindred souls, these misnamed "Mr. Walkabouts" seem to relish nothing more than stopping suspicious cyclists and giving dubious directions to lost tourists. If I had been feeling a bit like a lost tourist down in Shizuoka and Yokohama, following Taro along familiar Tokyo arteries has brought on a second wind; I will stay with him until the evening plays itself out.

It's around 3:30 A.M. and only empty taxis are cruising Tokyo's quiet streets. Taro weaves his Suzuki in and out of the orange and green cabs until hitting Shinjuku. Once a dull residential area, Shinjuku is now Tokyo's most dynamic government, business, and entertainment district. On its west side, beyond the rail station, skyscrapers are bunched around the new and massive city hall. With its two mighty cathedral-like towers rising into the night, the structure designed by Kenzo Tange reeks with all the ego and ambition of Tokyo itself. Some hate it but I love this Notre Dame on steroids.

Taro cruises along Meiji Avenue, a main artery arching through the gleaming districts of Shibuya and Shinjuku, ending up in Tokyo's dreariest neighborhoods. Indeed the impoverished and aging laborers living in the slums of Taito ward know of modern city hubs like Shinjuku and Shibuya only through secondhand accounts and newspapers. (I've met many of these ancient and forgotten men; they can't live in the modern Tokyo they built. They have no need for anything Shinjuku or Shibuya has to sell, while the vast rude hordes of affluent young shoppers would terrify these once-fearless builders of expansion bridges and elevated highways.) Besides Meiji Avenue, the only connection between Shinjuku's gloss and the slum's grime is in my head.

Computerized billboards dance colorfully over the closed stores and hangouts of Tokyo's affluent new breed. This commercial side of the Shinjuku Station looks like an elaborate soundstage for a *Terminator* movie set well into the next century.

In front of the Kinokuniya bookstore, Taro hops off his bike and waves me into an empty parking space. We stroll until we find a pay phone. He wants his elders to know that he is bringing a gaijin to their meeting. A giant video screen high above our heads reruns sumo highlights. Monstrous near-naked bodies grapple in one of the last arenas of machismo left in this constricted society. Taro picks up on my thoughts: "You like sumo?"

"I *love* sumo," I admit.

"It makes sense," he nods. "Sumo and yakuza are the last real men in Japan . . . I hope this country never has to fight another war."

I leave my car and get on the bike behind Taro. In a few seconds we're out of state-of-the-art Shinjuku snaking through "Piss Alley," a well-named maze of narrow wooden bars, stand-up ramen and T-shirt shops. With the wind whipping my hair in my face and the engine noise jarring my brain, I lose my bearings in this familiar area. Taro slows to a glide as we pass beneath a train trestle where a dozen homeless men sleep on the cool sidewalk. Their dirty, creased, white-whiskered faces appear strangely content, a condition perhaps explained by the empty containers of Ozeki One Cup, a cheap vending-machine sake, strewn about.

Taro picks up the pace, soon plunging us through the greasy puddles of a long passageway, behind a row of bars, porno theaters, and massage parlors. We stop suddenly as a trio of hefty rats scramble across the headlight beam and dive into a mound of plastic garbage bags. Taro parks the bike beneath a glowing paper lantern with the symbol for some kind of bird. Taro retrieves the Converse shoe box from the bike's storage well and stows his helmet. He smooths his hair, nods at me to do the same and takes a few deep breaths of the rancid air. Somehow my confusion about how to get back to the Mazda makes me insecure and tense, very tense.

An unlocked back door opens to a deserted ground-floor bar and a dimly lit stairway. The worn steps creak loudly as I follow Taro's penny loafers up to the second floor. He knocks four times on a cheap hollow door. A grunt comes from the other side. A teenager opens the door and bows his punch-permed head. We slip off our shoes and follow the kid across the tatami-matted anteroom. As a stained shoji paper door slides open, I feel like we are walking into a scene from any of the yakuza films I have ingested in recent years.

I love the utilitarian nature of a traditional-type tatami room. By day, it can serve as an office or drinking salon and, by night, a bedroom or hideout. Although I would later learn that the teenage chimpira was ensconced here, at the moment the room is a yakuza hangout for as long as his superiors want to stay. The two yakuza, who have been oyabun and kobun for twenty years, sit cross-legged on opposite sides of a low table. Above, a circular fluorescent tube glows, casting an anemic light on a large bottle of Sapporo beer and two bowls of polished black and white stones beside the game board. The game is go, a slow, complex game that seems almost as out of place as I do. Bluish cigarette smoke rises from a cluttered ashtray and hangs heavy in the unventilated room. Behind the men, two young Thai women dressed in cheap pinkish cocktail dresses steadily fan the backs of the players. Their exotic and expressionless faces hint of neither boredom nor amusement. I imagine that this mindless employment beat the hell out of their other option—fucking Iranian laborers and drunk salarymen.

The older man's white hair is slicked straight back from a smooth and shiny forehead. The smokey lenses of his wire-framed glasses hide any expression, although he greets Taro with a friendly grunt. He is an old-guard yakuza underboss in another Tokyo association, which I'll refer to as the "Kanto Alliance." He is also head of his own gang, which keeps small offices in Nakano-ward and Toshima-ward. His name is Lion and he's got a hard-ass reputation. But Taro says he's never seen that side of him.

My introduction is acknowledged with cool indifference by the men and curious glances from the girls. I nod twice and slump down near the door.

Lion wears only a white loincloth that twists around his waist, but he's hardly naked. The skin of his sagging breasts and belly is completely overlaid with dark tattoos of chrysanthemums and a bloodred carp (the latter is for bravery, as a captured carp never squirms on the cutting board). The name of a boss long since murdered is immortalized in Lion's cleavage. He isn't a tall man but possesses tremendous girth. I take Lion to be a graying late middle-aged man, yet (I am to learn) he is seventy-three. Lion's face is as smooth and fleshy as his stomach.

Lion also seems as calm and serene as the Buddha he resembles. Police crackdowns and gang wars, Lion has seen them all. He was born in the era of militarism and territorial expansion. He has smelled the charred devastation wrought by incendiary bombs. He survived to witness the economic miracle that peaked in the late eighties and seems untroubled by the recession of the nineties.

"Mura-san, please sit," Lion says to Taro, who has been standing all along. As exalted as Lion is, the old man is always respectful of young Taro. This yakuza elder has been in the racket long enough to recognize genuine talent and intelligence, characteristics often lacking in the yakuza rank and file. Taro relaxes and slides the shoe box under the wooden table. The chimpira scurries in with small glasses for Taro and me, and then, almost daintily, fills them with beer.

The other loined-clothed yakuza is a tautly muscular man named Honda. His massive back is tattooed with a traditional geisha print—except that her kimono spreads open to reveal untypically large, blue-nippled breasts. Rivulets of flowers and carp begin at Honda's shoulders and wind around his arms down to his wrists. He looks innately dangerous.

Honda's lean muscularity belies his fifty-plus years. His large head and frizzy hair give him the look of an Asian James Caan. A stubbly mustache and unshaven chin hint at an indifference to appearance. A curved scar on his left cheek adds to the creepy aura of a man who belongs off the streets.

Lion directs a belching grunt at the Thais, who stand and shuffle into the next room. A TV blares momentarily.

"Mura-san, always dressing like a high-class executive on a golf trip," Honda jokes (without smiling), before punching Taro's firm bicep and roughly pulling out his shirttail. The teasing gangster examines Taro's minimally tattooed back and grimaces. "But walking around with those half-assed designs! You make good money but you're still a baby stinking of piss!"

"Leave him," grunts Lion. "Let the kid look how he wants. He's got a little class! More than you ever had. And Mura-san knows how to conduct business." Lion turns to Taro. "I value your resource-fulness in these difficult times, with the cops hanging all over us."

"The laws and the shootings," Taro adds, while sucking air through his teeth in a customary Japanese show of concern.

"I think that's all over now," Lion says assuredly. "This kind of thing has to happen every few years. Though it went a little out of control this time."

"It was wild down by me," Taro adds.

"Well, you weren't hurt, Mura dear," jibes Honda. "So don't talk about that crap. We have some real business here and now."

"Mura-san," adds Lion in his gruff but sympathetic voice. "I know you have officially joined the group in Shimizu. That's good even if it's not my gang. It shows you're growing up. But you must get married! You're not a bosozoku anymore! How will you be promoted if you're still living like a child?"

Honda grins sardonically. "Yeah, get married already!"

Taro grunts and nods. Honda refills the glasses of Lion and Taro. Taro pours for Honda before kindly scuttling across the room to top off my glass. They raise their beers to toast *"Kampai!"*

With a wave of Lion's hand, the game board is cleared by the teenager, who slides the door closed behind himself.

Honda has removed a box of the .9 mm cartridges from the shoe box. "Beautiful," he sighs, and nods to me. "We really need these now." With that I realize he's under the impression that I'm the source of the lethal hardware.

Honda continues. "Americans can't make anything anymore but bullets and guns." Then he lifts a Beretta pistol from his side. I don't say anything in rebuttal, especially as I'm sure that the gun is Italian.

"Don't underestimate the Americans," says the older man, wagging a finger. "They won't be down for long. They're special people capable of anything, they're just not . . . well organized."

I nod in appreciation.

58

Firepower and Ice

"After the war, the kindness of the Americans helped rebuild straight businesses and our trades," Lion continues. "MacArthur let us crush the Communists."

Honda grunts deferentially—or perhaps it is impatience with an old story. He reaches out and hands Taro a white sock bulging with the expected gem-sized rocks of shabu. (Taro senses that the sock's weight is up a bit from the last time; he also feels some paper inside.) Taro nods to each man, and then quickly finishes his beer. He is clearly anxious to hit the road. Taro prefers to have the cover of night to run his contraband. (As there is no daylight saving in Japan, the summer sun appears before five o'clock.)

Taro rises and bows deeply, with the sock discreetly cupped in his hand. I don't want to go. I'm thinking that I may never see these fascinating men again. I'm thinking that for the rest of my days I may never be so intimate with such hard-core yakuza. So far it's the absolute highlight of my underworld peregrinations. But I stand with Taro, grunt my thanks, and woozily follow Taro down the stairs to the cool air. Once outside, he immediately opens the sock and fishes out a brown envelope. He rips it open to find that Lion has tipped him the yen equivalent of three thousand dollars. Then he immediately shoves the sock into a first-aid kit beneath the seat.

"That was some show up there, no?" Taro looks at me with an ironic smile. "Those two belong in a museum."

He rechecks the black tape on his license plate as he tucks some loose hair away from his eyes.

"You sure you want to walk?" he asks, grinning at my strange notion of strolling back through the dirty streets in the predawn hours. Then, with a shrug and a mock salute, he starts the Suzuki and gives it a few test revs. He roars down the alley and leans into a quick left turn, leaving me with the exhaust fumes and an incorrect recollection of where to find my Mazda.

THE NEW RECRUIT

I couldn't wait to meet up again with Lion and Honda. Taro had given me the men's telephone numbers, telling me to take my chances. Before anything could be arranged with those characters, a call came to my office at around noon.

"This is Takayama," said the voice of the legendary yakuza godfather. "I have read your proposal, and you should come as soon as possible if you need so much time with us."

This news that I would have total access to one of Japan's oldest and most-storied yakuza gangs brought tears to my eyes. Lion and Honda would have to wait. The next day I bought a platform ticket for ¥140 that allowed me to steal away on the bullet train (saving about four hundred dollars). In about three hours I was in the Kansai region, western Japan, talking my way past the ticket taker at Kyoto Station and out onto the streets of the ancient capital, presently ruled by the Aizu Kotetsu yakuza gang.

I had moved into an old house in a north Kyoto neighborhood near where the Takano River flows into the Kamo River. My first meeting with Takayama was at five o'clock at a fancy steak house in the Gion entertainment district. It was an early time for dinner, but when I arrived I understood. The doors of the steak house were guarded by two large men in suits and sunglasses. A third greeted me and led me through an empty ground floor, then upstairs to a private dining room where the gray-haired Takayama sat across from another bodyguard. I bowed and thanked him. It was nothing, the boss said, "I hope you like steak."

The New Recruit

I was grateful to be in the good graces of such a man. But to say Takayama was out of touch with the young men of his gang is to imply that he even gives a damn about them. When I mentioned I wanted to meet some young men of Aizu Kotetsu, I was introduced to subbosses in their late forties. But another lucky break came in the hefty form of Hara-san, boss of Hara-gumi, one of Aizu Kotetsu's largest subgangs.

Because Hara had spent most of the last year in prison, he had no trouble remembering our interview and the photo I had taken with him. Hara-san understood my need to balance the time I spent with a top oyabun like Takayama and that spent with a beginner. In fact, Hara said, a new Hara-gumi recruit would be arriving from Okinawa on the next day.

"Why not go ahead and meet him?" Hara suggested. "You can see how long he lasts before he runs back home to his mommy!"

Upon his release from juvenile detention, Koji's beleaguered mother ordered him to call local hood-made-good, Hara-san, in far-off Kyoto. A lot of old folks in Koji's working-class Naha neighborhood remembered the hell-raising Hara. As a burly violent kid, he had once been shot in the leg by American soldiers while trying to rip off an army barracks. That happened back in '72, the last year of the American occupation of Okinawa.

Later, at eighteen, Hara was freelancing on the losing side of a Naha turf war. He rashly took it upon himself to blast three slugs into the chest of a gang boss. Without an affiliation, Hara was convicted of murder and shipped off to serve a ten-year sentence in a notoriously squalid prison near Hiroshima. As the jail's youngest con, Hara suffered at the hands of brutal inmates and guards. Eventually, though, Hara made the proper yakuza connections—and future commitments—that ensured his survival inside the walls. One of those connections, a yakuza enforcer from Kyoto, was waiting for him outside the gates on the day of his release. It was the beginning of a new career in a new city. Now, many years later, it's Hara's policy to give any kid from his old Okinawa stomping grounds a second chance in his own Kyoto gang.

* * *

I am with a tall, olive-complexioned Hara-gumi man named Ken waiting for Koji at Osaka Airport. Ken, twenty-seven years old, checks the snapshot of this newest Okinawa recruit; a plumpish baby face stares back at him from under bushy brows. We circulate twice around the busy concourse before Ken spots Koji. Koji's showy crew cut and the colorful, old-fashioned bundle containing his few possessions, give him the aura of a bumpkin. Koji bows deeply and earnestly thanks Ken for waiting. Ken mumbles a short greeting to Koji, takes his bundle, and leads him to the baggage carousel. Ten minutes pass before Koji admits that the bundle is his only piece of luggage. Koji accepts Ken's explanation that I am the "boss's friend."

The early evening moon is blurred by the Osaka smog. Koji stares out of the passenger window of Ken's white Nissan Crown. He mistakes a huge oil storage tank for the famous Koshien Baseball Stadium, where the summer baseball tournament would soon begin. Beyond the highway railing, there is a forbidding landscape of huge industrial structures. Koji says, "This looks like America."

"America?" Ken repeats. "This looks more like Japan to me now than Mount Fuji."

"Mount Fuji?" asks Koji. "That's near Tokyo, right?"

"Of course, Tokyo," responds Ken, now easing off the gas and bringing the car to a slow stop behind a Honda Del Sol. The taillights of the stalled rush-hour traffic disappear into the dark horizon. Ken points eastward where the glittering Osaka monoliths can now be seen rising into the sky. Ken screws up the names of the major buildings himself. Actually, Ken doesn't get out of nearby Kyoto enough to know Osaka's landmarks or even how to get around here without checking a map.

"Kyoto's not like this," Ken admits. "Osaka and Kobe together have over ten million people. Kyoto's less than two million. So it's not so . . . much."

"I think Naha has only two hundred thousand."

"You'll get to learn Kyoto like you know Naha," Ken assures Koji.

The New Recruit

"I don't know," says Koji. "What's Hara-san like? He didn't sound like a yakuza on the phone."

"He's yakuza, but not like in the movies or television," Ken says solemnly. "He's hot and cold. He's relaxed like your best friend, he doesn't bark like a TV yakuza, but he's tougher than any oyabun in Kansai . . ."

The brick headquarters of the Hara-gumi has the dimensions of a Manhattan brownstone. There are four floors, but the first is a wide garage whose door is habitually left wide open. Inside this gaping cave stand a half-dozen motor scooters in various states of disrepair beside two hefty, Harley-style Japanese motorcycles. There's barely enough room for Hara's big black Benz. Outside, beside the front door, is a clean, square spot on the wall. It's the only evidence of an infamous plaque. For years, the implications of the Hara-gumi nameplate taunted the passing citizenry: "HERE IS A YAKUZA DEN, A CLUB FOR BOYS WHERE THEY'LL BE HARDENED AND TRAINED TO BE PROFESSIONAL CRIMINALS. THIS IS EVERY JAPANESE MOTHER'S NIGHT-MARE. . . . " Though the name plaque is gone, the security camera bolted above the front door remains as a subtler sign of what lurks within.

Koji looks tense as he slips off his sneakers and follows Ken up the Hara-gumi stairway for the first time. Though Kyoto is less oppressive than Osaka, the nightlife throngs we passed in Gion were imposing. Koji admits that he feels like turning around, but he has nowhere to go.

In the main room, a kobun sleeps head down on the reception desk, oblivious to the tiny closed-circuit TV screens beside him and the big Panasonic running baseball highlights at the far end of the room. The six guys who currently live in the headquarters are zonked out on old futons. Five of them are former Okinawans. Ken digs out another of these hand-me-down mattresses from a large drawer. He casually throws it at Koji's feet and says, with no apparent irony, "Welcome home."

There is no set routine for the 128 kobun in the Hara-gumi, most of whom work their jobs in packs of 2 to 4; 9 "executives" are like "young bosses" in other gangs. The majority of the kobun check in with their boss only every two or three days. Some never stop by until their name comes up for "office duty" three or four days each month. Office duty is a time to update the boss and perform various cleaning projects. These jobs may last an hour or two before the headquarters reverts to its customary mode as the laziest frat house in Japan. The big TV goes back on—the daytime soaps, cartoons, and samurai dramas (often starring the protoyakuza, Jinrocho of Shimizu). Reading matter consists of two-inch-thick comic books and a bunch of the men's magazines that report the yakuza news with voyeuristic glee.

Until the office manager receives the call signaling Hara's impending arrival, the office of the third-largest, but toughest subgang of the Aizu Kotetsu organization has an ambience of carefree relaxation. Sometimes Hara wakes up at his own apartment and sometimes at his girlfriend's place. If there is no rain, Hara often walks to a Chinese restaurant for an early lunch. Then he calls the office manager to tell him where the designated driver should meet him.

On his third day in Kyoto, Koji is thrown the car keys. Hara has requested that the new guy drive the Benz to the public bathhouse—and bring the American. Hara, the boss who has yet to speak directly to Koji, is ready to be picked up.

In the American Mafia, a boss's driver is often his right-hand man. This easy arrangement is anathema to a yakuza boss. In contrast to mainstream Japan's vaunted teamwork, yakuza gangs are largely personality cults. Such oyabun aloofness has ramifications all the way down the hierarchy from the top oyabun to the lowest recruit. One practical result is that Hara (like many oyabun) will be chauffeured by an inexperienced youngster who drives like shit.

After a few wrong turns, Koji comes to the Tony Lama boot shop, where he makes the turn that leads to the bathhouse. Hara is standing there in a gray suit, with the buttons of his doublebreasted blazer undone and his tie in hand. He is staring up at smoky clouds, perhaps assessing the odds of his afternoon golf lesson getting rained out. Koji is tense. As he jams the car into PARK, I notice that the back of his neck is slick with sweat. He looks unsure if he should get out and run around the Benz to open the door for Hara. I suggest that he should. An excruciating few seconds churn by as Koji gropes with his door latch. Rounding the fender to the passenger side of the car, he pulls himself up to watch the back door slam.

"It's okay," says Hara, interrupting Koji's string of apologies. "I open my own door unless it's raining and I've forgotten an umbrella."

"I often forget umbrellas," stammers Koji, as he reacquaints himself with the dashboard controls.

"Koji," whispers Hara, like a patient driving instructor. "Relax."

The car lurches forward. Koji, after a wrong-way encounter with a one-way street, manages to get us headed in the right direction.

To Koji, Hara must look like some kind of Mongol, not a fellow Okinawan. He is a stocky man with hairy forearms and big linebacker's hands. His head is nearly clean-shaven, with only a shadowy fuzz to protect him from the sun. His eyes are big, round, and expressive. He also has an ironic extroverted nature, so rare in a Japanese man.

Interestingly, Hara has honed a hip sartorial image. He favors baggy pants, two-tone boat shoes, loose designer shirts with bold coloring. The quick-to-flash grin beneath the round pate gives his face a more lighthearted appearance than his true personality warrants.

Hara, at thirty-six, became Aizu Kotetsu's youngest underboss. Few veterans are above flashing battle scars or waxing poetic about past battles in the underworld trenches. But Hara doesn't talk about yesterday's blood, he's ready to go today, now! Smooth-running business deals bore Hara. Is anybody screwing us over? Is anyone late with a payment? Then it's time to back a garbage truck through the debtor's front door. Or dangle some double-crosser by his ankles over the rushing waters of the Kamo River. Hara's obvious glee is disconcerting.

As we drive past a 7-Eleven and a Lawson's convenience store, Hara tells me to go ahead and click on my tape recorder.

"If I wasn't the boss, nothing would keep me in check," declares Hara. "Last week I was involved in a land transfer deal where I had to sit quietly through a dull meeting with three katagi. One man had a bag with twenty-five thousand dollars sitting on the seat right beside him. If I wasn't a boss, I would have just grabbed the cash and maybe even shot those guys—hell, they were dirty anyway. But I'm in Aizu Kotetsu, so I've got to behave!"

"You hear that yakuza gangs keep bad kids off the streets," says Hara. "Well, it's true . . . If I wasn't tied down with the duties of a yakuza boss, I'd certainly be on the streets—and it wouldn't be kid's stuff." I believe him.

For most kobun, Hara explains, gang activity is not a twenty-four-hour, seven-day-a-week kind of thing. The early years are a time to keep busy, trying one's hand at different jobs and scams. The first step might be working the floor of a pachinko parlor meeting shadier citizens of the neighborhood. The pachinko job can spin off into petty loan-sharking or drug-dealing. Every oyabun appreciates an enterprising kobun. Even a living yakuza god like Takayama says the most lowly kobun can approach him for business advice.

"But I don't know what questions to ask!" says Hara. "I'm a terrible businessman!"

"Hara-gumi is one of the biggest in Aizu Kotetsu. We're definitely the toughest but, I'm sure, we're also the poorest!" Hara laughs. "If I liked hard work, then I wouldn't be a yakuza, what would be the point? I've rejected the world of the salaryman. I can never be legitimate in the eyes of the mainstream, so why should I bust my ass building some kind of financial empire?

"Some yakuza live like salarymen, and some are like cowboys," says Hara. "If a kobun has some crazy business idea, I'll always say, 'Try it!' Even if one of them wanted to become an artist, I'd say, 'Yes, go ahead!' We'll figure out how to open a gallery and sell the paintings one way or another. I think yakuza would like to do business the right way, but we don't know what the right way is!

The New Recruit

So we do what makes sense to us or seems easiest; the easier the better.

"In my gang, we're mostly Okinawans," says Hara. "So Kyoto people really look down on us. They look down on everybody, but especially us because we're yakuza from Okinawa! I love it.

"Most of my kobun come up from Naha because they have friends in Hara-gumi. Sometimes I get a call from a mother with a bad kid like Koji, or a cop asking me to pull some troublemaker off his beat. If a young guy's got some spunk, our society doesn't know what to do with him. In America, I'm sure, this spirited type of kid could find a straight job. In Japan we take energetic kids and make them into criminals!" Hara sighs. I wonder if it's for himself or the newcomer Koji or both. For once, I don't ask.

As we pass Morinomachi Station, I notice a used-car dealer selling BMWs and Mercedes-Benzes exclusively. I ask Hara if they are the repossessed toys of hard-luck yakuza in these recessionary days. "No." Hara smiles. "All these cars probably belonged to citizens. Many small businessmen used their legal possessions, like their stores or homes, as collateral for easy loans. The payments were high and couldn't be maintained when the economy died.

"A lot of silly people acted like big shots during the bubble." Hara slowly shakes his glistening head.

AIZU KOTETSU: THE KYOTO CLAN

The cloudy days have prevented the heat of this Kyoto summer from reaching its usual notorious intensity. Old ladies in kimonos shuffle down the twelve-hundred-year-old avenues without their parasols. Opened windows suffice as air conditioners. It is a good time to be in town.

Kyoto was spared the bombing and devastation of other main cities during the war. Initially, the American War Department's appreciation of Kyoto's special place in the Japanese soul made it a likely strategic target. Luckily, that same awareness became the overriding reason they chose to spare the city. Kyoto's spirit of antiquity can still be found in well-preserved historical districts. The newer residential areas are divided between the upscale bedroom communities of Osaka executives and the isolated enclaves of the working class. Compared to Tokyo's subtler gradations of good and bad neighborhoods, Kyoto's poorest districts are uniformly miserable.

In this particular Kyoto neighborhood, cars are parked along the streets at odd angles, even pushing onto the sidewalks. This anarchic parking is the unique privilege of the *burakumin* underclass who live around here. The burakumin caste was invented hundreds of years ago when Japan was officially stratified into classes. The burakumin, people who worked with leather and butchered animals, were the lowest class. Though the system was abolished more than a century ago, and burakumin have no physical distinction from other Japanese, prejudice against them still exists. In Japan, special dispensation from parking regulations is what passes for affirmative action.

Near some railroad tracks, I find the dingy two-story building that is home to an ex-yakuza. Beneath an awning of corrugated green fiberglass, I climb metal steps to the second-floor flats. Long fluorescent tubes light the hallway where assortments of slippers and boots stand in formation beside five doors. Squat plastic washing machines silently wait beside three of the doors. A sixth door leads to the communal bath and shower.

Before their recent rise to affluence and glitz, yakuza found their pride and purpose in their myths and legends. Intellectual curiosity is rare within the yakuza ranks. But there is the occasional studious type who, if only by default, becomes the gang's in-house historian. Kobayashi-san, sixty-six, is a yakuza scholar lovingly obsessed with Kyoto's unique underworld.

After some intense rapping, the door opens. Kobayashi is standing in a light kimono and bare feet. At around six feet two, he is a remarkably tall man for his generation. He possesses the slim grace of an American movie star from the forties.

In deference to my foreignness, Kobayashi has set out a chair on the tatami by the yellowed shoji windows. Using two hands, Kobayashi slowly pushes the screen aside, revealing leafy branches. The foliage partly obscures a view of the rusty buildings across the way. Illuminated by the filtered sunlight, the sparely furnished room reflects the Zen aesthetic of a fine teahouse. Kobayashi-san's futon has apparently been folded away behind the fiberboard closet doors that constitute the side wall. A common type of bamboo curtain serves to screen the sink and gas burners from view. This is as simple and charming as any Japanese apartment I have seen.

He sits on the floor beside a neat stack of books and folders. I decline the offered chair, with slight regret, to join him on the soft tatami. He lights a Mild Seven cigarette. As he reaches for the ashtray, colorful pieces of tattoo peek from beneath his neck and out of the sleeve.

He opens with the statement that he is a war veteran. He suggests that he may have fought against my grandfather or uncle in the Burmese jungle. Very few men, he remarks, are both veterans and yakuza. He receives benefits every month. Though he "fought honorably," he says proudly, the government didn't want to give him his veteran's money. "Because of this!" He slides his sleeve back to reveal a splendid carp swimming gracefully upstream.

"Why can't a yakuza be a good soldier?" he asks, flinging out his cuffs. I assume it is a rhetorical question.

Though Kobayashi-san fought Americans, he now likes them. He is sad that most Japanese have forgotten how much the Americans helped after the war. He knows that Japan has always liked American culture, but is surprised that I want to know about the Japanese yakuza. He is happy that I don't take yakuza movies seriously, especially since most Japanese take them for the truth. "Kaicho," as he calls the Aizu Kotetsu boss Takayama, "is a better yakuza hero than any actor could fake. Indeed, Kaicho's looks give him a special dignity that cannot be imitated."

He continues, "Kaicho's rich hair and sideburns look like the mane of a lion. His thick eyebrows and sharp eyes are like an old samurai. His backbone is straight, as is his character. Kaicho is an easy man to respect. This makes his orders a pleasure to follow. There's never a second thought."

Aizu Kotetsu has a wonderful history, Kobayashi assures me. I tell him that's why I came to see him. He offers to do his best within a brief time. Closing his eyes, he begins:

"Aizu Kotetsu was born in 1888." His eyes open and turn to me. "This is not a guess," Kobayashi insists. "So today's clan is at the end of a direct line over one hundred years old. A yakuza clan is not a corporation that moves along just by itself. The oyabun is the clan as a clan *is* the oyabun. When an oyabun dies, the clan almost always dies. It is very rare for the same clan to survive the lifetimes of two oyabun. Yet Aizu Kotetsu has had four oyabun since 1888!

"The tale of this Aizu Kotetsu clan," Kobayashi says firmly, "is the tale of the greatest oyabun, Ubesaki Senkichi.

Aizu Kotetsu: The Kyoto Clan

"Our roots really go back to 1836, this is when Senkichi was born into a poor Kyoto family. At the age of sixteen, Senkichi was involved in a fight in which he beat up a punk who was a member of a gambling association. Senkichi was advised by the boss of a friendly gang to get out of Kyoto. As an excuse to leave Kyoto, Senkichi was handed the responsibility of escorting a blind girl named Orin up to Yoshiwara in Edo. That was a famous pleasure district in what is now Tokyo. Orin was to be trained, against her will, as a prostitute in one of Yoshiwara's brothels.

"It wasn't in the young Senkichi's nature to run away from trouble, but he did what he was advised to do. Well, not long into their trek, Senkichi and Orin fell in love. They returned to Kyoto, where Orin was hidden away in his parents' house. Senkichi hoped to earn the money to pay off the Kyoto boss who had struck the deal with the Yoshiwara brothel.

"The only way young Senkichi knew how to earn money was from organizing gambling. One evening, Senkichi had brashly run a dice game on the turf of a well-known gang called Owari-ya. The next night some Owari-ya henchmen broke into Senkichi's house and killed his blind fiancée. Upon his discovery of Orin's bloodied body, an incensed Senkichi appeared at the headquarters of Owari-ya seeking revenge.

"A notorious gambler named Senhachi happened to be visiting Owari-ya. Senhachi was impressed by the guts of this brazen kid who was about to be slaughtered by the Owari-ya guards. Senhachi interceded with his host, asking the Owari-ya boss to spare the hotheaded youth. When Senhachi later learned about the murder of Senkichi's blind lover, he was further moved and asked the youth to join his gang. He would be initiated through a traditional yakuza ceremony, known as a *sakazuki*.

"'But, before we can have the formal sakazuki,' the boss told Senkichi, 'you will need training!' Senkichi was sent to Gifu prefecture, Senhachi's native region. In 1856, after lengthy training in both the martial and gambling arts, Senkichi finally was initiated into Senhachi's gang.

"Senhachi was an exuberant gang boss who loved sake so much that he wore a sake skin outside his kimono wherever he went."

"What's a 'sake skin'?" I can't help interjecting.

"Ah," says Kobayashi. "I have been neglectful . . . " He rises in a single motion and glides through the bamboo screen. In a minute, he returns with a small tray holding two small ceramic cups. His other hand is turned to show me the hourglass-shaped flask. He kneels down and proceeds to pour sake in the cups. By now, I realize that a sake skin is like a Basque wineskin. Kobayashi nods in confirmation, then continues his tale:

"In the years right before the 1868 Meiji Revolution, there was turbulence in the samurai class. There was also trouble among the lower ranks of guardsmen. They were losing their jobs protecting damiyo, feudal lords, residing in Kyoto. A gang called Shinsei-gumi, headed by a man named Isao Kondo, found itself unemployed.

"Isao Kondo asked the gambling boss Senhachi for employment for the redundant Shinsei-gumi men. Though Senhachi accepted these men into his organization, he decided to put his favorite understudy in charge of these newcomers. Senkichi accepted the position and brought along three friends from his youth to assist him.

"This reorganized gang was now called Aizu Kotetsu-kai. Aizu, for the region where the gang originated, and Kotetsu, after Senhachi's favorite brand of sword. A stylized sake skin, another of Senhachi's trademarks, became the symbol of the Aizu Kotetsu.

"As the leader of this new gang, Senkichi had his back tattooed with the image of Ono-no Komachi, a famous beauty of ancient times. For their headquarters, Aizu Kotetsu-kai took over the Kurotani Temple in the Sankyo-ku section of Kyoto."

Another hour passes as Kobayashi slowly, deliberately, and with flashes of emotion brings me up to the modern era of the Kyoto gang world. The man has the soul of an artist and the bearing of a true gentleman. But his romantic interpretation of yakuza no michi, the way of the yakuza, doesn't seem grounded in anything I have experienced.

SHOOT TO THRILL

Koji quickly becomes comfortable with his life in Kyoto and Hara-gumi. As an oyabun Hara is no stern taskmaster. His personality, or what Koji has seen of it so far, bears no relation to his expectation of a domineering yakuza boss. Hara doesn't yell or ever seem to get angry. In fact, he is unshakably relaxed and smiles a lot. Koji has known lady schoolteachers more intimidating than his boss; it's almost disappointing.

Time has passed quickly and easily during his first Hara-gumi week. Being treated as a kid brother by his fellow Okinawans has made the adjustment even easier. Because Hara is sure the Kyoto police are tapping his phones, he encourages his kobun to speak in Okinawan dialect peppered with as much obscure slang as possible. Newcomer Koji fits right in with Hara-gumi's us versus them mind-set.

Koji's main job has been to ride around on the truck that makes deliveries and pickups of poker gambling machines. A lot of Koji's preconceptions have faded; yakuza life turns out to be undisciplined, laid-back, and even fun.

Since meeting at the airport, Ken has been acting as Koji's advisor and showing him the ropes. (Mostly he has shown Koji how to dress better!) Ken now tells Koji that the Hara-gumi executive board has scheduled his initiation sakazuki for the coming week. Koji is surprised. He thought that at some point he'd receive real training in yakuza arts. The other young kobun in the organization seem to have knowledge and skills still foreign to Koji. A lot of their talk centers on guns. The guys are continually debating the relative power, effectiveness, and feel of various pistols. Koji is getting anxious because he is on the cusp of official yakuza membership and has yet to fire a pistol. He complains about this particular omission. Ken merely nods.

Stars glimmer above the shallow flat plain of Kyoto. It is after 1 A.M., and, away from the bustling Gion district, the night is as quiet as any in the city's twelve hundred years. Koji and I are invited to pile into Ken's Toyota with three other kobun. Instead of the silk shirts they normally sport on weekend nights out, the guys wear T-shirts and Levi's. If you don't examine them too closely, they look like college guys heading up to north Kyoto's hundred-lane MK Bowling Center.

Ken fiddles with the car radio until locking in on Alpha Station, "Kyoto's music alternative." The DJ speaks in the Japanese/English lingo that passes for hip in collegiate circles. It's warm outside. Although the air conditioner works, all of the windows are rolled down. As the car slows for the big intersection of Kawaramachi and Imadegawa, one of the kobun points towards an unattended peddler's cart at the near side of Kamo-Ohashi bridge. Above the cart, a red paper lantern hangs from a pole.

The kobun, called Nara (after his hometown), pulls off his Hanshin Tigers T-shirt, exposing his tattooed back. He props himself up so his hips are inside the car and his upper body hangs outside. Nara's left hand grips the front headrest, his right draws a small pistol from the front of his belt. The light is changing as the kobun squeezes off three quick shots. Sitting beside me, Koji seems enthralled with Nara's audacity and the noise. But the shooter only looks embarrassed—he didn't even nick the lantern.

A lone taxi stuck behind us leans on his horn as Nara's fourth shot also misses the mark. The shooter yells back at the cab, then rolls himself out onto the street. Then we all pile out to watch the fun. Gun in hand, Nara struts back and forth in the beams of the cab's headlights like a Kabuki actor, dramatically, then playfully holds the pistol to his own head. Like most Kyoto cabbies, this old man looks to be a retiree in a second career. His white-gloved hand struggles with the gear shift, desperately trying to find reverse and avoid a heart attack. The cab stalls. Using both hands, as if giving the old man a lesson, Nara lines up the lantern once more. This shot does blow out the bulb, though the paper shell is still intact. A happy Nara bows deeply to the wide-eyed driver, then to Ken, who orders us all back in the car. For one levelheaded second, I consider taking off. I can't help thinking that a lot of this outrageous behavior is a show for the gaijin, but I dive into the backseat swearing I'll intervene the next time.

The four kobun hoot with delight as the car gets up to speed. Koji is in the backseat by the left window. Beside him, on my left, "Rambo," a squat, muscular kobun with a severe flattop, holds a pistol on his knee and shows Koji how to load bullets into the magazine. Then, with a quick explanation, he clicks the safety back and forth before handing it to the newcomer.

The car passes some used-car lots and rice fields as we wind our way up into the mountains north of Kyoto. Suddenly, Nara, the pompadoured kobun in the front seat, turns around with a stupid grin. He places his revolver to his temple and pulls the trigger. The click of the firing pin is loud enough to make us all jump.

"That's what *not* to do!" Ken yells back to Koji. "Who cares about his death, but imagine the mess we'd have to clean up. His mama would want to know what the fuck happened. Then cops are hanging around the headquarters bothering Hara-san . . ."

In the loose hierarchy of Hara-gumi, Ken is the most senior in the automobile. He has already served time in adult prison, whereas the others have only been through juvenile detention. "Don't fuck around! If you want to blow your brains out, go to Osaka, or anywhere outside our territory . . . You get it?"

"Hai." The pompadour nods without turning.

* * *

A green sign for the Kyoto International Convention Center is coming up on the left. Ken turns up the volume as the harsh metal chords of an old Guns n' Roses tune comes on. He doesn't understand most of the words but, I guess, something in the manic sound causes him to skid the car to a stop on the shoulder of the road. The doors swing open and, again, the kobun fall out like Keystone Kops. I consider intervening, but what the hell. Rambo pushes a pistol in Koji's hands and shoves him around to the passenger side. All four now crouch behind the car like they're ready to ambush someone—or something. But the road is deserted, pitch-black in either direction.

Ken sings out: "One, two, three—fire!"

A volley of lead bashes, rattles, and thoroughly punctures the big sign. It's insanely loud. Koji shakes his gun angrily before he finally remembers to release the safety and fires off five quick rounds, but only one hits the metal. He appears to enjoy the kick of the gun along with the whole anarchic orgy of noise and destruction. I don't believe that this is Koji's first time with it—he looks way too comfortable with the Chinese-made pistol.

Japan's tough laws against firearms do to gunplay what taboos do to any vice, making it many times more thrilling. As Koji will later gush, this spontaneous shoot-out was the most exciting experience of his life.

When the echos cease, Rambo pats Koji's back, asking, "Nice, huh?"

The sign is still legible but will probably be replaced within a week.

The car reeks of gunpowder and perspiration. Everyone's chest is thumping, and sweat trickles over Nara's veiny forearms. The loud music resumes as Koji watches the others loading more cartridges into their weapons. My nerves are shot; I wish this trip was over, but Ken keeps driving us away from the city. Reaching into a backpack at his feet, Rambo fishes out a handful of bullets. Without speaking, he again demonstrates to Koji how the cartridges are inserted in the clip.

* * *

We drive a few more miles before the car eases off the road onto a narrow gravel path. Ken clicks the radio off as we approach some small rustic buildings. He stops the car in front of an old-style house. A dim light glows inside. With the engine off, it becomes deadly quiet, except for the insistent chirping of crickets.

The door of the house opens and a bald robed man appears, holding a flashlight. Ken steps up to the door, and, when he's sure the man recognizes him, the young gangster bows. From what I later gather, the man is a deaf monk of some obscure Buddhist sect who lives here alone, caring for the old temple. The monk smiles at Ken and loudly yells, "Dozo . . . go ahead," while making a wide sweeping gesture with his arm.

"Domo arigato!" Ken yells. He then bows, takes a folded ten-thousand-yen bill from his jeans, and hands it to the expectant monk.

"I'll be going to sleep now," the monk announces. "When you leave, please be careful not to run over any of my raccoon and cat friends. They run freely around here."

"Yes, we'll be careful." Ken nods with a smile.

"Good-night, then!" the monk yells.

Koji slings Rambo's ammo-filled bookbag over his shoulder and follows the group to the wooden temple, which can barely be seen in the darkness. Either rats or cats are scurrying about inside. Rambo ducks beneath the raised temple floor, holding a disposable lighter ablaze.

"Got it!" he yells, dragging a small portable generator into the open.

"Is there any gas left?" Ken asks hopefully, as Rambo opens some valves.

"I think so," Rambo grunts, then puts his sneakered foot on the generator's frame and pulls the starter cord. The engine coughs twice, then growls to life. Ken climbs onto the back ledge of the temple and throws down the end of an orange extension cord. Rambo plugs it into the generator, and, suddenly, the yard is awash in bright light.

All of the kobun are squinting towards a dead-end path that has been cut fifty yards deep into the forest. At the far end of the clearing, wooden sake crates have been stacked. Inside the crates hang remnants of old targets. Rambo and Nara quickly replace those with fresh hand-scrawled bull's-eyes and intersperse them with photos of yakuza rivals and porno queens ripped from magazines.

Nobody can remember who was the first to use these temple grounds for target practice, but, as Ken cynically says, "A holy man will do anything for money." I've heard rumors of monks who hid crooks from the cops and, for the right amount of cash, gave them up. But a deaf pacifist monk who lets out his shrine for a pistol range seems almost poetic, in a perverse kind of way. Here on private property I feel more at ease. Although I'd love to participate, my obligation not to interfere keeps me standing back like a very lax chaperon.

Once his eyes adjust to the string of floodlights, Rambo notices a fat raccoon sitting on his hind legs atop one of the crates. Children and adults alike love the so-called Tanuki. The raccoon is a magical creature of Japanese folktales. In stories he can change his appearance but, because of his bumbling animal stupidity, always gives himself away as a mere raccoon.

When Rambo sees that the raccoon isn't going to run off, he raises his pistol. "Good-bye, Tanuki," he half whispers, before blasting the creature away. The plump body stands accusingly before flopping over. Calling a cease-fire, Nara walks up and nudges the furry lump to the ground. He proceeds to hang playing cards along the edge of a crate stacked at shoulder height off the dewy grass.

In a pedagogical tone, Ken explains to Koji the proper position for target shooting. "It's like hitting a baseball, there's only one right way." Ken smiles at Koji. "Let's see if you can have better luck than Tanuki!"

After two minutes of instruction, Koji looks confident he can at least hit the crate. For the next ten minutes, he joins the other kobun in a line firing at various bottles, cans, and playing cards. I can't tell who's hit what and who's just sending lead into the forest.

After the last reload, all four yakuza stand with their right arms extended and their pistols aimed at a line of Coke cans. Then Kenji barks out each of their names in turn, giving them one shot at the

Shoot to Thrill

cans. The first one to miss will be buying beers downtown. This is like some kind of lighthearted challenge between bowling buddies, except that each of the young gangsters is desperate not to lose. Especially a shaking, sweating Koji. I get down from the ledge where I have been sitting to move closer to the contest.

Bang! Nara's can is blasted. Rambo clips a Coke Light can. Ken's spins into the darkness. It's now Koji's turn. His aim is painfully slow and wavering. Finally, the gun goes off dramatically, blasting shards of wood off a dead tree in the background. The can, alas, is unscathed.

Koji's mentor, Ken, shrugs and smiles benevolently. But Koji seethes with embarrassment and anger at himself. His primal, if not Japanese, desire to be accepted by his group has been sidetracked by the miss.

As Koji stares angrily at the lone, taunting, standing Coke can, a fluffy white cat hops onto a crate. Two of the kobun are sweeping up loose shells as Koji lines the cat in his sights. Ken sees what Koji is doing and advises him in a soft voice to "breathe and squeeze." The cat curiously sniffs the top of the Coke can, looking like the coveted prize at a carnival shooting gallery. Seconds creep by, but Koji seems frozen in place. Ken, now exasperated, raises his own pistol and lines up the pale target in his sights. At that moment the generator coughs, both guns erupt, and the jumping cat is strobe-lit by the flickering bulb.

All is suddenly pitch-dark and silent.

Only when the crickets resume their chorus is the silence broken.

"Lucky cat," grunts Ken.

Koji says nothing.

I'm with Hara on his afternoon rounds but I don't mention the boys' night out.

"This is the wild yakuza business you've been asking about," he says, as he pushes open the door to a corner coffee shop. It looks like the many others that dot the urban Japanese landscape.

"Hello!" says a fiftyish lady wearing an apron and sporting a beehive hairdo. She brings over two glasses of water and rolled moist towelettes. A couple of weeks ago, two Hara-gumi kobun had dropped by the shop and gently badgered the owner into accepting one of the video poker games they had on their truck. The games had been rewired to act as gambling machines. (These machines are illegal, of course, but they're found all over the city.) After the first week the coffee shop's cut was around five hundred dollars. The kobun reported that, naturally, the owner was thrilled.

Two cups of coffee are soon placed on our table, which has a built-in video game and is leased from a legitimate vending company. A few minutes later, the owner appears from the back. Hara stands and pulls his business card from his shirt pocket. He greets the old man who holds the card up close to his nose.

"What's this?"

"I'm Noboru Hara." Hara smiles where others might have bowed. "I'm the president of my own company. I believe you've met some of my boys?"

"I don't know," says the stoic proprietor.

"They brought in that poker game about fifteen days ago."

"Yes!" The old man brightens up. "Yes—big kids! Good manners on those boys!"

"Thank you." Hara nods. "I trust they gave you your earnings from last week's total."

"Oh, yes," whispers the man, as if to keep the details from his wife. "It was very generous!"

"I was hoping you might accept four more of the games," says Hara conspiratorially. "We can return these unprofitable ones you've got here; you don't have to worry about a thing."

"Do you think there will be problems?"

"No, no." Hara smiles. "Do you know Terada-san who owns Happy Time Coffee Shop?"

"Yes, Terada," the owner responds. "We're in the same association."

"My company has had games in his shop for a long time. Terada makes some nice extra income."

"Really?" The old guy sighs, perhaps calculating what he's been missing all these years. "Yes, please, more machines!" He nods happily and leaves us.

Hara finishes his coffee just as the elderly hostess shuffles up with the telephone he requested. With his thick fingers, he punches in a number. "Hara here," he hisses to Koji, who has been cleaning the Benz's windows a couple of blocks away.

Turning to me, Hara shrugs. "This setup could earn about two thousand a week. Now most oyabun would keep this business for themselves, using their kobun to collect the money like clerks. But I'll just give this operation to some kobun who doesn't have good businesses. This is something that they can easily run and make money from. That's my style. I like to get things started and rolling but let a young guy develop it and keep it.

"I've found that an oyabun who keeps all the money for himself builds up resentment with his kobun," Hara adds philosophically. "They may 'yes' him to death and bow until they break their backs, but nobody wants to be an errand boy. I'm building up their feelings of responsibility and loyalty—duty—and I am also relieving myself of business headaches.

"I'm not really a businessman." Hara snaps a wooden toothpick against the table. "I don't like working, and I don't have a money obsession like some oyabun. Some are more like bankers than yakuza."

A brooding Koji delivers his boss (and me) back to the headquarters. Upstairs in his office Hara introduces me to his business advisor, a "college graduate" named Kaz. In the cash-drunk eighties, few yakuza had the expertise to handle their extraordinary profits. A cottage industry of small real estate agents and stockbrokers sprang up, ready to assist the uneducated hoods with their excess money.

At six feet three and now just 230 pounds, Kaz went to college to join the sumo team—and graduated with a business degree. He then learned real estate by helping to develop the southwest part of Kyoto out to Muko. Kaz is Hara's best friend and, because of his education, gets considerable respect. Hara strikes me, however, as more intelligent. A huge, outgoing young man, Kaz possesses a lantern jaw, the build of a bodyguard, and as sharp a mind as I've met slumming with yakuza. In English, Kaz greets me and proceeds to riddle me with questions about who I am and my interest in the yakuza. I feel like he is either double-checking my story for Hara or just putting on a show for his boss. I am taken aback by the phrasing of his last question: "What is the real reason you are spending so much time with Hara-san?" I tell him I want the truth about the way the yakuza live and work. Instead of learning about the yakuza by talking to the police and other journalists, I explain slowly, I want to see for myself. The big man seems satisfied.

Hara has already related Kaz's business tip to me—an "absurd" idea that reminds him of the whimsical, almost girlish nature of commerce he loathes. Last week the papers were wailing about the stunning 40 percent decline in Kyoto real estate value. Now Kaz is advising Hara to position himself to take advantage of the low residential real estate prices.

Today Kaz tells Hara that he has found such an undervalued property near Kyoto University. Kaz has already spoken to the manager of the nearly bankrupt loan company that owns the half-acre property. The guy is willing to sell it dirt cheap.

"But there's a problem." Kaz shrugs his big shoulders and lights a cigarette. He explains that the previous owners haven't vacated the house, even though they have no claim to it.

"No big deal." Hara runs a hand over his suede head. "We'll just get them out. I've got nothing against squatters, but when they've got to go, they've got to go."

Kaz sighs and smiles.

"What?" Hara nudges him. "Who's in there? Somebody's mother in a wheelchair?"

"No, it's some chimpira of N-gumi," Kaz says, naming one of the few Kyoto gangs not in the Aizu Kotetsu syndicate. For Hara this is another of the many local issues that transcend mere money concern. The presence of N-gumi in Kyoto has long irked Hara. If it was just up to him, N-gumi would have been run out of town years ago.

"I hate anything to do with N-gumi," Hara confirms. It is evidently the one topic capable of wiping the customary smile off his face. "They're low-class bums! If I even see their names in the papers, I get sick."

Turning back to a half-bemused Kaz, Hara nods emphatically. "Let's do it."

Later that day, a more relaxed Hara asks me if I enjoyed my trip to the countryside. Word has gotten back to Hara that young Koji performed okay in his first outing with a pistol, despite his final miss. But Hara doesn't put too much stock in the assessments of talent given by other kobun. He says he doesn't even expect young kobun to mature into productive gang members until after three or four years in the organization.

"No one here's a rocket scientist," Hara likes to say. "If anyone had half a brain, they probably wouldn't be in the yakuza in the first place!

"When a kid tries to do too much right away, more often than not he ends up in jail. That costs me money. I like a kid who's a listener, someone who can follow simple instructions without screwing up.

"My job is to match a particular job with the person. I don't send my nastiest enforcer to scare somebody; I know I might end up with a corpse on my hands, or at least a cop car sitting out front waiting for a bribe, a box lunch, or a warm body. That's the way it works in Japan. The cops here don't have to really investigate, they just pick a gang to pin it on and request the 'criminal.' And if the crime is really serious, the cops won't accept some young kobun handing himself in—even if the kid did it! Then one of us from the executive council has to do the time! That's the worst! It's sup-

posed to work the other way around: A young kobun is supposed
to confess to the crime of a higher-up! It's kind of a rite. But in those
situations I like a kid to volunteer; I never 'volunteer' a kid like a
lot of oyabun do. A really really new kobun wouldn't survive a day
in a real adult prison. No, a nice kid like Koji needs three or four
years on the street before he'll be ready for hard time.

"But this real estate problem is tricky," says Hara, scratching
the back of his hand. "I need someone with strong spirit, but not
too much." Hara points to his own dome. "Not too much brains
either like our little Rambo."

Kaz nods in agreement.

Almost two weeks have passed since Koji left Okinawa, and he has
already sent two sixty-thousand-yen money orders back to his
parents. Last week his mother received a visit from a Hara-gumi
"executive." This older yakuza was visiting his own family in Naha,
and dropped in on Koji's mom to report how well her son was fit-
ting into the Hara-gumi scheme. This reportedly delighted her.

"Before I entered the underworld, no one ever gave me a
chance," says Koji. "I was dying to learn a trade, or a skill that would
allow me to earn money and open my own small business. My father
was a garbageman but it's not what I wanted. I didn't think I could
do well in the yakuza. If you've only seen the yakuza in movies,
you don't get a real idea of what the yakuza is. Right now, I would
compare Hara-gumi to a club. That's what I keep telling my mom,
'It's like living in a clubhouse!' Actually, I'm starting to get a little
bored."

Hara decides to send the older kobun, Ken, to reconnoiter at Kaz's
bargain property. Ken decides to take the bus to Sankyo ward and
invites me along. He casually points out a few points of interest en
route to the Kyoto University stop. The sidewalks are baking in
the midday sun, so we grab a couple of cans of beer at a Lawson's
convenience store; Ken buys a disposable Fuji camera too.

Ten minutes later, we find the property in question. The house is a relatively large two-story concrete structure with a crude addition on its left side. The driveway leads to a new carport with a smoky Plexiglas roof.

I gladly agree to stay out front by a cinder-block wall. Camera in hand, Ken strolls casually around the house, even pauses to bow to an old lady who is hanging laundry in the next yard. Reappearing under the carport, he brazenly walks through the unlocked side door and out of sight. I nervously pace up to the corner of the block. I notice that all the neighbors' lawns and shrubs are in much better shape than the patchy grass beside me. When I return, Ken waves me into a small kitchen where a sink is piled with dishes. Playing Sherlock to my Watson, he shows me the open rice cooker with a few grains that are still moist.

Ken then explores the second floor. From a count of the scattered bowls Ken guesses there are four men living in the house. He snaps some photos upstairs and down, then takes a few more outside. As an afterthought, he hustles back into the house to grab some porn videos and a nearly full bottle of Courvoisier. We are halfway down the street when Ken holds up the cognac.

"A gratuity," he says. "That's the word!"

In an attempt to prevent trouble, Hara called a boss of N-gumi to inform him that, as a representative of the legal owner, he wanted the Sankyo-ward house vacated by six o'clock—today. "He was very sweet with me," Hara recalls of the conversation. "He said that I was probably right about the status of the property."

"But," the N-gumi boss added, "who hasn't had money problems these days?" Hara told him that he didn't give a shit about the world's problems, he wanted the N-gumi kobun out of the house by six o'clock. But the rival boss would not relent. He stammered something about double-checking the facts of the situation, and asked for Hara-gumi's fax number.

Hara isn't having any of these delaying tactics. Back at the office, Ken's report is digested and decisions are quickly made.

Rambo, the three-year gang veteran with big biceps and a perfectly level flattop, is psyched to deal with the squatters.

"It's just this kind of problem that gives me indigestion," says Hara, as he downs some chalky stomach medicine from a tiny bottle. The stuff must be good. A few minutes later, the boss is straightening his tie and going out to dinner. The rest of this operation has been left to the kobun.

At around 2 A.M., at the table in Hara's office, Rambo sits beside Ken looking over his pictures of the house. Ken advises him on the best way to approach the house so the N-gumi guys on the second floor won't see or hear him. Rambo's vague assignment is to scare the squatters into believing that they'll never get another good night's sleep in that house. Ken and Rambo debate a number of different plans, which escalate quickly. One of Ken's ideas involves six liters of gasoline, another hinges on the procurement of dynamite. Dynamite! This is not the type of "information" to which I want access. Ashen, I rise to leave, but the guys now explode with laughter.

Those extreme options turn out to be a joke on me, although the destruction of the house would be no big deal. Compared to the lot it sits on, a Japanese home has little monetary value. That's why so many are cheaply built and why developers will demolish even the loveliest homes without hesitation. If Rambo should raze the Sankyo-ward house, he might only be anticipating the inevitable.

Eventually moderation wins the day. "All we're supposed to do is get those assholes out of the building as quickly as possible," Ken reminds Rambo. "Boss said he doesn't care what you do as long as those guys get the message . . . but we don't want anyone to get hurt. This is a business deal!"

"We just want to let them know that they won't be getting any more sleep in that place." Rambo repeats Hara's phrase, to himself as much as to Ken.

"Yeah." Ken pats Rambo's shoulder. "You've got the idea."

"Just leave it to me," Rambo assures him, absolving Ken as well as Hara of responsibility.

Shoot to Thrill

* * *

There's a hint of autumn coolness in the Kyoto night, so Rambo's leather bomber jacket doesn't appear too strange. It is 3 A.M. when he kicks the racing-style Yamaha to life. I suspect Rambo doesn't have much more of a battle plan than a sumo takes into a match. (Sumo bouts rarely last more than ten seconds, during which the fighter is on autopilot, completely dependent on his instincts.) Only now as he hunches over his idling motorcycle does Rambo seem to focus on his mission and free his mind of distraction. He leaves one distraction in his exhaust as he roars off to Kawara-machi Dori—me.

About eighteen hours later, I get Rambo to reconstruct his night's work. He shows a surprising gift for detail:

Up by Kyoto University, the city blocks were deathly quiet. Rambo parked the Yamaha across the way and took a last look at Ken's photographs. He felt amazingly calm as he walked, helmet in hand, down the empty street.

When he found the right house, he squatted behind the wall and slipped the helmet back over his head. As Ken had guaranteed, the back door was open. Standing in the narrow kitchen, Rambo pulled an automatic pistol from the inside pocket of the leather bomber.

"I knew what I wanted to do," Rambo recalls. "But I didn't know how those fucks were going to react!"

In his helmet, sneakers, and baggy jeans, he climbed the narrow stairs. Because of Ken's recon photos, Rambo knew to turn right to find the communal bedroom. He could see four lumps snoozing on the tatami floor. Rambo stepped over one of the bodies as he reached for the string dangling from the overhead light. "I wanted the light on so I could make sure not to hit anyone!"

The light flickered on as Rambo jumped back to the doorway. One of the sleeping men awoke, asking drowsily, "What? Who?"

Rambo started firing. The others sat up, then rolled up against the wall. "I shot way over their heads." Rambo laughs. "They weren't in any danger but, I swear, there was someone crying!"

Rambo had blown a hole in the wall that, a week later, he will actually help repair. When a couple of Hara-gumi guys return to the headquarters after assessing the damage, they say the room reeks of urine. With mock bows they compliment Rambo on scaring the piss out of the squatters.

Rambo is happy.

GOLF: JAPAN'S BLOOD SPORT

"Do you like golf?" Hara asks.

We are cruising north, with Koji driving confidently now, on one of the typically straight Kyoto avenues. The air conditioning blasts as I look out at the grassy bank along the upper reaches of the Kamo River. Old ladies in lightweight mesh kimonos sit watching gaggles of shirtless preschoolers splash in the shallow current.

"I should take you on a tour of Kyoto's yakuza offices," Hara muses between sips of an Asahi beer. "There must be over hundreds in Kyoto—more yakuza offices than 7-Elevens!"

I am curious. "Aren't all the gangs in Kyoto, Aizu Kotetsu?"

"Most," he grunts. "There are a few Yamaguchi-gumi, like that N-gumi. We should wipe them out, push them into Lake Biwa and hold them under until the bubbles stop."

Now on a twisting road through the eastern mountains, Koji carefully keeps two hands clamped on the wheel. He slows down as we pass clusters of dingy small homes that are built a few feet from the road. An ambience of squalor hangs heavy over these hamlets. The hills rise steeply behind the hovels and block almost any chance of direct sunlight.

"Burakumin," sighs Hara, sensing my puzzlement.

I now recollect that these villages are unique to Kansai, often remaining nameless on maps and beyond the pale of the Japanese consciousness. In such rural plots, as in city slums, these burakumin families eke out their meager subsistence. For many of the young men, joining the yakuza is the only way out.

A dozen more miles and we finally reach the S. Country Club, another hallowed shrine in a country addicted to golf. The gates are quickly pulled open by an old man garbed in navy blue coveralls and a wide-brimmed straw hat. The smoothly paved drive curves through a dense forest that is eerily dark on this bright summer midday. We pass crumbling stone Buddhas along the side of the road. Then the trees give way to the manicured lawn of a Tudor clubhouse. Walking by the practice green, I'm happy to see two white men in a foursome preparing to tee off. I was concerned about leaving the touristy confines of Kyoto, where gaijin are commonplace, not "dangerous."

We are met by Yoshimoto, the number two man in Hara-gumi, and, says Hara, "a state-of-the-art gangster." With his luxuriant hair, lean, six-foot frame, and disarming good looks, "Yoshi" is the perfect picture of modern Japanese masculinity. If only he had a decent family background, he could be the youngest member on some board of directors. But he was raised in a poor Korean section of Osaka where his stellar appearance, 90 percent of the success game in Japan, went unrewarded. Hustling golf matches, taking advantage of the successful, is one of Yoshi's compensations.

Hara is right. Yoshi seems to be the true embodiment of the tabloids' "new yakuza." He has the ready smile and confident appearance of a fast-track salaryman. But rather than a gimmick like an Italian suit, it's Yoshi's natural bearing that gives him a sophisticated air. Yoshi is "new" because he vacations in Hawaii and hustles golf instead of dice. But unbutton his shirt and examine those tattoos; unlock the trunk to his Jaguar and find his trusty Glock. You'll find the "new" yakuza hasn't evolved at all.

Hara and I watch Yoshi tap casual but precise putts on the practice green. He is wearing white golf shoes, pressed khakis, and a long-sleeved white rugby shirt that he keeps buttoned to the neck. This is the preferred style of dress for tattooed golfers who don't want to shock the membership. "Three-quarters of the citizens I play with don't realize I'm a yakuza," says Yoshi. "The other quarter of the corporate honchos I play with don't care if I'm connected." Many of these company officers are obligated to golf with business associates four or five times a week, and are happy to bring in a yakuza as a partner—especially with a two handicap."

Yoshi doesn't change in the locker room, nor would he undo the second button of his shirt even on the stickiest of summer days. A human body so completely marked (I have seen several) exudes a hostile otherworldliness that makes one gasp. When the face and manner are as charming as Yoshi's, the effect hits you doubly hard.

As the son of a Chinese father and a Korean mother, Yoshi knew from a young age he could never be part of the mainstream. He committed himself early on to being a gangster, and gradually to complete body tattooing. His design even reaches beyond the normal dimensions of a yakuza bodysuit. Surreptitiously he lifts a cuff to show me that his arm tattoos are engraved down to his wrist, well past the usual mid-forearm limit.

As Hara's tattoos end above his biceps, he sports a conventional short-sleeved golf shirt along with a broad smile. He's been taking twice-weekly golf lessons from Yoshi since the cherry blossoms last April. These days, a yakuza boss who can't handle a driver is as worthless as an old-timer who couldn't wield a sword. Hara is earnest but skeptical about his chances of becoming a decent golfer. As a kid he didn't even play baseball; "I only liked fighting!"

Japanese caddies are women. In the rural farming communities where golf courses have displaced rice farmers, their resilient wives have learned the difference between a sand and a pitching wedge. They wear large, sun-blocking bonnets wrapped in a gauze-like material that's tied under their chins. They bend, but don't break, beneath the burden of excessively loaded golf bags. A rural Japanese tradition, saddling women with the most exhausting work on the farm, is continued here.

I drive the cart during Hara's nine-hole adventure with shanks, hooks, and divots the length of throw rugs. We finish at the clubhouse bar's shaded tables beside the practice green. The boss orders "whiskeysodas" and Yoshi begins to tally the scores. "Don't bother with mine," Hara orders, with a short chopping motion of his hand. Yoshi folds the card as a very tall, strapping man walks up to the table. I will learn he is the assistant pro, though he acts as obsequious as a kobun. The pro greets Yoshi with a big smile and acknowledges Hara with a sharp, short bow. I watch Hara's demeanor change instantaneously from the casual hacker to that of a no-nonsense boss.

Apparently this assistant pro often acts as a liaison between club members and Yoshi. As a golfer of near-professional skill, Yoshi can be utilized in a number of ways. In Japan, as elsewhere, it's considered rude for a host to beat his guest, who is usually a business client. The good host, therefore, may partner Yoshi with an inferior guest to make their combined scores competitive. Conversely, an inferior duffer might pair up with Yoshi in order to shut down some hotshot executive rival.

Until recently, it was common for companies to hire scratch golfers to do nothing but play with top executives. With staff cutbacks, Yoshi is the new freelance hired gun for many Osaka VIPs. They might call him the night before or at six in the morning for a round. Whether he's asked to play straight or throw every third hole, Yoshi is never paid less than thirty-five hundred dollars, on top of any side bets won during the day.

The proposition for Yoshi is simple enough: to play next Monday as a partner to the host, and discreetly beat the guest opposition. The reason for this ambush is intriguing, whispers the gossipy assistant pro. Even Hara is curious, and invites the man to sit down and tell us more.

It gets too complicated for me to follow. Later I will understand why the plot is so compelling: It involves Japanese mores, shady businesses, and shaky real estate loans—quintessentially post-bubble. When the boom economy went south in 1990, trillions of yen were lost from small, insufficiently secured loans. Legions of bank VPs and bright, young loan officers had their careers stalled or killed.

One such man, Mr. A, an executive at a major Kobe-based bank, has been handed an ultimatum by his boss (who also has one foot out the door). Mr. A must recoup 25 percent of the balance from Mr. B, a toiletries manufacturer, who has defaulted on an eighteen-million-dollar loan. It had been secured in 1987 with Wakayama land holdings, which have depreciated by 75 percent in five years. Now, questions have even arisen concerning Mr. B's actual ownership of the land. If Mr. A doesn't recoup the money within two weeks, he'll be permanently demoted to a position with a comatose subsidiary already in bankruptcy. Essentially, Mr. A's life will be over.

Mr. B, a known golf freak, has been invited by Mr. A to play on Monday. Mr. B is bringing an associate who played college golf for Kobe University, serious stuff. Mr. A needs a man like Yoshi to pose as his associate and play any role necessary to hustle Mr. B into a huge gambling debt that Mr. A can use as added leverage for the monies owed his company.

"It's stupid the way some katagi think," Yoshi will say later. "They invent complicated plans that delicately dance around a problem instead of being direct. It's like a Kabuki plot that needs a lot of dramatic motion to get across a simple idea. Dealing with these salarymen makes me wonder how Japan has become number one in business. If A-san cannot collect money owed to him, he should simply hire someone to do it for him!"

The grinning assistant pro assures Yoshi that Mr. A will pay him five thousand dollars and cover all betting losses and winnings. Also, it's important that Mr. B not guess that Yoshi is yakuza. At this, Hara interrupts to suggest that I be brought along as some sort of "college friend" of Yoshi's. Yoshi nods in agreement before asking me to "carry the putters" for the round. But, I suspect, there is something "high-class" and "stylish" about a gaijin hanging around. Perhaps I may deflect any thought that Yoshi is a yakuza. The assistant pro leaves.

"Hey," Hara says, laughing, after finishing his drink, "you thought yakuza life was just finger cutting and dice!"

That evening Yoshi calls a yakuza friend, a bookies' bookie, who is an important earner for an Osaka branch of the Yamaguchi-gumi. This man takes over four hundred calls (and faxes) a day from bookies all over Kansai and is a one-man on-line gangland grape-vine. He instantly recognizes the name of Mr. B as a notorious Kobe high roller. He also knows that Mr. B recently collected on a $120,000 high school baseball parlay from a Kita-Osaka book-maker. Of course, the guy has contact with the Kobe-Osaka under-world but he is not quite a yakuza groupie. As far as Yoshi's friend knows, Mr. B is a legit businessman, or at least "as legitimate as that kind ever are."

Waking up in predawn darkness I dread the day ahead. It isn't just the tedium of watching more golf, but the event doesn't seem the least bit promising for material. Pulling on a Lacoste polo shirt pur-chased for the job, I pray for rain or another gang war. Ten min-utes later I am out on the empty streets, hunting for the lucky cab for what I imagine will be a $130 ride. By the time we roll up to the club, it is daylight and $130 is a passing fancy.

Even with the warmth of that mild Monday morning, Yoshi, taking no chances, wears a long-sleeved cotton turtleneck. Mr. A is surprised by my presence but easily accepts my ruse of being a former exchange student. I am supposedly spending the summer in Kyoto visiting old teachers and school chums, such as Yoshi. Mr. A, with nicely moussed, graying hair, looks like a TV anchor-man. He is of that breed of cosmopolitan Japanese who always say, "I'm sorry I don't speak English"—in perfect English. If men like Mr. A are on the verge of career failure, things must be bad out there. Certainly the man is serious; not one word concerning the situation or plan seems to pass between Mr. A and Yoshi, just per-functory comments about the weather.

The two opponents stride towards us with the resolve of MacArthur sloshing through the Filipino surf. Mr. B is a squat fifty-year-old whose beefy arms hint at power, offsetting his beer gut. His thinning hair is slicked back away from his squarish wire-framed glasses that feature strips of black plastic across the top of each lens. This style of frame, with the faux eyebrows, is the preferred model this year for all Japanese men of respect.

Golf: Japan's Blood Sport

His preppy companion is tall, lithe, and in his early thirties. He betters my résumé, allowing that after graduating from Kobe University he spent a year at Oxford. He speaks confident, if stilted British English. It strikes me as odd that this accomplished young man would be in the employ of a small company like Mr. B's. "Kobe's" practice swings are also confident and hint at some problems to come for Mr. A and Yoshi.

I am impressed by the zeal with which Yoshi seizes the role of emcee. After easing his tee into the turf and gingerly setting his ball, he smiles and addresses the men. With a disarming frankness, Yoshi suggests a high-stake, combined-score bet for the first hole. Mr. A feigns (I think) a mild look of surprise at his partner's bluntness. Mr. B, however, barely hesitates before accepting the terms. I watch the foursome from the cart, which is parked on the gravel path. The distant green of the first hole, a long straight par four, is still shrouded in morning mist. Yoshi's ball clicks off the head of his graphite driver. Though it never gets more than a yard off the ground, the ball carries deep into the haze. Kobe's shot soars high and deep with the power of a professional, finally rolling to a stop thirty yards beyond Yoshi's. This doesn't look good.

Mr. B now takes his choppy, homemade swing, sending the ball low, but with enough force to roll about as far as Yoshi's. After anxiously glancing at me, then Yoshi, Mr. A proceeds to shank his shot. It disappears into a thick grove of bamboo trees as forbidding as a Vietnam jungle. Mr. B graciously insists that Mr. A do it over "this one time."

"Dozo, go ahead," urges Yoshi. Mr. A's second shot is straight enough but noticeably shorter than the others. The men then make grunts of mutual approval. The two caddy ladies in big gauze bonnets silently retrieve the drivers and shuffle down the dew-covered fairway.

As the men walk after their shots, I drive ahead, then veer off to the left, easing the cart along the path lightly shaded by the outstretched arms of fine-leafed maples. I know Jack Nicklaus and other Americans have done well designing courses in Japan, but I doubt that any gaijin had a hand in this one. The few touches of traditional Japanese landscaping I can find seem to be entirely accidental; a foreigner would have been more "Japanese."

I long ago decided that few people reject their native culture like modern Japanese. A recent editorial in a Kyoto paper chided the locals for their pell-mell destruction of traditional Japanese homes in favor of banal prefab boxes. Thank goodness for our foreign residents, the writer concluded, they're the only ones who want to live in our traditional buildings. I had, in fact, been staying in an ancient, thin-walled, tatami-matted house with an ancient squat toilet that was technically an outhouse. It was fine for the summer, but in the cold I just couldn't imagine paying that kind of price for tradition.

Staying abreast of the other players, I stop the cart beside a fragile bamboo fence. Peering through some overgrown shrubs, I discover what looks like a teahouse—or more likely, the home of a grounds-keeper. Old brown planks run vertically across the left half of the façade, while the right side is a mossy organic green. A roof of tattered gray thatch hangs low over the door and a closed paper window. As my foursome draw their state-of-the-art clubs from their logo-covered bags, I turn back and sadly contemplate the marvelous teahouse. It could have dropped from the sky for all the sense it made there beside a goddamn golf course. I'm tempted to explore the grounds of that ancient building and immerse myself in a less modern, more "Japanese" Japan. But, of course, the thing about being a Westerner in Japan is that your very presence usually dilutes the authenticity of the experience. Although, I have to admit, the authenticity quotient of my underworld action seems high. Almost too high.

Even if I could enter the teahouse's cool confines, I can hardly turn my back on my hosts. Unlike my girlfriend's father in Ibaraki prefecture, who refuses to even meet me, these tattooed outlaws have taken me into their homes and their lives. They have welcomed me at their table, and even pay me to carry their putters.

Golf: Japan's Blood Sport

* * *

Both Yoshi and Mr. A hook their second shots into adjoining bunkers while the staunch opposition hits the green in regulation. Yoshi blasts a wave of sand over the collar, sending his ball high and accurate. It drops a couple of yards beyond the stick, bites into the green, and rolls back a couple of yards to about three feet from the cup. Mr. A's wedge shot just clears the lip of the bunker but manages to bounce onto the green. After some confusion I give the four men their proper putters. I then remove the flag and walk off to stand with the caddy ladies. They respond to my whispered "hello" with simultaneous bows.

Mr. A three-putts a six. Kobe birdies with a long putt. Mr. B needs a lovely, curving second putt to nail par and he gets it. I'm sure Yoshi is faking his anguished expressions as he lines up his simple three-footer. He finally sinks it for par and responds to the shouts of "nice shot" (in English, as is the Japanese convention).

Carrying putters is a breeze compared with lugging their obscenely heavy golf bags. A scorecard is clipped onto the steering wheel but I am not really paying close attention. Sometimes, between holes, the men ask me for the next yardage from the red tees, and I read it off the card.

Kobe wears a severe expression, except on the occasions he speaks to me in his best British public school English: "It's dreadfully hot here!" or "We act so bloody serious. Japanese cannot enjoy anything, even a game feels like work." He flashes me a big ironic smile after his English asides. I ask him what he does for a living. He says he is involved with some vague European investment in Kansai in connection with the new Osaka airport. God knows what his connection with Mr. B is, but Kobe could sure play golf.

As the sun rises, the grass dries and the thin shadow of the flagpole draws closer to the cup. The heat makes the cicadas roar, and the players reach constantly for their hankies to mop their sweaty faces. The caddy ladies stoically chug down the fairway and wait for the men to catch up. They continue to home in on wayward balls as if by radar.

After three holes I am losing track of strokes. With each appearance on the green, I'm feeling more and more like an intruder. I also sense that something is up, although everyone appears collected, if a bit grim.

As the men drink cold beer at the ninth hole break, the caddy ladies finally get a rest, sipping cold green tea. I can't believe we're only halfway. I watch Yoshi tallying scores. Sitting with his legs crossed, his sweaty turtleneck drawn taut on his back. Perhaps only I notice the dark patterns revealing themselves through the moist cotton fabric. Though Yoshi had at first suggested the betting terms, with each succeeding hole, he has become more reserved, often deferring to Mr. B's gaming preferences.

Mr. A's putting remains inconsistent. Things get no better on the back nine. Since putting is the only aspect to which I am paying attention, I assume things are rough for Yoshi's team. Kobe possesses a consistent long ball but is lousy around the green. Even with our morning start, the heat has now reached a point that should send middle-aged smokers like Messrs. A and B to the clubhouse. After they hit off at the seventeenth tee, the portly Mr. B holds up his hand and tells me to wait. He slides in beside me—all sweaty, red-faced, and exhausted. I drive us along the fairway, slanting towards his ball, which is far down on the left side.

"How do you like Japan?" Mr. B asks me.

"Great." I nod to him. "A lot like America. Baseball and golf . . ."

"Is that so? And how do you know Yoshi-san?"

I recite the bit about knowing Yoshi way back when I was an exchange student.

"Is that so?" he asks, wiping his brow with a soiled handkerchief. I stop near the ball, and stomp on the parking brake so the cart won't lurch when Mr. B steps out. But, as we are ahead of the walkers, the man stays beside me and fires up a Winston. The crescendo of cicadas peaks again, then slowly diminishes to silence. The air is so still that the cigarette smoke lingers in the cart. The heat and dead calm of the sweeping vista envelop us in a Zenlike trance. Another kind of Japanese man—a poet or a gangster—

might have waxed emotional about the summers of his youth in some rural village. But Mr. B just takes a final puff of his Winston and mashes it on the sole of his spikes, cursing, "It's too goddamn hot for this shit."

After I gratefully reset the pin in the eighteenth hole, I zip the cart over to the pro shop. The assistant pro is grinning.

"Everything OK?" he asks, handing me a nice clean towel.

"I don't know." I shrug, turning off the cart.

The assistant pro hands me three folded ten-thousand-yen bills. I thank him in my best Japanese but he is preoccupied.

I walk back to the players, thank them for the honor, and bow a bit. I have interrupted a heated discussion, but they all smile and shove bills at me. I protest briefly, before I accept the money forced on me. Yoshi asks if I will wait for his clubs to be delivered to his Jaguar. He gives me the keys so I can start the car, run the air, and "answer the telephone."

I compliantly sit in his driver's seat with the cool air and the radio blasting. The bag has been trotted over by a teenage kid with a brush cut and bulging biceps. He honors me with a forty-five-degree bow. Then I hand him two ten-thousand-yen bills to deliver to the caddy ladies (who I am sure haven't been paid as much as me).

Hanging around yakuza, you can't help but get in the money chain. I have earned about eleven hundred dollars just by lurking at the periphery of a shady golf match. Suddenly, the car phone flashes and clicks. I hesitate before answering the call.

"Did they bring my bag?" Yoshi asks in an even tone.

"Hai."

"In the big pocket at the bottom of the bag," Yoshi instructs, "there's a pistol. I want you to put it in your pocket and walk into the bathroom through the locker room . . . and bring my keys. If I ask for my keys, give them to me and go. If I ask you to change ten thousand yen, say 'no' and give me the gun." He clicks off.

* * *

As whimsical and ill-advised as my adventures have been, I have as yet to get in any situation that my assortment of police business cards wouldn't extricate me from (I hadn't taken courtesy meetings with police officials for nothing). In my wallet, I possess the cards of a key Kyoto detective and the Osaka cop in charge of their antiyakuza resource center. If I should get busted, there is little chance I will get dumped into the dank hell of a Japanese detention center. But gunplay on a summer day might be getting a bit serious.

For some reason (like because I can't call Yoshi back), I feel I have no choice. Bending over the trunk, I rummage through a nest of loose balls and wooden tees. Finally I find the pistol, a snub-nosed .38, cool and heavy in my hand. It bulges noticeably in the front pocket of my khakis, so I pull out my oversized shirt.

I find the locker room neat and empty. In the next room, a massive painting of Mount Fuji looms over two aqua-tiled baths that are built into the floor like small swimming pools. By the low water taps, on a dry section of the floor, two of the men sit on plastic stools. They are still dressed but with slippers on their feet. I now notice that the men, Mr. A and Mr. B, are facing a squatting Yoshi, who is mostly blocked from my view. Kobe is standing off to my left with his arms clasped behind his back.

Yoshi looks up at me, saying *"chotto matte,* wait a second," and his words echo around the tiled walls. Kobe smiles and bows at me. He points out that I haven't removed my sneakers before coming inside. I should go back and do the slipper routine, but I am thinking that I might soon be running from the scene. Then Yoshi says something, and the two seated men turn to me. I see several stacks of shrink-wrapped bills on the floor. I also see that Yoshi has removed his shirt. "Come here," he calls. Mr. B looks up at me with a crooked smile. "Can you break ten thousand yen?" Yoshi asks me.

"I'm sorry, I cannot," I say gravely.

"Can I have my keys?" Yoshi asks.

"No," I answer dumbly, transfixed by the sight of his ornate chest. Only by nervously rustling through the bills in my pocket do I feel and remember the car keys. I sheepishly place them in Yoshi's waiting hand still wearing the black golf glove.

"Domo, thanks," I grunt, then bow and backpedal out of there. Back at the Jaguar, I nudge the gun out of sight under the seat. Then I draw a picture of a pistol and an arrow pointing beneath the seat. I leave the note on the brown leather and nudge the gun out of sight.

I want to split. The sun is harsh in the parking lot and I think I should be back in Kyoto. I yell at the kid who had brought the golf bag, and he comes running. A city teenager wouldn't have his own car, but kids like this always do. When I ask him if he could drive me into town, he shrugs and sucks on his teeth (Japanese hemming and hawing). Yet I knew he couldn't say no if I offered him ten thousand yen. In less than a minute the kid rolls up in an old Nissan Sovereign and soon we're on the highway heading back to Kyoto.

11 P.M. Trying to forget the confusion and complexities of the locker room incident, I head for a bar. I drop into—or rather, rise up to—a popular gaijin hangout that overlooks Gion from fifteen floors up. I sip a Long Island ice tea, contemplating a window view of a clear, Kyoto evening.

There are neon-outlined buildings rising above a motley mix of oddball structures with aluminum wings, chrome façades, and mirror walls—walls that enclose some of the most raucous and depraved of nightspots. Yet, one block away, the Tokyo tackiness gives way to a Kyoto calm where the street is so quiet, you can hear the rush of shallow streams. From these Gion sidewalks you can see, even eavesdrop on, geisha parties that glow with that ephemeral Japanese essence.

Supposedly, the tourist trade has things so warped that any bumpkin with a credit card can access a near-geisha experience. At least, that is the opinion of my girlfriend, who describes geisha as "hostesses in kimono who are too fat to work in Ginza."

But geisha are still lovely to me because they're doing their part making Japan seem like Japan. At about five-thirty in the evening, when the *geiko-chan*, the junior geisha, walk the streets of Gion in their exquisite white masks, the tourists get giddy. They snap a dozen photos and then cajole the girls into posing for a dozen more.

When night comes to Gion, the streets swell with slow-moving taxis and men on foot. There are local salarymen working through the crowd, but, more than any Tokyo party district, Gion attracts the yakuza poseurs in bad golf shirts, white slip-ons, and clutch bags. Short, round men with dark glasses and gold bracelets strut about the area in cross-generational groups. Though Kyoto is almost next door to Osaka, many younger Osakans look at Kyoto like it's a hick town, which it is in many ways. Osaka's hip salarymen prefer cosmopolitan Kobe as their party destination.

But the older elite of Osaka, Japan's money city, can't get enough of the traditional bamboo and teak geisha houses of Gion. Neither can I. These Gion evenings along the Kamo River are timeless. On either side of the Shijo-Ohashi bridge, wooden decks are built high on steel braces cemented into the cobblestone banks of the river. Here businessmen sit jacketless on the tatami sipping whiskey, receiving compliments, and reveling in the geisha attention. Below the monied classes, down where the cobblestone slopes into the water, university students swoon, neck, and stare at the stars. A Kyoto night away from yakuza may not be the wildest, but it can be just as memorable.

When the clock hits midnight it is technically my birthday. I tell the barkeep who pours me a drink and one for himself, charging me for both—another custom to remember! I finish my drink, and, a bit older and tighter, I take to the streets.

Tokyo isn't a place where you accidentally run into friends but Kyoto, maybe. It seems that a meeting of Hara-gumi "executives" has just broken up. Dressed in flashy silk shirts and led by the shiny-domed Hara, the mob elite boozily greets me on Shijo bridge.

"I was just asking your golfing partner about you," teases Hara genially.

"I said we had a nice time," jokes Yoshi, who seems a lot more relaxed than he was when I deserted him.

Golf: Japan's Blood Sport

Upon hearing that it is my birthday, Hara insists on taking me to the best joint in town. We stroll to a hostess bar called Chanko, which is down a flight of stairs off a Gion side street. Mama-san, the manager of the place, is Korean, and so are all the hostesses. Some of the girls are so fresh off the boat from Pusan that they don't speak any Japanese. Most of them are stunningly beautiful, with long legs, high cheekbones, and an unexpected aristocratic air. The transplanted Okinawa yakuza have said that Kyoto treats them like gaijin. Do they like Chanko because they relate better to these foreign hostesses?

"No," says Hara, clinically, "it's simply more secure than dealing with Japanese girls who may understand us."

The Hara-gumi men take over a wall of sofas and a row of facing chairs. At the next table a group of three businessmen are quietly leafing through the pages of a karaoke songbook. The colored lighting playing off the silvery wallpaper fills the small room with holiday cheer. A bevy of fresh-faced Asian ladies come over and join us. A gorgeous "senior" hostess (about twenty-five years old) slides in next to Hara and begins massaging his neck.

One of the salarymen begins crooning at the video screen where a young couple are shown walking hand in hand through Hibiya Park in Tokyo. I may be the only one listening. It is a popular, maudlin piece. Against the white noise of our merry band of thieves, the paunchy man sings doggedly on:

It's better if the sake is not too hot or too cold,
A quiet woman is best; a dim light is better,
If you drink in tears, my heart is weeping.
If you feel lonely at midnight, I'll just start singing.

(Perhaps, as they say, something gets lost in the translation, especially when you transcribe on a napkin. . . .)

One of the hostesses begs me to sing "Hound Dog" but I coyly decline. I occupy myself by picking apple slices and strawberries off a replica of the Disney castle built of fruit. Four of the hostesses are busily dropping ice cubes into dozens of highball glasses before mixing perfectly uniform Bushmills "whiskeysodas." The Mama-san laughs at my quaintness when I ask for sake: "It is just not what anyone drinks anymore!" She returns, however, with a precious bottle of Kagoshima-area sake, which she generously pours in a rocks glass. With the sake in my hand and the lovely Korean women, a birthday party has never looked so good. I have to admit I am kicking ass. Indeed, I came, I saw, and ingratiated myself.

A big grinning man in a dark, double-breasted suit walks into the club. It's Kaz, the business manager for Hara-gumi, of whom Hara thinks so much. Kaz also commands respect from every level because, above all, he looks and acts like a yakuza boss. A case in point: Kaz compliments my taste by ordering sake for himself as well. At the end of the evening, everyone but Hara is drinking sake.

Although he greets me in English, he asks me in Japanese if I enjoyed my golf outing.

"It was too hot."

"Most Japanese don't play games to have fun." Kaz laughs.

Yoshi leans over to mumble something to Kaz, who suddenly stares at me and raises an eyebrow. Then Yoshi nods at me. "It's OK. You probably saved me from getting in more trouble."

"What do you mean?"

"I'll explain." Hara holds up a silencing hand at Yoshi while giving me an indulgent smile. "After losing his match, Yoshi wanted to splatter the brains of the big-shot asshole all over the locker room. But you misunderstood the code word or something. Hey, even I have trouble with Yoshi's Osaka accent. Anyway, you didn't need to get involved in something like that . . . "

"Did I screw up?" I ask, replaying the confused locker-room scene in my head.

"No, no, no," Kaz chimes in. "You did a good thing. Yoshi is a hothead sometimes."

"Didn't the deal work out?" Now I'm really curious.

"Yeah, everything's fine," Hara says, as if I had done something wrong. "But Yoshi was—I don't know if you understand the expression—it means something like 'horny for blood.' That was Yoshi's condition, but, really, you did OK."

Golf: Japan's Blood Sport

*   *   *

"I suppose you want to start being paid," Hara says to me, as he sips iced coffee in his office several days later. The guys in the Hara-gumi headquarters are so used to seeing me around that they have toned down their once-effusive greetings to the more casual grunts they accord each other. The kobun named Matsui takes to inviting me along on his daily rounds about town. Matsui is tall and lanky—and very enthusiastic about yakuza life. Two years in prison mean nothing when you can fall right back in the groove with your yakuza brothers.

Although he had lived as a free man in Kyoto for over six years before his imprisonment, Matsui drives around the city with a renewed sense of wonder. He is constantly asking me to read from my English-language guidebook. I suggest he buy his own guide in his own language. But he shakes his head, as if that were unthinkable in his circles. It strikes me that the strain of anti-intellectualism in the yakuza may even exceed that of the average salaryman.

"Nobody in the gang knows anything about the history of this city—nothing," Matsui assures me. "We come from Okinawa, where the education system is not very good. Once a guy comes to Kyoto, he's already done with school. We learn how to make a living and how to behave, but nothing about the long history of Kyoto. The only history we learn is that Aizu Kotetsu hates Yamaguchi-gumi . . ."

"According to the newspaper," I interrupt, "Aizu Kotetsu signed a peace treaty with Yamaguchi-gumi two months ago."

"See!" Matsui laughs and slaps the dashboard. "That's how stupid I am about my own business."

Around noon we are sitting on a raised tatami platform in the shade of a shaved-ice concession stand. There are scores of Japanese tourists nearby, milling about and taking turns posing in front of the immense Kiyomizu Temple. The temple, according to my guide-book, "seems to grow right out of the nearby slope of Higashiyama and has attracted Buddhist pilgrims for thirteen hundred years."

"It's a good place to bring chicks," muses Matsui. "And that reminds me. Hara-san asked me to invite you to come out with us this evening."

I assume he is talking about another night of singing karaoke and carousing with the Hara-gumi executives. It's fine with me. These yakuza know how to have a good time, and they always pick up the tab.

"Yes, thanks," I say.

That evening as I duck into the backseat of Hara's Benz, I feel underdressed in my jeans and T-shirt. It also strikes me that the three men in the car are the Hara-gumi I know best. Because he is still in the novice phase of yakuza development, Koji is driving, with Ken in the passenger seat and the big boss Hara beside me in the back. They are all dressed in suits. With his freshly shaved head and unstructured jacket, Hara looks much hipper than his underlings. They simply look like the young hoodlums they are.

Although the Maharaja nightclub of Tokyo is no longer that city's most popular disco, the Maharaja is still king in Kyoto. And it is Maharaja's, at the foot of the Yasaka Temple in Gion, that is our destination . . . after one quick stop.

Over the past few weeks Koji has developed a defter touch behind the wheel. His eyes are always moving from his own side-view mirror, then straight out the windshield, up to the rearview mirror, to the speedometer, then over to the passenger's side mirror and back. His head doesn't move. He accelerates and brakes with a smooth, professional ease—a remarkable transformation from his first lurching attempts.

Hara is antsy, rubbing his palms against his knees. He breaks this nervous routine by clicking off the radio that has been whispering a Hanshin Tigers game. We drive down past the car dealerships in southern Kyoto, where the city's quaintness gives way to the same omnipresent landmarks of Lawson's, McDonald's, KFC, and pachinko halls that seem to define the urban corridor from Tokyo to Nagoya to Osaka.

Golf: Japan's Blood Sport

Hara grunts something to Koji, who cuts a sharp left onto a side street, and then a right into a gravel lot. I see a few bicycles locked to a chain-link fence but not much else before Koji cuts off the headlights. Ken and Koji are staring straight ahead at the back door of what I think might be a closed pachinko parlor. I can't read any of the Japanese painted on the wall. I assume we are picking up another guy for the disco. Ken turns back to speak but he is cut off by his boss, who tells him to shut up.

Then the building's interior lights go out and a hunched, haggard man in a loose-fitting suit emerges. He looks around for a moment, then turns to lock the door.

"Now," Hara whispers. Koji clicks the headlights on with the high beams. The man looks back, surprised but calm, as he raises his arm to block the glare. Hara and Ken simultaneously open their doors and get out. My stomach begins to churn as I watch the scene unfold. There is something comical, though, about Hara's squat figure in the baggy suit and black-and-white saddle shoes, with the halogen light reflecting off his dome. He looks like a killer clown. The man in the lights is still squinting when Hara clamps his hairy hand around the guy's arm. First his keys fall to the gravel, and then, with an easy shove, the man is sent sprawling.

If bar fights between young bucks are the only brawls you've ever seen, the beating of an aging and defenseless man looks particularly brutal. The man rolls back and forth trying vainly to block Hara's awkward kicks that thud into his ribs. Ken dances around the man's legs, taking opportune shots to his groin and thighs. Hara seems to start laughing, saying something to Ken, who is now breathing heavily from his exertions.

From my vantage point, the man is difficult to see, but he still has the strength to raise his arms above his head. The assault stops momentarily. It looks like Hara is telling some kind of long-winded joke to Ken, whose openmouthed, hangdog face appears to be waiting for the punch line. Then Hara looks back at the car.

"C'mon," Koji says to me glumly.

We approach the smiling Hara, who now looks, at best, like a paunchy weekend hunter standing over a wounded deer. I look

107

down at the man, who isn't as old as I thought, or as small. I don't know his offense, if he is a yakuza, or what. I can't imagine what the hell kind of thoughts are going through his scrambled brains. I imagine an American looking up from a New York mugging only to see a Japanese journalist.

"This is the fun part," Hara announces, as much to me as to Koji, who looks as stupefied as the victim. Ken has returned from the Benz toting, of all things, an aluminum baseball bat. The man forces out a plaintive wheeze that earns him another shoe to the head.

Hara takes the bat from Ken and hands it, grip first, to Koji, who holds the bat with his hands apart, like Ty Cobb. Then, like a Little League coach giving batting instructions, Hara points to the midpoint of his own thigh as the best place for Koji to aim. "But swing at the side of the thigh!" Koji looks confused, glancing at the man, whose moans are growing louder. I can't slink away, so I watch Koji and cringe, hoping he will swing forcefully enough to bust the femur with a single, relatively humane attempt. But Koji freezes, holding the bat in that awkward Cobbsian fashion.

"I don't like baseball," he says, then imploringly adds, "I've never played baseball—ever."

The man coughs blood onto his face, and then rolls over, vomiting onto the gravel. I feel the same way in my own gut; I want to get out of the whole fucked-up situation as much as Koji does. Then, in a fit of disgust, Ken pushes Koji aside, snatches the bat, and raises it high above his head. But Hara intercedes. He raises his hand and orders Ken to put the bat away. The bald yakuza smiles at me. "Maybe you shouldn't be here for this kind of thing. We don't want to make a bad impression on you."

Later that night in the club, I have to ask Hara about the incident and whether the reprieve he gave the man, a run-of-the-mill debtor, was an example of *ninjo* (yakuza sympathy).

"Ninjo?" He laughs. "No . . . Just call it public relations."

A few days after the baseball bat incident, I stop by the Hara-gumi office to find about thirty kobun in front of the building. Hara is yelling instructions to a carpenter setting a wooden plaque into the brick beside the front door.

The crowd looking on includes Koji, Yoshi, Ken, Matsui, Rambo, Nara, and the business manager, Kaz. The sun is beating down and Hara, looking a little silly in a pinstriped Hanshin Tigers baseball cap, guides the carpenter "higher, higher," then "left, no, a bit more to the right—right—perfect! Right over the old spot."

The square piece of heavy pine is then pushed firmly into the plaster. On the plaque is engraved "HARA-GUMI HEADQUARTERS."

Yoshi steps forward and throws up his arms, leading the group in shouting "Banzai! Banzai! Banzai!" and then gleeful applause.

Hara-gumi is the first gang in Kyoto to rehabilitate their public sign. After the new laws were passed last year, every gang removed yakuza symbols from their property. They all tried to look, if only superficially, like legitimate outfits.

"Who the hell were we trying to kid?" Hara laughs. "Everyone knows what we are. The cops know we're yakuza. We know we're yakuza. You know we're . . . So why not show it?

"And, if anyone complains . . . " In a pretend hitter's stance, Ken lifts his front leg in an imitation of the great home run hitter, Sadaharu Oh. " . . . it's batter-up time!"

LUNCH WITH THE BOSS

A lunch of soba noodles in delicious beef broth has been served in the third-floor conference room of the Aizu Kotetsu. As is customary, the oldest and most revered yakuza boss in western Japan, T. Takayama, sits at the head of the table. Next to me is a hulking fortyish underboss who, along with another older underboss, is pulling his three days a month of "SP" duty. Although no one seems to know the two English words for which SP is an abbreviation, these men—big-time bosses in their own right—are essentially bodyguards for their patriarch. Dressed in formal suits and ties, with their AK lapel pins gleaming, these middle-aged men aren't properly outfitted or trained to be legitimate bodyguards. This tidbit is confided by one of the more relaxed SPs. Supporting the SPs is a full-time detail of younger security specialists. SP duty is purely symbolic, reminding these criminal princes that Takayama is their king. Surely SP duty is humbling. To be plucked for even three days from one's fiefdom to hang around Takayama and suffer his utter indifference, must be humiliating. Takayama's royal aloofness, maintained in the midst of his underbosses (even as they hand him a drink or a phone), is rooted in his complete belief that he is a god to his men. Perhaps he also understands that if he cannot trust these men in his own office, he is as good as dead anyway.

110

Lunch with the Boss

The one time I witnessed Takayama-san speak directly to an SP was illuminating. At the end of one of my interview sessions, Takayama-san was leafing through his date book. September 3 was V-J Day, which in Japan is a solemn dirge of a holiday called Obon Yasumi, featuring much wreath laying and hand-wringing. I was ignorant of this when I requested another noontime meeting, and the boss seemed equally oblivious to the day's significance as he marked down the time.

But then, two or three beats too late for a truly spontaneous reaction, a rotund SP in a plaid suit exploded. He could no longer contain his rage at this American, who had monopolized more than a week of afternoons and evenings of a man whose importance he could not comprehend. Besides asking endless questions, many of them presumptuous and often tactless, and rudely accepting every one of Takayama-san's obviously rhetorical invitations to accompany him to his home, to dinner, even to the hyperexclusive Golddigger Club in Gion, this American now wants to continue his inquisition on Obon Yasumi!

I can only guess what this man was really thinking. Like the ideal Japanese housewife, a yakuza underling is supposed to silently anticipate his boss's needs and desires. But a wife and husband have daily contact. A silent SP sentry has just three days a month. Hence, his outburst was a real gamble. The delay in his attack reflected his indecision, but his wild tirade embodied real emotion, real anger. Not that I was sullying a sacred holiday, but that familiarity and endless talk had reached the point of disrespect.

"You cannot do this!" boomed this wide, fleshy-faced SP. "Don't you know that is Obon Yasumi! Can't you understand what an important man Kaicho-san is? You have taken enough of his time!"

Four wide-eyed men pushed through the door as the red-faced SP castigated me. "Explain to him!" the man pleaded with another SP. "He doesn't know what he's asking from the boss, a great oyabun who is like a god!" And back to me, "You're American, you don't understand!"

My heart was in my throat. I was afraid that perhaps I had been rude. I knew some of the underbosses resented my daily visits. One had said exactly that over his car phone while driving me to Otsu where I was to see Takayama-san's home. But it never bothered me. Actually I was glad to pick up some bad vibes: this tension made things feel real. I wanted some suspicion, resentment, and even a bit of hostility from these men. They were tough guys, after all. These were supposed to be the dregs of Japanese society, there was no reason they shouldn't be stupid, racist, and irrationally mean.

But had I screwed up? Had I fallen out of Takayama's favor? As the waves of aggression rolled over me, I was paralyzed by a terrible thought. If I fell out of Takayama's favor, the whole project would be dead. The presumptuous notion that I could infiltrate the gangs and write about them authoritatively was rooted in the belief that I knew how to get along with them. I used whatever novelty they saw in meeting a young American reporter to get close to them. Then I tried to show I wasn't coming in cold, I knew yakuza fundamentals and more. I knew the old stuff, the latest conflicts, the legends, the rising stars, the rules of their games and the rules they lived by. I knew to be straight with them, to be much more honest than would be proper with regular Japanese. I knew my Japanese sounded like mush, but I thought it made me sympathetic.

If the angry bulk was correct in assessing my rudeness with Takayama-san, however, I had failed. After three years in Japan I had perhaps internalized that uniquely Japanese belief concerning the fragility of human relationships and the idea that they could be irreparably destroyed by a single transgression. Think of what it takes for a yakuza to atone for a mistake: The guilty man must cut off the end of his finger!

But no. Takayama waved off the complaints of his bodyguard, saying that he had planned on giving me as much time as I needed—and he did, truly. Although the extent of these conversations are not reflected fully in these memoirs, the emotion, inside dope, and general wisdom imparted by Takayama-san constituted the foundation of my underground knowledge on which I based virtually all of my opinions and insights.

A few days after the explosion, the SP's point is well taken. I owe the boss. Towards the end of our soba noodle lunch, the sixty-four-year-old patriarch of Kyoto's Aizu Kotetsu clan turns to me. "You're a journalist. Shouldn't you be reporting on the Tokyo demo?" "Demo" as in "demonstration." Tokyo as in far and expensively away. But "yes" is the only answer. "Yes" is the only response Takayama ever hears. Not that it doesn't make perfect sense. I have been hanging around his office as plans are laid to send Aizu Kotetsu representatives, along with certain sympathetic Japanese newspapermen, to attend this demonstration against the controversial new antiyakuza laws implemented that summer.

Lunch with the Boss

The next morning, I am packing my bags for Tokyo and brooding a bit. I feel that I owe Hara more than I am able to give. At some risk, this active boss has virtually taken me to his bosom, even let me play with his kobun and fondle their guns. Where my sessions with Takayama have been cerebral and theoretical, my time with Hara has been real action in real time. I called the man last night to thank him for his hospitality and his unexpected accessibility. But Hara wouldn't hear of my gushing statements of gratitude. He even topped himself by offering to send a car to drive me to the station this morning.

Sure enough, as I dash out the front door, there is the familiar black Mercedes waiting at the curb. Ever alert, Ken pops the trunk lid and gives me a half bow. I feign surprise, but Ken just grunts and puts my battered bags away. Quickly we are off to the bullet train, and I take the opportunity to check up on the rest of the Hara-gumi guys. Ken responds laconically as I ask after Rambo, Nara, and the other kobun. Only when I get to my favorite rookie, Koji, does Ken show any particular feeling. He sucks air slowly through his teeth. "Since three days ago"—Ken glances over to me—"Koji has been in jail."

I am in shock. My precarious Japanese vocabulary crashes. I swallow hard and manage to spit out, "What the hell is Koji doing in jail?"

"Hara-san says, 'Koji is doing his duty' . . . "

"Please explain . . . ," I persist. "What did he do?"

We are waiting for a few cabs to clear the curb near the station entrance. Ken stares straight ahead and sighs audibly, as though he's explained this to me a hundred times before. "Koji did not do anything himself," Ken says, as he puts the car in park. "There's a member of the executive council whom you don't know. He's the number three man who never comes to the office because he runs his business out near Otsu. Anyway, somebody owed him money, and this somebody decided he wasn't going to pay up. This guy ended up hurt and unconscious on the shore of Lake Biwa. He was discovered by some schoolkids on an outing, and when the Nagahama cops ask him what happened, well, this moron men-

113

tioned our number three boss by name and by gang, and then Nagahama cops want a body. And they got one, named Koji."

"I'm surprised Koji would choose to serve out someone else's sentence," I say with a sinking heart.

"He didn't 'choose'—this was something he had to do," Ken explains. "But he's young, and it will only be five or six years . . . unless the guy dies. Then Koji will be in until he's forty or something."

"Dies?"

"The guy's in a coma now."

OBSOLETE HONDA

For three years, the trendy shops and neon bombast of Tokyo's Shibuya district have been an almost daily part of my life. But today, parking my scooter beneath the same catwalk where I've always hidden it, I'm not that same loose cannon hunting some crazy youth culture fad that might photograph well. No, this afternoon I'm scratching a back, washing the other hand—I'm returning a favor. Like the obsequious newspapermen who I had seen file through Takayama's office to pay their respects and ask his blessing, I approach the demonstration as a representative, however vague, of the Aizu Kotetsu yakuza syndicate. Although I am still a reporter, I'm not in my normal role as an unkempt and unruly freelancer looking for scenes. But, alas, I meet a small, disheveled man who says the demonstration has been postponed until the next Saturday.

Pacing around the fountain in front of Tokyo's Asaguya Station, I must look like a lost tourist. Off to my right is a charming stretch of full leafy trees that strikes me as lovely and serene, in direct contrast to the job awaiting me. Six weeks have passed since I first encountered Honda, Lion's lieutenant and Taro's drug connection.

I am now having second thoughts about this private interview. Beyond the tattoos and tough talk, the impression he gave me was that of a tightly wound man who exuded the scent of violence.

But I'm disarmed and a bit disillusioned by Honda's second, and now street-dressed appearance. The gangster in his blue polo shirt and matching cardigan looks for all the world like a successful daddy waiting for his daughter's ballet class to be let out. His oversized S-class Mercedes is the only hint of a shady character. The car definitely impresses me and draws several admiring glances from late-night commuters. In the now-stagnant economy, both citizens and yakuza have been divesting themselves of imported behemoths. Honda's panzer tank of an automobile proves he is still a man to be reckoned with.

After a few pleasantries I decline Honda's offer to visit a local hostess club and, rather boldly, suggest we talk in his apartment. We silently drive to his flat, which turns out to be only slightly larger than his car. Although it's a typical Tokyo "six mat," about 108 square feet of living space, it feels much too small for Honda and me—and the hulking man who suddenly emerges from the apartment's tiny bathroom. Dressed in just a T-shirt and boxer shorts, the bruiser warily steps around me to get to a satin shirt hanging on the wall. Honda, sorting his mail, waits for him to button up before reassuring each of us that the other is mutually harmless. I rise from the carpet to bow while the big man grunts, "Sit, sit!"

For "security reasons," the big man can't tell me his name but volunteers that he is "not a yakuza but a rightist." He also announces that he has lost his pants. He then shrugs and plops down on the floor, exposing a palm-sized patch of inflamed red skin on his inner right thigh. I know Honda deals shabu, so I presume that the scarlet patch is the result of a decade of needle pricks. With shaking hands, he manages to light his cigarette.

As Honda continues with his mail, I follow up on his pal's "right wing" declaration by asking his opinions on two of the Far Right's favorite issues: reclaiming the northern islands from Russia and trashing Japan's American-written constitution. "I'm not into that political shit anymore," he spits, before taking a long drag off

Obsolete Honda

his Marlboro. "It's not the same as it used to be. Now the right is just little punks too weak to commit themselves to the hard life of a true Japanese patriot. No! They just want to extort money from any citizen for no reason! Back in my day we had a reason, some kind of political purpose, before we'd put the squeeze on some-one—or we made one up! You gotta have a reason . . . any reason . . . just some kind of reason . . . You gotta give a reason . . . "

Honda just snickers at the drug-induced ramblings of his buddy, and not at his struggle to get up on his feet.

It's a bitch for fat Japanese men (a rather recent phenomenon) to get off the floor. Being wired on speed and holding a cigarette makes it even tougher for this nameless Buddha. Eventually he achieves a fully erect standing position. He turns back to the plas-tic bathroom, grabs his sweatpants, and tugs them on with diffi-culty. Honda and I share a silent moment of amusement. Surely, the man would be happier in a roomy American split-level or even a New York studio apartment—he's just too big for Japan.

"If you want to be a yakuza," the rightist resumes in a more confident tone, "you should go live with Sato-san, the famous boss of Tokyo's big Matsuba-kai gang. Then you would learn! You'd have to wake up before the sun, like a monk, and cook breakfast for your oyabun . . . And you better hope he likes it!" He pauses to look into a wall mirror, pats his wavy permed hair into place, and brushes imaginary dandruff off his shoulder. I watch the manic hulk grab a set of keys off a side table.

"Do you even know what *natto*, the Japanese bean paste break-fast, is?" He points down at me, a small, slightly terrorized figure with a tape recorder and a note book in my lap. "Yes, you'd spend the day working chores like a woman! You couldn't ask a lot of stupid questions! You'd learn by watching and by doing! Then you would really come to know yakuza no michi, the true path of the yakuza! Yakuza no michi can't be taught like baseball!" He jabs his pawlike hand towards the TV.

"Even gaijin can learn yakuza no michi!"

"Enough!" Honda barks, interrupting what he must have con-sidered nonsense.

117

YAKUZA DIARY

Honda's outburst startles the fat man and he seems to recon-
sider his place. "I am sorry, Honda-san," he says in fairly formal
language punctuated with a short bow. "Forgive me." He doesn't
look at me as he drops the keys in his pants pocket and walks to
the door. As he props himself against the wall to slip on his shoes,
he seems to struggle with another Japanese custom. The metal door
slams behind him.

Honda is now absorbed with the process of feeding two big
turtles he keeps in a large tank. It is like a well-appointed tropical
resort, with a swimming area that gives way to a purple gravel beach
supporting two plastic palm trees. Relatively speaking, the two
turtles had a five-thousand-dollar-a-month Tokyo living space.
Below the turtles there's a smaller tank where dozens of goldfish
swim in hazy water.

Honda dips a small net into the goldfish tank and corners a
single fish, then gingerly scoops it out. He places the net on some
newspaper and then, with thumb and forefinger, picks up the tiny
fish. In his other hand he brandishes a medical syringe with a two-
inch needle, which he carefully inserts into the head of the wrig-
gling fish. Honda eases in the plunger, forcing air (as he explains it)
into the fish's brain, killing it instantly. He dangles, then drops, the
limp form into the tank, where it's slowly noticed, but then quickly
devoured by one of the turtles. As more fish are dropped in, the
hungry turtles knock shells, like tiny sumo, hustling for the food.

Honda lords over his miniature execution ground with the
quiet manic glee of a nasty boy—more precisely, an *unobserved* nasty
boy. This feeding ceremony doesn't end until fourteen fish have
been served. Then Honda lights a cigarette and stares at the turtle
tank for a full minute before turning to me. I click on my tape
recorder, wishing I had a video camera. Honda's ensuing soliloquy is brilliant, erratic, sweaty, ice-cold, and scary:

"My father left my mother before I was born. I was raised by
my grandmother, who worked cleaning up at a pool hall in Iriya
in Shitamachi, Tokyo. She worked six days a week from nine in
the morning till midnight, when she had to scrub the toilets. When
I was small, I was brought to the pool hall every day. I don't know

118

what happened to my mother. I was told she died, but I was never shown her gravestone at O-bon, an August holiday honoring dead ancestors, when my grandmother and I would wash the tombstone of my grandfather.

"My grandparents had come to Tokyo from the snow country in the mountains of Niigata prefecture. They came down here after the war. Some people from their hometown had sent messages back about the nice lives they had made in Tokyo. My grandfather was inspired by these notes to pack up and move to Tokyo. In truth, conditions in Tokyo turned out to be worse than back in the sticks. But my grandfather would have been ashamed to return, so they stuck it out. It turned out that their friends in Tokyo—or their sons, at least—were selling morphine and had their wives working in brothels serving American GIs.

"Anyway, my grandfather stayed and became one of those blade sharpeners who walk up and down the streets singing out, 'Oh bring out your dull blade and I'll make them sharper, as sharp as a samurai's sword.' He was an honorable man, but died in 1957 without any pension for my grandmother. That's why she had to work.

"Growing up in a pool hall, you're going to meet a lot of yakuza. I was a kind of chimpira until I left school at fourteen. I knew arithmetic pretty well from all those years adding up pool scores and making change at the hall. And I learned everything about gambling and bookmaking from the older men. Lion-san came to know me and took me into his organization. But my yakuza career really began in 1977 when I asked Lion-san if I could form my own gang.

"Lion-san was doing well, the gang was making piles of money. Lion owned three dozen safe-deposit boxes at just one of the neighborhood banks. He wore this big ring of keys around his belt loop that made a *sing-ling-ling* noise when he walked. His wife used to call him 'The Bellboy'! You should know she's from Osaka; only an Osaka lady would joke that way! This was a happy and relaxed time for Lion, he wasn't such a strict oyabun then.

"I had lost some years in jail and had been promoted to *wakagashira*, young boss. But most of the Lion-gumi's new businesses were just investments that didn't need a lot of men. But I needed warm bodies for my own rackets. I also needed more time for my own operations. I really needed my own gang. . . . "

For a kobun to form his own gang is a natural way for a yakuza organization to grow. A kobun with special "heart" or intelligence is expected to break off from his parent gang to open his own office and take the title of oyabun himself. An ambitious yakuza has got to be a self-starter and pretty goddamned confident to make the change. A gang of, say, sixty kobun may have only two or three with the ability and guts to form their own gumi. These "best kobun" will seem indispensable to their own oyabun, of course. But it's the duty of an oyabun to know the moment when his star pupils are ready for leadership. He then is obliged to order them to leave. For a kobun to presume to ask his oyabun to let him go may look very bad. But they will always share their father-son relationship, and the kobun will continue earning his boss lots of money. Still, the overture can be construed as a selfish, wholly un-Japanese act. Thus Honda was filled with trepidation entering Lion's office to request permission to form his own gang.

Honda continues, "I told him that it had always been an honor to be a member of Lion-gumi, that I was thankful for all that I had learned and for what I had become. Lion-san looked up from his newspaper like he thought I was crazy to talk like that so early in the morning. Then I simply said that I knew I was ready to lead my own gang that would serve Lion-gumi's as well as my own needs.

"'You want to be an oyabun?'

"'Hai!'

"'Then call Seki-san.'

"Seki-san was a neighborhood citizen who made wreaths and calligraphy displays for weddings, openings, and funerals. So 'call Seki-san' meant plan the sakazuki that would celebrate the birth of Honda-gumi. I fell to my knees and bowed all the way to the floor. I was relieved that oyabun wasn't insulted. I went down to my girlfriend's snack bar and bought a bottle of Chivas. It was the happiest moment of my life."

* * *

Obsolete Honda

Sakazuki is a ceremony performed by yakuza for various important occasions. When a new young kobun first joins a gang, a simple sakazuki takes place. A peace agreement between two warring gangs may be sealed with a more elaborate sakazuki. The most extreme sakazuki occur when an old, revered oyabun of a major syndicate retires and passes the leadership to a new boss. This big-time sakazuki can become a huge holiday with the biggest, richest, most famous bosses converging on the grounds of a single temple or headquarters. The overwhelming show of yakuza man power, cohesiveness, tradition, and outright arrogance leads the TV evening news and gets big photo spreads in tabloid newspapers and magazines. It also makes the authorities uneasy.

The yakuza have often been players in Japan's largest movie studios, so it's not surprising that milestone sakazuki ceremonies are documented by professional film (now video) crews as both personal keepsakes and for the gang's archives. It's a rare yakuza boss who doesn't groove on the atmosphere of a major sakazuki fête when the nation, including everyone in the old neighborhood who thought he was dirt, is watching.

"I have a photograph," Honda continues. "I'm wearing a gray suit and white socks! Lion-san looks fat and healthy sitting on a cushion on the tatami beside a single pyramid of oranges. With his dark glasses he looks like a movie oyabun! A retired yakuza named Kurotani acted as the *azukarinin*, the master of ceremonies or guarantor. Most gangs have some older member who knows how to perform a sakazuki the right way.

"I was thirty-four when Kurotani spoke the words that I still have memorized, 'Lion-san, you have been in the world of outcasts and gamblers for thirty-five years. You have lived in the spirit of Jinrocho of Shimizu and practiced chivalry and patriotism with the selflessness of a true yakuza. Your kobun Honda-san asks that you indulge him by letting him take the mantle of leadership in his own organization.'

"Kurotani poured sake from a jug into a small ceramic dish and, with two hands, held the dish before Lion. Lion took the dish and after the prescribed two sips, handed the dish back to Kurotani.

"'Honda-san,' Kurotani said to me, 'will you remain true to your mission, to your heritage, to your oyabun? Will you practice the traditions of a gambler and an outcast in the spirit of chivalry? Will you treat your kobun strictly but with compassion? Will you do nothing to soil the name of your oyabun?' Then the dish was filled three-quarters full of sake and handed to me. I drank it all with one sip . . . and Honda-gumi was born."

He pauses for a minute, as if he were drinking it all in again. Then he blinks a few times and clears his throat. "Gang headquarters are everywhere. In Tokyo's major districts, like Shibuya and Shinjuku, there are about 250 and 500 yakuza offices, respectively. There may be several gangs in a single building. For the most part, yakuza working among citizens take great pains to be good neighbors. But when gang trouble erupts, a lot of the gunplay goes down in the hallways of these 'mixed' apartment buildings.

"In 1978 I rented a suite in a new office building in Asaguya, one with windows that were like huge two-way mirrors. My office had a nice view, but no one could see inside—it was made for a yakuza! I had business cards printed up with my gang name and address. I decided to call myself 'president' instead of 'oyabun.' 'President' sounded more modern. 'Oyabun' always sounds like an old man, and I still felt like a young man. I lost a lot of my youth in prison, but I was still immature—in a good way. I was ready to make money and make something of my gang.

"My first thought was expansion. There were massive construction projects going on all over Tokyo, even in neighborhoods that nobody had ever shown any interest in since the war. I would walk up to a site that was just breaking ground and asked the boss if he needed men. 'Of course,' he said. 'It's my biggest problem. You get me some bodies here by six A.M. and I'll make it worth your effort.' So I rented a van, and on the next morning I went over to Taito-ward slums, picking up raw laborers! I told you I was in conventional yakuza businesses! Managing day workers isn't exactly the glamour of the stock market!

Obsolete Honda

"Within six or eight months of my sakazuki, I had seven kobun in Honda-gumi. Two of the original guys I had known from the Asaguya shopping street; the others were their buddies from the neighborhood and juvenile detention. That business about young kids being 'recruited' into the yakuza! Let me tell you, it's more like they show up and hang around until you've got to give them a job, just to get them off your back.

"It helps that new guys usually have friendships with the other kobun from before they joined the gang. Everyone works together better that way. That's why this world's got the salaryman's beat: Yakuza are mostly buddies who would've been together without a formal gang. It makes everything run smoother and more enjoyably. Of course, when real friends become enemies, it can make some real trouble within a gang! But that doesn't happen often.

"My Honda-gumi was a typical small Tokyo gang. Six of my kobun slept in the office, where there was a small kitchen. They would eat and clean up before I arrived around ten A.M. One of the kobun, called Aoki, was older and didn't live in the office. He simply had to check in with me. Aoki had finished high school and kept my books on a computer he made me buy. That made my life easier.

"I was probably the first yakuza to be computerized. Back then, I sure as hell never heard of any boss near my level who received a weekly printout of all their business! Most yakuza don't like to write anything down, but Aoki assured me that no one could get at our records.

"After a while it seemed that everyone in my gang was at Aoki's place learning about computers. Nobody was out hustling. This began to make me nervous. So one day I had Aoki print out what I needed. Then I took the computer and monitor and smashed it in Aoki's garden.

"After that, Honda-gumi was never really high-tech. I favored the plain concrete kinds of activities that weren't too complicated. My business philosophy was based on the idea that there's always room for one more ramen shop, serving Chinese noodles. I'd drive around Tokyo looking for a stretch that looked like it could support a new ramen shop. You don't need much space. Often there's a usable storefront available down an alley or in an apartment lobby. I found out that the restaurant supply business is a well-oiled machine and as interconnected as the auto industry. We can build a ramen shop in five days!

"Like most citizen businesses, those suppliers worked extra fast when hired by yakuza—not because of any threat, but because they knew they'd get paid right away. A couple of my kobun could handle themselves in a kitchen, so, before hiring a real ramen cook, my boys would work the place for a few weeks to gauge the traffic. If it looked like the place would make it, I'd go out and find real ramen men. If not, I'd cut my losses by selling the place cheap or just shutting down.

"Once, when a ramen shop went bust, I turned the place into a discount shop where I could fence the electronic stuff I'd gotten through some credit card scams. I soon learned that I could sell things for regular prices as long as the place appeared to be a discount store. Japanese housewives belong to incredible gossip networks: if they think they're getting a bargain, the word spreads all over their buildings and neighborhoods. When the lease was up, I finally shut the store, and some women were begging me to stay open! I always believed it was better not to squeeze something to a dry husk. As stupid as the typical Tokyo beat cop is, eventually someone's going to ask too many questions. Tokyo seems like such a big city, but I like to think of it as a thousand small villages put together like a puzzle. The chance to re-create the same business in place after place is infinite! My own boredom is what kept me moving half the time.

"I have to laugh when yakuza say, 'We're just like citizens— trying to make a living, raise a family, and support our country.' The basic difference is that when the average citizen has a business problem with someone, he doesn't scream at the guy and wave a pistol in his face! Japanese hate confrontation and fights.

"The younger yakuza go to violence too fast. The older guys may whisper threats, may even get into shouting matches, but they don't pull guns! Yakuza now have guns, like guns, and use guns. I'd say yakuza go out of their way for this kind of fight, even if it means hurting their income.

Obsolete Honda

"As a last resort, even I have used a gun. I guess there's something wrong in the yakuza brain, that keeps us from acting like regular people. We used to spill blood only among ourselves, but now I think the general public is justified in their fear of us. Everyone seems to be afraid except foreign journalists like you!"

I ask him what other foreign journalists he means.

"There was an American writer who sold me ammunition a few days ago."

I tell him that American writer was me. I add that I was just along for the ride and that I was not truly selling him the ammo.

"I see." Honda smiles like he's catching me in a lie. "Then those bullets were just a gift?"

I don't feel like attempting to explain the truth because that would entail contradicting him while I'm trying to show him respect and keep him talking, so I ask what he may have in mind for "my" bullets. With that, Honda rises to disappear in the bathroom for as long, I assume, as it takes to inject himself with shabu. Whatever the downside of the drug, Honda returns wide-eyed and ready to talk.

"I'm not planning on killing anyone soon," Honda says without sarcasm. "I hope I don't use any of your ammunition or anyone else's for the rest of my life. Does that disappoint you?"

It's okay.

"I remember who I have shot," Honda says. "There are yakuza who say they don't know exactly how many men they've killed because ninjo, their heart, keeps them from shooting someone right in the head or sticking their sword through the heart. But that's crap! If you're going to get someone close up, then you're going to shoot to kill. Anything else is stupid. In the old days you'd only get a seven- or eight-year sentence for murder, but now it's fifteen!

"Yakuza don't hire hit men like the Mafia. Only an elderly boss would ask a kobun to do his dirty work; most yakuza—bosses down to chimpira—do their own shooting. I have killed three men in my life. Two I won't talk about. Those two I regret.

"The third was a fat stupid bum named T., who had become a regular customer at my girlfriend Megumi's 'snack,' which was more a saloon than a snack bar. T. said he first came to Tokyo to train in sumo. He said he was from Gunma prefecture but his heavy hick accent sounded even more rural. He sported a complete yakuza image with these fancy Hong Kong suits, gold rings, dark glasses, and even those huge sideburns sumo used to have.

"Because he was fat, T.'s age was difficult to figure. Maybe somewhere near fifty. I didn't know. Anyway, he was a good tipper who sat on the same stool every evening from six to nine-thirty. Every bar needs a few regulars like that. Also, he was the kind of a colorful loudmouth who gave the place a party atmosphere, even when there was hardly a soul in the joint.

"I didn't mind all his big talk about his sumo victories and injuries. After five or six months, he began to run a tab at the bar. The first time he paid off after two weeks. The second time it took longer, then he paid the exact amount down to the last yen—without a tip. All the time he was pumping my girl for information about me, about Honda-gumi, about my car (it was an Eldorado back then). Listen, I was rarely ever at the snack bar, maybe right before closing, a couple times a week.

"In the middle of the next tab run-up, which was really starting to bother my girl, T. started bragging about his yakuza connections. Megumi knew never to admit to strangers that I was connected, even though, back then, I looked like a gangster right out of the movies. T. tells her that he was going to set up a meeting with some liquor supply people he knows. He says these guys will save her lots of money. He was saying this stuff to a lady! A Japanese woman is always going to be well-mannered and say 'yes' to everything! All along she was hoping that he was just shooting off his mouth, and there's not going to be any wiseguy suppliers coming down to the snack. She didn't bother me with T.'s offer.

"One day a couple of slobs drop three cases of Chivas Regal at the snack. Megumi did the right thing and called my office. I got over there with a couple of my boys ready for trouble. I didn't know whether these guys were yakuza or phonies or what. We just sent them and their scotch packing.

Obsolete Honda

"We left, but I went back again that night. T. was there. He offered me a drink but I said 'no.' I took out the delivery guy's business card and pushed it to T. He looked at it and shrugged. I told him that denying he set up the liquor scam would make things worse. Then he changed his mood, saying he just suggested that some friend of his call Megumi about buying some cheaper whiskey. He said he had only told Megumi that he could save her some money. I was thinking, 'Who does this jerk think he is—going to save Megumi some money!' But I didn't say anything.

"'I told Megumi that some boys might stop over to talk to her,' he said. Now I wanted to kill him because he was lying and trying to pass his mistake off on a woman! What a creep! I was so mad, I couldn't speak when he then called out to Megumi. 'Didn't I tell you, Megumi-chan? Did I say something to you about some boys?'

"'Don't talk to her, old man!' I yelled. 'Don't hide behind a woman!' I was getting angrier.

"Megumi, who was at the far end of the bar, was walking past us to get into the back room. T. suddenly jumped up and grabbed her with his arm around her neck. Quickly he reached beneath his jacket and pulled out an old *katana,* a short sword!" Honda stands up to demonstrate with a Kabukilike stance. Then he drops his arms and relaxes back on the carpet before continuing.

"I saw the madness in his eyes, so I didn't move, I just told him to relax. Inside, I'd already decided to kill him, but, I thought, I must stay cool on the outside. Megumi looked very calm for someone with a knife at her throat. You never know how people are going to react. 'Get the hell out of here!' T. yelled at me. The other bar customers quietly backed out the door. With every second the situation was getting worse." Now Honda slowly uncoils from his seat and strikes a new pose before continuing: "I stood up slowly with a big grin and— one, two, three—I grabbed his arm with my left hand and whipped out my pistol. *Bang, bang!* The guy got two new eyeholes and he and his katana crashed to the floor. Megumi didn't say anything, even with T.'s blood on her face and hair. Maybe she was in shock."

A smile came over his face: "It's usually good to shoot somebody in the head because it's easy to make it look like a suicide. If

127

Tokyo police think there's a small chance that an unnatural death can pass for a suicide, they'll call it that. They don't waste time with investigations that could confuse their conclusion. Two bullet holes make it harder to explain.

"I pulled open T.'s shirt to see if he had any yakuza markings, but he was just fat. I called my kobun, Aoki, who came and helped me wrap the dead pig. He had brought this red-and-white striped fabric used for festivals. I joked that he should've found the black-and-white fabric used for funeral decorations. We even had a couple of drinks, then we drove the body across town to the freight yards in Sumida-ward. I pushed my gun under the body, so the cops wouldn't have to think at all. When I returned to the snack, Megumi had cleaned all the blood from the walls and floor. She was burning the bloody rags in an oil drum in the alleyway, but she hadn't cleaned the blood off her face and dress. I left the fire burning, drove her home, and gave her a bath. Then she felt better. After I put her to bed, I sat in the bath for a long, long time."

Honda lights a cigarette as I switch cassettes to keep him talking. Then, as if cued by the *click* of my RECORD button, Honda begins another chapter: "I try never to have personal conflicts with anyone. I'm a stand-up guy who doesn't screw around with my kobun or the citizens who work for me. I am successful in my businesses because I don't bleed them as soon as they turn a profit. All my bills are paid on time; I don't jerk people around. Let me tell you—some bosses, once they get money, never pass it on to those who helped them get it. Some young kobun who's busting his ass washing dishes in his boss's club or doing some other shit job is never gonna ask his oyabun for his pay. And your average citizen, of course, doesn't have the balls to demand his money. I'm not talking about a loan company or some fat land developer, but little people. You see I was trying to be more than a good boss, I was trying to be a good guy.

"Still I was just a stupid Shitamachi kid. Making small profits and being Mr. Niceguy isn't all there was to business. Making money grow and keeping it safe, those things I never figured out. Especially when Lion-san always reminded me that those days were special and the easy money wouldn't last. Ten years ago, the stock market was like a pachinko that always came up sevens. Once I met with this stockbroker who was offering guaranteed big returns on my money. But it wasn't my style. My businesses were nothing fancy, just straight-up yakuza trades. I don't grab turf that isn't mine or go out of my way to hurt anyone who doesn't earn it. I even let some jerks off the hook who didn't deserve it.

"In 1989 I was still doing pretty good. Honda-gumi had thirteen kobun, two offices, and three six-mat apartments for the kobun. We were the number one group under Lion-gumi, and I was starting to make big plans in my head. I finally married my old girlfriend; we had a son and a girl. I kept two mistresses and sprung for their apartments. Eventually, I laid off one talkative mistress. I was an oyabun, of course, so I needed to be discreet.

"But when you have a son, you start seeing things differently. I began wondering, When he gets older, how will I look through his eyes? I'd heard all the stories of yakuza whose kids are embarrassed at school or whatever. I was yakuza, and that couldn't change. But I wasn't into putting girls on the street and taking their money. I wasn't into any real sex business or sleazy blackmail or drugs. I mostly relied on my special talent for small business. Everything I touched did pretty good. Of course I didn't pay taxes, and I was breaking the law a hundred little ways, but I was no menace to society.

"Those dirty land developers who I helped with evictions were always tempting me with inside offers on this or that. But I was an old-style yakuza. Making money with money didn't fit in with my idea of what a yakuza boss does. If a business didn't need any workers, then how was I helping my kobun?

"Part of the yakuza life is having something to do and a place to go. A young guy comes to me because he's been thrown out on his ass by his family and nobody else wants him. This kid is honestly looking for something to do with his life and his youthful energy. His desire must be strong, or he wouldn't come to some man like me—a big creep with nine and a half fingers and a gun in his belt—asking to join my gang.

"Hey, these young guys aren't the kind of robots who want to wake up at six to take the train for two hours to get to some boring job. These young guys have spirit; sparks shoot out of their assholes. They're always eager to do anything, they hate doing nothing! Most kobun would rather sweep the street with a toothbrush than wait in a car for a few hours. They keep their boss moving. That's why a boss has got to provide different chores and jobs; that's what I've always believed this oyabun duty was all about.

"Every Sunday it is my obligation to pay my respects to my oyabun at his house. . . . You been there, right?" Honda asks me.

"No," I say, assuming the room above the bar was not Lion's home. "I met you and him in Shinjuku . . . that's not his home?"

"No!" Honda huffs like I should know better. "I mean his house in Meijiro. Anyway, I'm talking about a few years ago, back when I was a young boss, the number one kobun in Lion-gumi. But, when you talk to your oyabun, your success doesn't matter, you're still a kobun. During my weekly meetings, I kept his cigarettes lit, his drink fresh, and let him win at go. For the first hour, I would just sit answering his questions about my wife or kids—anything except yakuza business. Sometimes he would tell an old story from his gambling days or about war time. Yakuza had it rough back then, they never had money for extras like new clothes or a nice meal. But they had a strong yakuza spirit. They weren't always worrying about real estate and keeping different types of companies under control. Lion-san was a gambler running dice games anyplace he could find that was away from the cops. Only citizens, mostly laborers, were allowed to play. The yakuza just ran the game and paid off all bets. There wasn't any guaranteed profit; they could go bust with just a short run of bad luck! I used to love hearing about those old yakuza—before the big money, big cars, the golf. . . .

"During my meetings with Lion-san, he would test me by asking about my kobun. He wouldn't ask, 'How are your boys?' he'd be real specific, like, 'Is that skinny Murata making any progress?' He remembered all the names of my kobun and their jobs; he was like a computer. If I didn't know where one kobun was working at a given time or some other small detail, he would shake his head.

Obsolete Honda

'Your kobun must be your main concern.' He'd say, 'They're not just employees—if they don't feel the heat of your breath on the back of their necks, they'll become wild and dishonor you.'"

At this, Honda's voice trails off until he just stops talking. For a few seconds he stares at the television, which is rerunning the same baseball highlight show that was on when I arrived. He's staring, staring, staring . . . until he's back.

"I told you I was a moron," Honda declares. "I always have been, and that's not going to change now or ever. Anyway, in 1989 I was doing all right, better than that, really. I didn't know life could be that good. My kobun were doing pretty well, too. But one of them got a little ambitious. This kid, Suzuki, who came from the country and had some big ideas about real estate. He got these ideas from some chimpira in a Shinjuku gang. They were all in on the latest real estate craze for parking lots. The real estate market had started going soft, and big building projects were getting canceled all over town. Landowners stopped making plans for rebuilding, the need for mass evictions looked like it was going to dry up." (These "removals" are better known in yakuza circles as *jiyage*. During the real estate boom Japan's strong tenant rights spurred many property owners to hire yakuza to clear out old buildings for development. Using methods ranging from payoffs to bodily harm, yakuza forced stubborn tenants out.)

"Then some new tax loophole was discovered that made property owners want to level everything and put up parking lots. Maybe you've noticed? One day there's a row of houses, the next days there's a fenced-in parking lot with no cars. With a money-losing parking business the owner didn't pay any property tax.

"Anyway, suddenly there was a new demand for jiyage. The big real estate companies wanted all the tenants out fast, before the law got changed. These men weren't going to be happy until Tokyo was one big, money-losing parking lot.

"My kobun Suzuki learned the ropes with the Shinjuku group. Of course, he had come to me first, and I told him to go ahead. I was interested myself because I'd been hearing a lot about real estate work over the years. But, since I was based way out here in

Asaguya, I never saw any of the big-money property deals that went on inside the Yamanote line. I could do just about any kind of business anywhere in Tokyo, but land sharking is something else. You need solid connections in the old-boy network of straight businessmen as well as in the yakuza.

"It was in Shinjuku where I first saw you with Taro Mura-san?" Honda looks at me and I nod. "That's not Lion-san's office, it's just a place he's had for a hundred years."

Honda continues: "Suzuki began doing pretty good in Shinjuku. Maybe you've heard stories of how land sharks force tenants from apartments with jackhammers and threats, but the truth is that it's usually much more simple and well-mannered. Basically, two men will go by the apartment early, say, five-thirty or six, and knock on the door and say 'good morning.'

"That simple 'good morning' is usually enough to get people moving. But the one big problem we had, has stayed with me. Suzuki had received a contract to evict a woman and her young son from a broken-down apartment building in Nishi-Shinjuku. I had spoken to the developer, who said this mother was being hardheaded and unreasonable. He said he had offered them five million yen and promised a bigger new apartment, but the woman refused to leave.

"I suggested to Suzuki that he go over with some candy and have a nice conversation with her. Well, he didn't report back to me right away. It seemed like a week until I saw Suzuki again. He reported that the woman was crazy. He said she took out her lease and read all the provisions that made it legally impossible to force her out. So, between the developer and my own kobun, I had this picture in my mind of a feisty, tough woman who wants to fight it out.

"So, I told Suzuki to take the operations to the next level. I wasn't specific . . . I just told him to take care of it."

Honda takes a break to light another cigarette. He has long since stopped looking at me as he speaks. Instead, he stares blankly at the silent television screen. He takes a long drag.

"What Suzuki did was break through the door and fire blanks in the house. This caused the lady to have a heart attack and die.

Obsolete Honda

I found out maybe an hour later when the developer called me all freaked out. 'Why did he kill her?!' the developer kept screaming.

"I thought he had gone crazy, but quickly I learned the truth. Before Suzuki had gone over there to frighten them with the blanks, he had never made any contact! There had been no previous visit, not even by the developer. They both had been bullshitting me. The morning Suzuki busted in firing the pistol was the first and last notice!

"I had to go to the apartment myself to take care of the mess. It turned out the kid was only nine years old, and he wasn't the woman's son, he was her grandson. Their apartment was small. It reminded me of when I was a kid living with my grandmother . . . I took the kid to the ward office. I said I was his uncle but I couldn't care for him. I heard he ended up in some temporary home. All this so some greedy developer can put up a parking lot. But the number one reason was my laziness as an oyabun. I hadn't been keeping the close eye on my kobun that Lion-san had told me was so important. I kicked Suzuki out of my gang. Now he's caught on in a gang in Chiba. It was my fault really, but I never meant to hurt an old lady or a kid. . . ."

Though I've seen a Japanese man beaten to a pulp, I've never seen a sweaty, shaky wreck like Honda. Then, as though waking from a dream, he shakes his head and lights a cigarette. I know that Japanese housewives often use English teachers as de facto therapists. With their rudimentary English they like to unburden themselves of dark personal secrets and taboo marital complaints, unspeakable in Japanese. Although Honda's catharsis is in his native tougue, perhaps it's the foreign ears that make the difference.

The nicotine calms him enough to order me to stop the tape. He rises to his feet and looks at the wall clock that says 12:45. As he turns to the door he asks where I live.

"Hiro-o," I say, as we slip on our shoes. I can't help thinking that the long ride home will be awkward, but a cab ride would be over one hundred dollars.

"I'm going to Shirogane-dai," Honda says. "That's near you. We can go together." Standing at the door, Honda seems a much smaller man than the confident yakuza five hours earlier.

Together we walk from his apartment building. It's warm and the country quiet reminds me how far away we are from where I'm going. I drift off the footpath to the gravel space where I thought he had parked his big Mercedes.

"No, no, no." Honda waves me to the road.

"What?" I ask stupidly.

"I lent the car to my friend, you remember?" Honda says, with more hope than conviction. His sheepish grin and my memory tell me otherwise. I know he is trying to save face. The big car that so impressed me isn't his at all. I walk in silence beside Honda as we stroll down some twisting side streets. Eventually we reach a two-way avenue where a glowing Family Mart convenience store is the only sign of life. Now I walk behind Honda, whose heel-scraping, yakuza shuffle echoes in perfect rhythm until an empty cab stops at his side. In the cramped backseat, I am closer to Honda than I want to be. The man has lost his money, family, his honor, and even his automobile. Does he realize I know the car isn't his?

One doesn't talk about underworld business in the presence of prying cabbie ears, so I listen to Honda sing along with the radio. It is a typical heartbreaking *enka* ballad; the bits of lyrics I copy on my notebook cover read, "I told you I would wait by the stream where we first met. . . . My tears fall into the rushing waters. . . . Ten years have passed, but I wait here still. . . . " Honda begins to sing softly as the taxi cruises unimpeded from dark Nakano-ward through the lights of Shinjuku, where those brazen neons flash over forlorn sidewalks. The song gives way to a weather report, but Honda continues singing between yawns, "Ten years have passed, but I wait here. . . . " As the cab swings past the glassy new Shina-nomachi Station, I feel Honda's shoulder press against my own. He drifts into a sleep induced by a four-hour autobiographical soliloquy and, I surmise, the need for a shabu fix. I know his supplier lives in Shirogane-dai.

A right turn is enough to nudge Honda's sleepy head atop my shoulder. His stiff permed hair brushes against the side of my neck. This killer leans against me like a sympathetic lover.

The taxi turns right on Meiji Avenue. A police officer is standing beside his bicycle contemplating what looks like a drunk salary-man sprawled on the sidewalk. With his foot the cop nudges the body, only managing to flop the guy into the gutter.

The taxi meter flashes horrifically past ¥11,000 ($120) before braking at Tengenji-bashi right near my place. I tell the cabbie to stop. Honda grabs an armrest to pull himself off me. He looks around.

"Tengenji-bashi, Hiro-o," I say, reaching for my wallet.

"No, it's okay. I'll take care of this." The killer rubs his eyes as my door opens. To argue would be insulting. I nod to thank him again.

"Are you from a newspaper?" he asks, forgetting my original introduction as a freelance writer.

"Something like that." I smile.

"Hmm . . . " He stops himself and lets his arm drop limply to the seat. After a long moment, the cabbie pulls the door closed before cutting over to the turning lane on the way to Shirogane-dai.

I was to end the summer with hundreds of notebook pages documenting conversations with over a dozen Tokyo yakuza. Mostly I used initial meetings to facilitate further meetings, where I could watch them doing their real jobs and living their lives. My routine was to pull the best lines and recycle the cassettes with the next subject. A wily old-time veteran journalist had once told me never to bring a tape recorder or even a pencil to an interview: you'll remember everything worth a damn, he assured me. In the moments after I left Honda, as I sat in the lighted hallway (so as not to wake my sleeping significant other), the old-timer's advice rang true. What were supposed to be just quick notes on the body language of the washed up gangster became something like a case study. I felt the tapes had become superfluous, but, against my policy, I broke the tabs to prevent reuse.

TWILIGHT OF THE LION

After Honda's rather dramatic confessions I was looking forward to meeting Lion one-on-one, although I didn't expect a performance to match that of his underling. Honda hardly seemed a yakuza anymore. His solo shabu distribution business wasn't worthy of a yakuza of his former stature. When I called from the station, it was Lion's wife who instructed me on where to find the old yakuza boss.

Beside the tracks of Yamanote line, near the Otsuka Japan Railroad station, a *tsuribori* has been erected. Here, each spring, long plywood platforms are placed alongside narrow ditches of about one meter deep. These long troughs are lined with blue vinyl, filled with water, and then stocked with hundreds of homely carp. If these fish had been more spectacularly colored, like their well-bred and revered brethren, they might have enjoyed a pampered life in a traditional Japanese garden somewhere. No such luck. Instead they are fated to be the proverbial fish in a barrel.

Judging by the success of pachinko parlors and tsuribori, the Japanese are, perhaps, the world's most easily entertained people. Tsuribori fishing strips away the element of chance and skill as well as a natural setting. The salaryman on a lunch break—or with a stolen hour on a sunny afternoon—rents a short pole, a bait pail, and

Twilight of the Lion

a low stool. It seems more of a meditation technique than an activity. The men sit on their stools well apart from each other. Silently, these passionless anglers drop their lines and reel in their quarry.

Retirement has proved difficult for these salarymen who entered the business world back when the yen had to be propped up to boost the struggling postwar economy. I wonder if these old salarymen soldiers feel any personal pride in the new Japan's economic hegemony. Of the numerous traditions that Japan Inc. has driven to near extinction, respect of the elderly is the most lamentable. The fate of these forlorn retirees is a common, though usually comedic theme in television dramas.

Eventually I find Lion, sporting the wide-brimmed hat his wife had described. It is the type that home gardeners wear for sun protection and, I believe, to separate themselves from common laborers. Aside from his unique hat, Lion is set apart by his sumolike girth bulging over his belt. Elderly Japanese believe that excessive fat is a sign of good health. Perched at the end of a row of wrinkled old citizens, Lion's physique is a ringing endorsement for the yakuza lifestyle. The man had made a strong impression on me when I first met him on the night visit with Taro Mura.

I bow and sit beside one of the few senior citizens in Tokyo without an identity problem. Lion's powder blue golf shirt has the required long sleeves of all yakuza sportswear.

"I try to slow down in the summer," Lion says. "I'm uncomfortable driving around town with the heat outside and the air conditioner blowing inside. It's like there's no middle . . . so I like to slow down my pace.

"This is the mildest summer I can remember. But as I've always slowed down every summer since 1955, I'm slowing down in 1993 . . . I'm the boss, who's going to stop me!?"

"Why in 1955?" I ask.

"That's when I made Lion-gumi." He smiles. "And I had sakazuki with my first three kobun."

"Was Lion-gumi your idea?"

Lion laughs. "No, no. This was the old days, not like now when a chimpira gets tattoos on one day, then wants his own gang on the next! Back then, your oyabun gave you life; you couldn't dream of living outside his magic. My association with my oyabun gave me happiness and pride.

"I was like many boys in the poor areas of the Shitamachi. My father worked like a dog either in factories or some kind of heavy labor. He drank, hit my mother, and fell into sleep with his arm around his sake. None of the boys ever saw their fathers sober. The only other men we knew in our area were the peddlers and the police. The cops never impressed me. I thought they were phonies. Their loud talking and bad manners seemed undignified. My memories are from the years right before the war when the police seemed very powerful. After surrender they were much weaker . . .

"You want me to make broad statements. But I cannot paint all yakuza with the same color. The Japanese yakuza is not a baseball league. A yakuza in Hokkaido may hold a very different belief about his life than a yakuza in Tokyo or Kansai. In my heart the way of yakuza is clear, but it is often distinct from other oyabun. I cannot say that those who believe differently are wrong. I may be wrong.

"You want to hear my little ideas? Do not force me into your present picture of an oyabun."

I nod.

"Those big oyabun at the top of Yamaguchi or Sumiyoshi or Aizu Kotetsu-kai are not typical. I have met them and knew their predecessors. They have more responsibilities than I can imagine. An oyabun usually worries about a few city blocks, not entire prefectures. That is the way it is for most oyabun and kobun."

I ask how the big organizations like the Yamaguchi-gumi came to power.

"Taoka-san made the modern yakuza after the war. In the time after surrender, most Japanese were confused and had heavy hearts. But Taoka-san refused to follow. He saw that the time was right for a new start. He had big ambitions. He understood that if you could unite all Osaka-area yakuza, it would put an end to all the small fights that disrupt business. You see, back then, these small battles between gangs were the main activity of yakuza life. The businesses of yakuza used to be limited to a certain amount in a certain area. Before Taoka-san's rise, if a gang wanted more money, they tried to take over another's turf. Yakuza didn't have any idea about making businesses that could develop and grow. The yakuza world was limited by our customs and our small brains, but Taoka's revolution built a yakuza world without limits. The Yamaguchi-gumi's size and strength forced others to unite to save themselves."

I ask about the recent gang war.

Lion dabs his face with a handkerchief and suggests we continue at his home in one of Tokyo's most exclusive residential districts.

"I can only speak for myself. Lion-gumi is in the Kanto Alliance. Here in Tokyo, we have always been on top of each other. Of course, I had known other oyabun before we made the Kanto Alliance. We would meet to settle problems and to discuss general issues. Even if our kobun fought, we enjoyed each other's company because we had similar feelings and goals. In those informal meetings we were equals. But creating the Kanto Alliance forced us to create a hierarchy, putting one above the other. This was a problem because we were all oyabun. The oyabun who had taught me was my only boss. Though he was dead, in my heart I believed it dishonored my oyabun to pledge support to another yakuza. Others had reservations too. So we made the association without sakazuki. There was no money involved but we gave up our independence."

I wonder how the responsibilities of an oyabun have changed. Are his duties today different from those of his oyabun?

"An oyabun is a father. It may appear that kobun live to serve their oyabun: Kobun fight for oyabun, they earn money for oyabun, they speak politely to oyabun, they light oyabun's cigarette! But, the truth is an oyabun really serves the kobun. A kobun is a kobun forever. At sakazuki an oyabun adopts a kobun. The boys who join the yakuza are bad kids, that's why they want to be yakuza in the first place. We get the people everyone has rejected. A kid from

Tokyo University doesn't decide to try yakuza life! But a bad kid in others' eyes may be a decent kid and he may be an intelligent kid. But the boys who came to Lion-gumi were trouble. Many of them were beaten by their fathers or didn't have fathers. They had been told they were shit all their lives. They were rebellious and dangerous. They'd been in bosozoku gangs or in juvenile prison. Then these tough-acting boys would come to me, but I'd see the weakness and sadness in their hearts.

"Also, there are kids who are crazy. I mean low intelligence, sometimes retarded. Japan has no place for these types. Their parents are ashamed. But an oyabun must take in these boys too. Is this a way to hire employees for a big business?

"But these are the boys who are yakuza. If they can do even minimal work, then they can stay with me forever. The kobun who don't have good abilities stay close to their oyabun. They have great loyalty. Kobun who are clever tend to be away earning a living. An oyabun should stay aloof so as to treat each kobun pretty much the same.

"It was basically the same for my oyabun. His business was really just gambling, so he couldn't accept kids who couldn't do that work. There were not so many easy ways to make money then. Also, before the war, it was risky to be yakuza. The police were strong and vicious. My oyabun told me that an 'oyabun's job is to watch over his kobun without looking.'"

An air of quiet gentility separates the neighborhood called Meijiro from the griminess and bustle of pedestrian Tokyo. Large houses are shrouded beneath ancient trees, and their high walls lend privacy and protection from the unwashed. (These homes are the private delights of their owners—apart from the neighborhood, not for the public.) On the street, the high summer sun allows the old ladies to flaunt their lightweight mesh kimonos and quaint parasols.

A rolling aluminum fence has been left open and a small white Akita yelps from inside a modern rambling house. Traditional wooden houses were virtually all burned in the American incendiary bombing of 1945. The ones that survived have been built out by their owners—expanded on the ground floors with small bedrooms jutting haphazardly above. In country towns, old-style homes with their tiled roofs stand out in the middle of open fields. But Tokyo mansions camouflage themselves with ornamental trees, rampant ivy, and shadows. Old wood warps and fades into the browns and grays that are the aesthetic of old Edo. Tokyo is a city of Japanese immigrants. The real Edokko, those families that go back to when there was no Tokyo, are the ones who (I imagine) live in the big old houses in Meijiro.

Lion's wife greets us at the door with a singsongy "hello" and bows. Her eyes sparkle behind round wire-framed glasses as she ushers me in. Neat in a flower-print dress and apron, the *Ane-san* (the boss's wife, in yakuza argot) of Lion-gumi is the picture of a upper-middle-aged Japanese housewife. Her black hair is pulled back into a tight bun.

Lion excuses himself as I am led across a smooth wooden floor through a large dark tatami room. The Ane-san slides open the bright backlit shoji paper door revealing a short Japanese back porch. A square cushion is laid on the buffed wood for me to sit. The backyard is a gloriously overgrown retreat whose thick foliage blocks the sunlight and keeps out the heat. The Ane-san carries out a tray with a tall bottle of Kirin beer and a small glass. She kneels beside me to pour the beer, apologizing for Lion's tardiness.

I am left alone in the cool garden that seems more English than Japanese, though, somewhere in the bramble, I hear the familiar intermittent trickle of water. Then there is the sound of footsteps coming from the other side of the shoji. A young kobun, about twenty-three, zips open the door. Without stepping out onto the porch, he bows and apologizes, saying his oyabun will be out soon, after changing clothes. A short time later Lion emerges from the house in a gray kimono. On his feet are black socks sewn with a gap between his big toe and the rest. His wife follows with another Kirin and an extra glass. I fill the glass for Lion, who grunts a thanks as his wife smiles, bows, and slips inside.

Though the man appears relaxed, I sense a lingering suspicion about what the hell I am doing. If I had approached Lion through some other channel, say, an introduction from a tabloid journalist or another boss, he might be less leery of me. I had surprised him, literally, in his underwear in the middle of a drug-for-ammo exchange. He says that he knows I'm not some kind of police but the fact that my own business card shows no affiliation with any company or publication gives him pause; "I know you're not an enemy, but I'm not sure you're a friend."

He runs his fleshy palm over the top of his head, smoothing the gray hair back from his face. The kobun appears in a neat brown suit with slippers on his feet. He apologizes, falling to his knees on Lion's left side. Then he holds out a cigarette, which Lion snatches and examines through his smoky glasses before placing it in his own mouth. Lion turns to the kid, who lights the cigarette with a silver Zippo. Lion puffs on the tobacco, then barks at the kobun, "Ashtray!" Almost simultaneously, the shoji slides open and the Ane-san holds out a black plastic ashtray to the youth. She smiles at me; the kobun bows and thanks her.

"When I began, I was more nervous than him," Lion says, placing the cigarette on the lip of the ashtray. The kobun daintily picks up the cigarette, taps off the small nub of ashes, and replaces it, with the length of the cigarette angled towards his boss's hand. "A young kobun must learn to anticipate the wants of his oyabun. He must walk on eggs and do some guessing, like a new bride!

"Let me tell you, when I first joined I was terrified of screwing up." He smiles, showing his straight, yellowish teeth. "My mother and sister were depending on me to catch on with the yakuza. During 1944 and the years after, there was very little food, almost nothing; everyone was hustling, trying to buy, steal, or grow food. Oh, Tokyo was a mess . . . those B-29s flying high like black swans. I used to think to myself, They're so wonderful, great! Great! I didn't blame the big black swans for the fires they left behind. There was such a mess on the ground, down where we humans were living in shit. Ah, but very high in the sky! That must be different!

"The air-raid sirens blew almost every day," he says, sipping the beer. "At night it was quite scary. Even so, many times my mother and I argued whether we should leave the warm kotatsu to run to the shelter. When the ALL CLEAR signal blew, I'd climb to the roof to watch the flames where bombs had hit. That was thrilling; fire never scared me.

"But, in the daytime you could see those American planes high in the blue sky. Me and the other boys would cheer in the streets! People would run wild to the shelters. But we'd jump around in our old, ripped-up clothes, yelling 'Go, go, go!'

"We were brazen because there weren't many men around," Lion continues, picking up the smoldering cigarette in his thumb and forefinger, looking wistfully at the rising bluish threads of smoke. "One young man, a Chinese who couldn't serve, slapped me for our cheering. I was fourteen and big—I would've been drafted if the war had continued—so I punched the Chinese. Then I stepped on his head with my wooden geta. He couldn't get up. There was blood on his face and running from his ear. Soon the cops showed up and took me to the station.

"'If this man wasn't a gaijin,' the police chief said to me, 'I'd throw you in real prison!' Then he called in a fat pig cop named Ishikawa. I'll never forget that name! Ishikawa took me into an empty cell with a wooden table that I had to lay on, stomach down, with my pants off!

"The fat pig was a real sadist," recalls Lion. "He beat me with a long bamboo pole. It wasn't thin like for fishing but thick. He swung it like a baseball bat! I was crying and could feel the blood dripping from my numb ass and running down the inside of my thigh. I couldn't walk for days or sit for weeks. They just left me in a holding cell to rot away.

"At some point a man was thrown into my cell. He was wearing a Western suit and a fedora. I thought he was a schoolteacher but he had a long beard that wasn't allowed for teachers. He slept on the dirty straw for a full day before waking to find me staring at him. He roared, 'What the hell are you looking at?'

"He scared the shit out of me!

"Now, it wasn't like I was in a real prison, it was just a lockup in the back of the police station. But my mother didn't know where I was; I knew she must have been worried. The bombing was getting worse, and it was becoming very chaotic out in the streets. It kept the police very busy just keeping everything under control. They didn't seem to be processing me or the man called Gifu.

"When Gifu sobered up from his drunk, I hadn't had food for three days. I told him this, and he pulled some money from his sock. He gave some to one of the cops, and, in five minutes, we were eating soba and pickled daikon! I was thrilled and appreciative to this Gifu. This was a better meal than I had been eating on the outside. After we ate, Gifu became more friendly, asking me about my family and if I had any education. Then he asked me, 'What are you doing after the war's over?' I was dumbfounded because I had never thought about the war ending. I had grown up during the war years, I couldn't remember much of anything before the war.

"I told him I had no plans for after the war. I didn't know how I was going to get out of that cell. 'Oh, I can get you out of here,' Gifu said. 'But are you sure you want to leave? A jail's not so bad compared to what it's going to be like when Japan surrenders.' That's when I was really shocked. I had never heard anyone mention the possibility of defeat. It knocked the wind out of me!

"The cops brought in a washbowl and a towel. Before washing, Gifu took off his jacket, tie, vest, and shirt. His body was covered by tattoos. I had never seen such a thing! I was more shocked than you were when that kid Mura-san brought you to my place in Shinjuku!" Lion laughs while mashing out his cigarette. "Now, Gifu wasn't as old as he seemed to me then. He had a strong body with heavy muscles. He brought me close and explained the meaning of the different designs on his back and arm. There was some little story for each picture. It was like listening to fables!

"Gifu was a gambler who had come from Mitake City with a traveling gang that moved between Nagoya and Tokyo. But the draft had thinned out the gang, so they settled in Yokohama's Chinatown for the war. But their boss died, and most of the gang went back to Mitake or some hick town down there. But Gifu had met a gambling boss called Tsunami, you know, like big wave. Tsunami-gumi had managed to stay afloat during the war. They had a big piece of the black-market action between Tokyo and the northern suburbs in Chiba and Ibaraki. From the amount and type of goods that were appearing on the black market, Gifu could tell that Japan was going to lose the war. During the few days Gifu talked about his travels and gambling, I was in a happy trance. I had never had an adult man treat me so kindly. I had fallen under his spell. But, when he again told me we would lose the war, I couldn't keep from crying . . .

"On my fourth day with Gifu, there was a terrible bombing raid that I thought would crack the earth open. The police didn't find time to process either one of us. I believe the cops had actually eaten the canned meat they had picked up Gifu for selling. When the bad bombing of August ninth shook Tokyo, they let both of us out to work on a bucket brigade. Before I went home, Gifu took the address of my mother's house. That was the last time I would ever see him . . .

"My mother cried when I walked through the door of our shabby apartment. I felt like I had been gone for five years, not five days. My mother and little sister were scrawny and hungry. I turned back outside and swore I would find them something substantial to eat. I didn't find food right away, but there were soldiers recruiting men to load dead bodies onto carts. A bomb had destroyed a factory in Funabashi. They didn't give me gloves, but they had us wrap our faces with cloth. There were headless bodies, arms, legs, and such scattered about a huge ruined area that was still smoldering. I was disgusted, but I didn't show it to the soldiers bossing us. The other men they had enticed into doing this work were feeble old farts. 'You're lucky you haven't been drafted,' said one of the soldiers who was helping load the body parts onto the truck bed.

"'I want to fight,' I told him.

"'Don't be stupid, this is almost over and you should be thankful.'

"The soldiers paid me eight yen, which was more than the old men got. I bought some soba noodles and whitefish to bring home to my mother. We ate well for six days. One morning there was a banging on the door of our shack. I saw my mother drop to the floor and bow formally. I thought it must be the cops or the army coming to get me.

"She must have thought the man standing at the door was some kind of official. The man, however, introduced himself as Tsunami. Considering the backdrop of our half-charred neighborhood, he appeared immaculate, almost divine. Tsunami-san was wearing a nicely pressed dark suit with a bow tie and a carnation in his lapel. This was in August, at the absolute lowest point in the war for Tokyo, and this man had a flower in his lapel! Ninety percent of the city had burned to the ground, and there was a dapper man standing in our door with a fresh flower in his lapel! No wonder my mother fell to her knees." Lion laughs, then coughs a bit. As if cued, the door slides open, and the Ane-san hands a glass of water to the young guy, who places it at Lion's side. Then the door slides closed.

"So there was Tsunami-san standing in the wreckage of our street, asking if he could come inside. He looked at me. 'Are you Hiroshi?' I said I was. Tsunami-san sat at the tiny table and from his pocket took out a box of fine green tea! We hadn't seen anything so luxurious even before the war! He gave it to my mother, who had tears in her eyes.

"'Where's your father?' Tsunami asked me, while my mother prepared the tea.

"'In China,' I responded.

"'Then you must take care of your mother,' he said, then slowly drank his tea without saying anything. Frankly, I didn't have any idea what he was thinking. The world felt very confused and uncertain, and so was I. However, the moment Tsunami-san entered our home, it was as if the sun had burst through the smoke and clouds. I didn't realize it at the time but, for me, the war was over . . .

"After he finished his tea, Tsunami-san asked my mother if she would allow me to come work for him. She said that she would be happy if I had a job because I hadn't been too successful in school. 'Oh really,' Tsunami-san said to her, 'I have heard that he's quite bright.' That really made me feel like a man! Before he left,

Twilight of the Lion

Tsunami-san gave one hundred yen to my mother and told me to be at his house at five-thirty in the morning . . . "

The Ane-san brings us another big bottle of beer. She smiles as she picks up the empties and says to her husband, "Why don't you take a break from your old war stories?" She teases the elderly man, who I realize has become tired from all his talking. I feel that perhaps I have overstayed my welcome, but the Ane-san earnestly asks me if I would like to hear about the yakuza life from a woman's point of view. I am happy to oblige her.

"It's feast or famine if you're involved with a yakuza," the Ane-san booms in her Osaka accent. "There were days when we had twenty-seven bank accounts! The bankbooks were kept in a hidden drawer at the bottom of our closet. I ran a snack pub, where he would hide piles of money in pots or rolled into small ceramic sake bottles. Some days he'd be so flush with cash that he'd close the snack and force me to go and spend some of it. I'd ride down to Ginza and attack the fancy department stores; they have the finest kimono and sashes in Wako and Takashimaya. After ordering many of the traditional Japanese things I liked, I'd buy the latest European dresses and shoes. After a time, I realized that if I never wore any kimonos I had bought, I could later pawn them for the maximum rate.

"Although we moved into a high-class apartment building in Omotesando, I could never enjoy a peaceful life. His kobun were always tracking through for one reason or another. They put on their best manners around me, but, by that time, I was tired of the young men. I bought the snack so I could get away from their daily activities. Then his kobun started coming to snack! They thought they were helping me and showing respect! They could kill you with their manners. My husband had to ban his kobun from entering the snack, but then he began using it for secret meetings and hiding money . . .

"You may have heard that yakuza cannot marry 'nice' girls, so they settle for 'bad' girls from the water trades. But this is no kind of set rule. These days many educated young ladies work part-

time as hostesses. And would you lump a trained hostess in the same
category as a soaplady? We women who have worked in nightclubs
get to see what silly, weak boys many so-called great business and
government men really are. Every night you're wiping their mouths
and tucking in their shirts, really putting them together! So, to us,
yakuza who make good lives have a manly appeal, even though
they've had none of the advantages. Yakuza may be crude and stupid
about the world, but they know how to scratch a living out of any
situation. Yakuza don't judge a girl badly if she's in the business of
entertaining men, and we don't care if he speaks poorly or has a
finger missing.

"Unlike citizens, marriage with a yakuza is very, very rarely
'arranged.' It's always based on mutual feelings of attraction and
understanding. The lifestyle may be extravagant or simple, but the
life will have more interesting challenges and truer happiness than
regular folks . . . I like to believe this."

Lion smiles indulgently during his wifes's assessment of her life. I
realize that she must be fifteen years younger than her husband.

"So it hasn't been so bad, Ane-san?" he asks.

"Not bad." She smiles at the gangster.

MARRIED TO THE YAKUZA

The talk with Lion's wife encouraged me to follow up on leads I had with women in the underworld. Virtually every gaijin woman I knew had yakuza connections, whether they knew it or not. If they were working at one of the half-dozen hostess clubs that specialized in having white girls pour the drinks and chit the chat, the young women likely thought their respective "Mama-sans" were the owners and sole boss. My connections told me that four of the six gaijin hostess clubs had owners who were tattooed. But yakuza wives are the most compelling female characters in the underworld.

While the unsophisticated yakuza man may live with a truer affinity for traditional Japan than practitioners of the tea ceremony, Kabuki, or sumo, when it comes to women who marry into the yakuza, the irony is greater. They do not follow their instincts into the underworld—they follow their men.

The backgrounds of these young women are strikingly similar to those of their boyfriends and husbands: lower working-class, high school dropouts with one or two parents of Korean or Chinese extraction. It's no stretch to say that in their youth many future yakuza wives were the tough-talking "bad girls" of their schools. Their youthful rebellious posing, speech, and behavior are thoroughly modern, which is why their eventual transformation into the matriarchs of yakuza gangs is so dramatic and ironic.

In the early years of marriage it is not uncommon for a young wife to do her time earning money as a bar hostess or even as a prostitute. In the yakuza value system a woman who sells her body is not looked down upon, nor is her decision

149

considered a stain on her character. Once the husband starts making decent money on his own, the life of a bashita *will become bourgeois, with shopping and socializing as the main activities. As a yakuza matures and moves up to subboss, and eventually runs his own gang, his wife adjusts to a very traditional mode.*

Unlike the wife of a salaryman, whose world is small and mean in a tiny apartment with a single child, the bashita's *house is expansive: Her living quarters occupy a complete floor in the building that constitutes the gang's headquarters. She becomes part den mother, part cook, as each new kobun joining the husband's gang swells the size of her household. Much like an aristocratic matriarch of an old-fashioned country estate, the yakuza wife must keep kobun busy with jobs around the house and grounds; she may buy food in bulk from various merchants who deliver to the door; she must help prepare huge meals and be able to impressively entertain her husband's cross-generational underworld associates.*

In extreme situations, for example, after the death of an oyabun, a yakuza wife may find herself taking over the actual day-to-day business and eventually naming her dead husband's successor. But the yakuza-connected women I knew were not the wives of future underworld stars and seemed to share with all women connected to the yakuza a fundamentally un-Japanese insecurity regarding every aspect of their lives.

The striking blonde at the newspaper kiosk on Sakurada Dori looks like a successful gaijin bank executive except that she's buying lottery tickets. I've never seen a foreigner playing the arcane Japanese lottery. My interest in learning the lottery system provides an opening for conversation. Liz Sato, an American, introduces herself, and after a dozen or so leading and increasingly personal questions, she admits that she's desperate for money. She also admits that she and her Japanese husband are involved in the underworld. I am floored to discover that her husband is a yakuza and in prison to boot. My eager interrogation amazes her. "I can't believe you're interested in this yakuza shit.

"Like most yakuza my husband was stupid enough to find his way to prison." Liz sighs. Sato, a midlevel thirty-three-year-old yakuza, is serving a five-year jail term for narcotic trafficking. Although Sato was obsessed with guns, his main moneymaking scam entailed visiting about eighty doctors a week for his "acute migraines." After initial consultations, he was able to collect eighty weekly prescriptions for Valium, Halcion, and the like. These light tranquilizing pills had become the favorite buzz in Tokyo night-clubs, selling for up to ten thousand yen a pop. His lucrative trade had kept him busy all day and half the night, dashing about the streets of central Tokyo in his Cadillac. When he was finally caught and sent away, he left behind five pistols and a rifle scope in the rice cooker.

Liz did what she had to do to maintain her high-flying Tokyo lifestyle. There was the expensive six-room apartment, the Chinese domestic, and the garage for the Caddy. Then there was the cost of indulging every whim of her ten-year-old biracial daughter (including a home fax machine the kid needed to send fan mail to her favorite "idol" singers). Liz chose to become a call girl.

Liz's personal and working lives are now totally enmeshed in the yakuza culture. She is especially tight with other gaijin women married to gangsters. These fellow travelers, from places like Bangkok and Manila, find themselves in the double bind of being a despised minority while wedded to the ostracized criminal class. All of Liz's Japanese friends were yakuza wives who, according to Liz, were also estranged from their own parents.

"They rejected the marriage partners chosen by their parents," Liz said. "It was a stupid romantic fantasy that drew them to the wild yakuza type. Most end up being alone most of the time. Yakuza husbands are always out on the town or in jail. But never around."

Several days later, Liz and I are sitting on the rough-hewn concrete bleachers of a speedboat stadium on the banks of the Edogawa River. Spread-out newspapers serve as place markers for those gone to the betting windows. These tabloid pages bake in the ruthless summer sun, slowly turning yellow and brittle before my eyes. Most of the bettors are hiding in the clubhouse shade, sitting on the back of their heels in what's known as "shit squat" meditation. The crowd is thoroughly plebeian and predominantly male. A few young women have accompanied their gold-chain-flaunting boyfriends. These women smoke thin cigarettes held between their middle and ring fingers. Their nails have been varnished in a trendy tough-girl style with alternating colors, while their faces glow powdery white beneath tinted bangs and dark sunglasses.

In speedboat betting, you've got to pick both the first-and-second-place finishers in order to win. A knowing handicapper tracks the past performances of both the drivers and the outboard engines that are switched in each heat. The outright winner isn't too difficult to nail, it's the number two boat that's the pain in the ass.

The races take place every half hour. Drivers in helmets and life preservers kneel in four-foot-long boats with the huge engines wailing at their backs. The pack of six whip around for a couple of practice laps before lining up at the start, and then they take off for real. Blaring engines rock the stadium's foundation as the boats jam their noses into a tight bottleneck at the first turn. The first two to emerge usually win the race.

Holding court at the far side of the betting windows is a particularly animated tout to whom I had been drawn. This licensed boat-racing prognosticator literally sings out his analysis as he pushes little magnetic boats across a metal board (without quite showing who would finish second). For a hundred yen I buy a folded strip of paper with his predictions of the one-two finishers. His numbers might've actually won, except that one of the tout's favorites capsized. The boat's white hull bobs and glistens in the dark water left choppy from the wakes of the others' final lap. Two ambulance boats roar up to the hull where men in wet suits, after some time and difficulty, manage to flip the boat right side up. I hear some yakuza types laughing that the driver is probably dead, and, if he isn't, he should be for fucking up their parlays. (This is according to Liz's translation.)

"This kind of gambling is total bullshit," Liz declares, ready to leave after just four races. "Tonight I'll show you the real deal."

That evening, we wait for a taxi in front of the Wendy's where Azabu Juban's shopping street meets Sakurada Dori. Liz's blond hair hangs limply in the humid evening air, as the door of an orange cab opens for us. Liz gives the driver an obscure address in Shinagawa ward. Before shifting the car in gear, the confused driver makes Liz repeat our destination three times.

"I'll direct you when you get near the station!" she finally spits out in perfect peremptory Japanese. At last we roll away from the Tokyo Tower (that garish Eiffel copy) and down from our "high class" neighborhoods to the landfill district.

Liz's beeper hasn't sounded since an afternoon rendezvous with a drunk British banker at the New Otani Hotel. It is now about eight-thirty; the Tokyo Giants game blares on the cab's radio. Jesse Barfield comes to bat and smacks a 2–0 pitch for a double, a good omen for gaijin.

Tokyo is much more charming at night. Except for the monsters of Shinjuku, the scale of this city's buildings are very human. Though often disparaged, I like the low-rent humility of the ferroconcrete structures that constitute the majority of Tokyo dwellings. These boxy, postwar homes and restaurants have become as typically Japanese to me as any slope-roofed temple or teahouse.

There are five or six big cars idling near a small, red, wooden Shinto archway that fronts a vast cemetery. Our driver stops at the bumper of a black Lincoln. I can see a group of men smoking at the doorway of a dirty building that looks like a small warehouse. A rusty corrugated steel roof throws shadows on a faded sign above the entrance. The smokers courteously stand back to let us pass. Inside we're greeted by loud rock music and voices shouting roulette numbers and perfunctory apologies.

Along the far side of the vast room a line of bulky sewing machines have been pushed aside so the boys can play. A grid of shaded bulbs is strung from low steel cross beams. Hard thrashing guitars blare from potent speakers set on tripods off to the side of the gaming area. A long-legged waitress in heels and a one-piece bathing suit struts past balancing four drinks on a small tray. We step into the crowd of men around blackjack tables.

Liz's blond hair now glistens; a few heads turn to look at her. I watch a man hit a sixteen and bust. The dealer, a neat young man in a tuxedo shirt and a black tie, with a black vest, apologizes before snatching up the chips. His eyes are on the gaijin, however.

"Liz-san!" yells a middle-aged man sitting on a padded stool at an adjacent roulette table. His nose is crooked, but his smile is disarmingly kind. With a bejeweled hand, he waves her over to his side.

"I'm so surprised, Liz," the man says earnestly.

"I hope so . . . " Liz smiles tentatively. "It's okay that my friend and I are here? Someone invited us."

"Yes," the man, called Tabuchi, assures us. "Of course!"

"Thank you very much." Liz gives a little bow.

"Who is your friend?" Tabuchi grins at me, reveals a gold tooth where his left incisor should have been.

Liz introduces me as an "American who likes yakuza."

"Likes yakuza?" He sucks air between his teeth like a man stumped by a riddle. "He must be the only person who likes yakuza without being paid to like yakuza." This sounds like a knock against Liz, who's known in these circles in her call girl capacity. But that wouldn't be right, because yakuza understand that sometimes a woman has to use her body to make money.

"Sadly," Tabuchi continues, "there are no yakuza here!" Liz laughs as Tabuchi turns to the roulette table and picks up a pink chip. Then, facing me, he spreads open his hand, leaving the chip in the middle of his palm. Two sections have been cut off his pinkie, and one from his ring finger. The skin that covers the nub of his pinkie is oddly shaped, with a slight dimple in the center. I don't think he is trying to shock me.

"Take this," he says. "For good luck."

I pick up the five-hundred-yen chip from his mutilated hand and thank him.

"But Americans don't need luck, do they?" Tabuchi smiles. I say that I need lots just to pay my rent each month.

"Give me a number!" Tabuchi commands, as the guy in a tux asks for roulette bets to be placed. I hesitate because, even at the thoroughbred track out in Yamanaka, old Japanese men often ask me to hold their betting slips for luck. They always lose and I always feel bad. But, to keep face, I suggest two bets, 28 and red. In front of yakuza, it's important not to waver like a woman or a child. I try to look confident as the small white ball whizzes around the wheel, popping into the teens before settling in red-21. The color doubled Tabuchi's thirty thousand yen against ten thousand yen; he loses on the number.

"I'm sorry," I say, smiling.

"It's nothing," says Tabuchi, who then shouts for a waitress. "So you like gambling?"

"No, no!" a tipsy Liz interjects. "Yakuza is his hobby!" Tabuchi laughs, then facetiously asks if I recognize anyone in the casino, because he "thinks these men may be yakuza."

"No, I'm sorry," I joke, looking around at the hairy wise guys. "They look like katagi."

"Katagi!" Tabuchi cracks up. He pats me on the side of my arm and tells me to enjoy myself. Two big "katagi," both over six feet three, suddenly appear at Tabuchi's side. Though their brawny faces remain expressionless, they have an air of impatience. I've seen this before, a distinct older-child-indulging-senile-parent attitude of kobun towards their oyabun. This faux coddling passes for affection in their circles. It's an indulgence older Japanese men appreciate after playing the stoic for forty years.

Liz and I share a spot at a blackjack table with two men and a woman. Despite the temporary lights, the casino looks as legitimate as any of the "casino bars" around Tokyo that cater to citizens. Many of the casino bars in Roppongi have hired gaijin friends of mine as dealers and waitresses. They operate on principles similar to those of pachinko parlors: You exchange won chips for some kind of marker that can be traded for cash in-house or at a nearby outlet.

Yakuza casinos, however, are strictly for the amusement of the wise guys. Most yakuza business interactions, from loan-sharking to bookmaking to drugs, take place between yakuza themselves—in a sort of self-perpetuating, minimal-effort lifestyle. These underground yakuza gambling halls have always been around and will remain after the current fad of casino bars has faded from the mainstream. The thirty or so "citizens" at the Shinagawa casino are the half-connected businessmen, yakuza wives, girlfriends, high rollers, and assorted mob hanger-ons like myself.

Drinks keep coming. Our pile of chips goes up and down. A half hour passes without a steady run either way. The man beside us is wearing a loud shirt made of silk Hermès scarves. On the ring finger of his right hand is an incredible feat of watchmaking, a woman's Rolex set in a bulky, diamond-studded ring. I can't help glancing at the monstrosity each time his fingertips tap the table for a hit. Finally, his eyes catch mine.

"You like it?" His hair is neatly parted on the side. His soft pleasant face, despite his gaudy shirt and ring, seems every bit the nice average salaryman.

"Very stylish," I say, taking a closer look at the thing. "Stylish."

"Was it a gift?" Liz asks sweetly.

"No." He smiles, holding the ring up to his own face. "I had it made in Switzerland."

Then Tabuchi walks up to us, his gold tooth shining through from his ever-present smile. "Have you had good luck?" he asks, more to Liz than me.

"So-so," she answers.

"And you, Miyazaki?" Tabuchi looks to the guy with the ring, who has a dozen high piles before him. "You're having the luck of the seven gods. We shouldn't allow professionals in here."

Miyazaki grunts humbly under his breath. Evidently Tabuchi is a man to be respected.

Tabuchi speaks into Miyazaki's ear.

"OK," Miyazaki responds, before pushing his chips towards the dealer. The tux counts the chips by breaking them down to piles of ten. As Miyazaki stands to smooth his silk shirt, the dealer puts down a small stack of white chips. Miyazaki throws a chip back to the dealer and briskly turns from us.

Tabuchi pats Liz on the shoulder and tells us to follow Miyazaki. The casino sights and sounds fade as we walk into the darkness at the back of the building. Two double-breasted studs stand at the bottom of a stairway. As we walk by, they each greet Miyazaki with a grunt and bow. Miyazaki ignores them, as the men seem to ignore Liz and me. Another sumo-type stands at the top of the stairs. This one seems suspicious of us but doesn't move anything but the pupils in his narrow eyes.

Stepping into the bright upstairs room is a shock. We seem to have walked into a period soap opera. I have observed such guys in their offices and homes, but I have never felt so intimate with them as at this moment. We remove our shoes and step onto new tatami; its greenish hue and pungent scent reek of Japan. The mats and the shoji screens along the walls are obviously new. Miyazaki, himself looking amazed, explains that this office was transformed into a *toba* (a traditional gambling den) that day. The dozen gamblers are oblivious to the décor, their eyes are on the stacks of ten-thousand-yen bills being wagered. There must have been over fifty thousand American dollars in yen laying there on the floor.

The game is *hanafuda*, flower cards. It's a matching game vaguely like gin rummy but played with stiff, plastic-backed cards featuring birds, flowers, and trees instead of the dry numbers and suits of Western cards. When shuffled properly, the rigid cards smack together with sharp clicks, a sound that warms the heart of a yakuza. More than a game, hanafuda is an orgy of half-naked yakuza reveling in their mythic roots and ancient customs. In preparation for such an occasion I have learned the basics of hanafuda. But the few hands I played with my girlfriend were hardly adequate training for the nuance-laden rite I am watching.

Twelve men kneel around a large red cloth that has been folded to serve as the playing surface. Six of the men are shirtless, their assorted tattoos flowing into one another like panels of a continuous art nouveau mural. The glaring light of two circular fluorescent bulbs intensifies the deep reds and blues of the ornate designs against the white of unmarked skin. Four of the more extroverted players sport hari-maki, the old-fashioned cloth money belts, wrapped around their midsections. Two older gents aren't even wearing pants, but flaunting tight loincloths that reveal their painted buttocks. This manly nakedness harks back to a not so distant past when Japanese laborers toiled and relaxed with little clothing and less shame.

Liz and I sit below a fan that oscillates loudly to negligible effect. A shirtless dealer, about six feet from where we sit, is covered with reddish serpentine dragons, swimming in blue-black waters. A golden reptilian head gazes from his thigh, with its mouth open, eyes askew, and red tongue lashing out.

Another tattooed man does the dealing on the opposite side of the cloth. Large blue petals fan symmetrically over his pectorals, then wind down in art nouveau style to frame a bellyful of crinkled chrysanthemums. The man's eyes scan the cloth before he mumbles something and lifts a small cloth revealing a single card. The dealer lets the other players see this card, then leans forward on his knees to collect the bills lost by the players around him.

The other dealer begins to chant in a low tone that isn't loud but carries well. I can't make out a single word, however, as he apparently announces another round and asks that bets be placed. He repeats the same obscure phrase five or six times, then ends with a flourish of formal thank-yous and apologies. A man crosses in front of us and sinks into a shit squat, leaning forward on the balls of his feet. His arms hang limply between his legs. I recognize the mini Rolex ring of our tablemate from downstairs.

"You like?" Miyazaki asks me, nodding towards the players whom he's blocking from my view.

"Yeah," I say. "But it's difficult to understand."

"No, this is a child's game."

A skinny teenager in a red Lacoste tennis shirt appears at Miyazaki's side. He bows and hands a whiskeysoda down to Miyazaki. The kid's face is smooth, almost angelic. In a high, prepubescent voice, he thanks Miyazaki, and bows again. Miyazaki takes the drink without looking at the kid, who remains standing at attention. Miyazaki turns towards Liz as he swallows his first sip.

"Aachh!" Miyazaki growls, glancing down at his drink, then up at the kid. "This is shit! I said my 'usual'!"

"I'm so sorry, sir," the kid bawls. "But I poured the Johnnie Walker . . . "

"Stupid, this isn't Johnnie Walker!" Miyazaki rants, passing the glass back to the trembling youth.

"Of course, I screwed up!" he stammers, almost spilling the drink. "It's my mistake! I'll get you another!" He bows and spins away.

As if nothing has happened (but perhaps for effect), Miyazaki turns to Liz with a bogus smile. "You're Ito's foreign friend?" Though he uses the nice word for "foreigner," it is crude that he brings up Ito, a yakuza who is one of Liz's regular customers.

"Yes, I've known him for a long time," Liz responds coolly in her sweetest Japanese.

"He thinks he's better than he is," Miyazaki sneers.

"I don't know." Liz shrugs.

"He's Korean, not really Japanese," Miyazaki grunts.

"Are you sure you're Japanese?" Liz jibes, looking into Miyazaki's lecherous eyes. "You look a bit Taiwanese to me." I admire Liz's mastery of the language and her tough yet flirtatious demeanor in the face of this pompous creep. It's part of her job, I'm thinking, but what a distressingly bad job.

The kid returns with another drink. He stands silently for a few seconds before repeating his formal greeting with shaky bravado. I feel bad for him because he has been callously roughed up simply to impress Liz.

Miyazaki accepts the fresh drink without acknowledging the kid, though the boy stands by nervously as Miyazaki resumes his wise-guy wooing of Liz. Miyazaki launches into some kind of story that I can't follow because he has inched closer to Liz and is speaking in a dirty-joke whisper. Liz giggles a few times as Miyazaki drones on and on with the anecdote. As the kid's leg is partly blocking my view of the game, I stare up at his now-placid face. He is no longer standing rigidly like a soldier but seems more like an anxious dog hoping for a reassuring pat from his master.

Liz laughs at the conclusion of Miyazaki's tale. Leaning forward, she puts her hand on Miyazaki's long-sleeved arm, teasing. "Really? You're telling the truth?"

"Yeah, yeah, yeah," Miyazaki insists, sipping his drink. Miyazaki's sudden transformation from a blasé stud to a contemptuous tyrant, then back again, seems to show some outright schizophrenia, but none of the other men react to the outburst. It is simply another oyabun-kobun dressing-down, which they've all seen before. The kid soon disappears, and Miyazaki maneuvers over to Liz's left side.

One of the street-clothed players slowly stands up from the hanafuda, adjusts a tie clip, and buttons his blazer. He lights a ciga-rette, exhales the smoke, then bows curtly. He is closely attended by a taller, younger man who kneels down at the doorway and actually slips the older man's tasseled loafers onto his waiting feet. Thus shod, the elder strolls briskly into the hallway, leaving his footman alone to rummage for his own shoes and catch up.

The tattooed dealer on the far side sings out like the side-walk sweet potato seller whose sonorous melody wakes me on winter mornings. Without looking away from Liz, Miyazaki responds to the dealer's call with an automatic baritone grunt. It's the guttural assent with which young sumo and Japanese soldiers sound the affirmative before heading into battle. Miyazaki whis-pers something to Liz and smiles. He stands and walks around from our shadowy end of the room to the vacated space at the red cloth. He stands at the spot, looking down at the scene in a meditative gaze. The dealer begins shuffling the hanafuda cards, making that staccato clapping that now sends shivers through me.

Suddenly, the dealer interrupts his siren song and looks up at a noticeably sweating Miyazaki. The shoji screens are props, of course, and they can't be slid open for a cooling evening breeze. It's unmercifully hot and stuffy in that converted office, and, appar-ently, that's why Miyazaki begins to remove his shirt.

Like a child, he watches his own fingers unfasten each button from his neck to his belt. Then he pulls the front of the shirt from his slacks and opens the last button. He drops his arms, letting the cloth fall off his torso. A young man behind him gathers up the hang-ing shirt and pulls the remaining tail out of Miyazaki's pants.

Besides me, no one else seems to take notice of Miyazaki's slow, methodical disrobing until the dealer eventually looks up at the half-naked figure and raises an appreciative eyebrow. Moments ago, this man stood with his everyman Japanese face in a tacky shirt and cheap slacks: he now appears as a kind of branded denizen of hell.

Married to the Yazuka

Miyazaki's blatant monotone tattoos show none of the humanity and subtle touch of a master tattoo artist. Dark blue stripes, vines, and blotches twist wantonly around his arms and trunk, enveloping all but his hands and face. This isn't a man or even a criminal; it is more a shadowy beast. In feudal Japan, criminals were branded for each offense with a simple black line around the arm. By that reckoning, Miyazaki might bear the marks of all the crimes committed in the name of Hirohito.

Finally Miyazaki sits. He pulls a wad of ten-thousand-yen bills from the ribbed waistband that he wears beneath his pants. The other players casually puff cigarettes and sip drinks, indifferent to the monster in their midst. Miyazaki apparently is known for his deformities and treated deferentially.

Any man who has been in a public Japanese bath has seen the various forms of body tattoos. In subject and detail, they vary infinitely but a certain traditional aesthetic is rigorously maintained. My mind reels.

Not that I wasn't warned about such preconceptions. A Tokyo boss once told me: "No yakuza is the same as another yakuza, not like you might say one salaryman is like another. This is a world of outcasts, misfits, and losers. As society's rejects, we can understand each other's problems. We have formed these organizations because we are different from citizens. Though we unite because we are different, that doesn't mean we necessarily have anything else in common. The tattoos give us the illusion that we are of the same breed. But that's just on the skin." The pun was unintentional, I'm sure.

Over the next hour, many men from related gangs drift into the room to watch the hanafuda. Each time, the spectators acknowledge the newcomers with silent bows. A mountain of shoes builds up in the doorway until a young guy begins sorting them into rows. Suddenly, he springs up to let a stooped figure shuffle past. The quiet mumbling of the gambling is disturbed by the cacophony of booming greetings lavished upon this bent elderly man. One of the shirtless players springs up to execute a full, ninety-degree bow.

Gingerly the old man raises his right hand to acknowledge the men. His sparse white hair has been shorn to the length of toothbrush bristles, while tinted glasses darken his barely opened eyes. He's dressed in a conservative suit with a dark red tie and a white shirt. A thick wooden cane hangs loosely from his left wrist, as if he doesn't really need it.

The old man's short steps stop for a moment. He looks around nervously, like a pensioner who has just paid his half-fare but found every bus seat occupied. I get my numb ass off the cushion and catch the eye of the old man's hulking attendant. I whisper something to Liz about leaving, and she stands too. The younger man comes over and brushes off our cushions before thanking us. The game resumes, drawing the attention of the old man, who now looks very tiny. The geezer hands his cane to the bodyguard, then steps beside me with a grateful smile that, again, renders him as harmless as any other Japanese senior citizen to whom you give up your bus seat.

"You have a good manner," he says to me in halting schoolboy English. "It is a fine how do you do!"

I keep a straight face, smile, and thank him in English. His assistant grips the old man's left elbow and nods at me to hold the right. Together we lower the ancient onto the cushion. With an appreciative grunt, the assistant thanks me. I wonder if the old man can even see the game between the broad backs.

I look for someone to thank before leaving, but the room is packed. I don't see Tabuchi. And Miyazaki is busy at the center of it all. There's a bunch of men around the doorway, but Liz and I manage to find our shoes and leave.

The air feels blessedly cool downstairs, where the dealers are now folding tables and stacking chairs. All the action has evidently moved upstairs, where some sixty sweaty and mesmerized men are crammed watching a few others play cards. I have no more business hanging out there than I would have crashing a Mitsubishi board meeting.

Before we reach the exit, a large man yells out and runs up to

162

us, out of breath. It's the old man's assistant. He says something to me but I don't understand. Liz asks him to repeat himself. He does but I need Liz to explain that in return for my kindness in helping the old man sit, the assistant wants to give me a hundred thousand yen from his boss (as in employer, not oyabun).

Liz winces as I turn down the money. But in thanking the man I explain that I am researching a book about the Japanese underground and would like to meet the old man for a discussion. "Book?" The man turns away, as if to look at me again would mean he'd have to hit me. Liz sees impending danger and grabs the man's arm to assure him that we had spoken to Tabuchi, who knows that we're no threat. She gives him my boilerplate guarantee that I am interested in yakuza only as a part of traditional Japanese culture, not as criminals per se. But he looks unconvinced. So, as a sign of good faith, I give him my business card with my name and address. He doesn't return the gesture. Instead he turns my card around, examining the English on one side, and then the Japanese on the other.

"You live here?" he asks.

"You or your boss can call him anytime," chimes Liz. "Your conversations will be completely confidential." Before she can give him the hard sell, the man grunts and turns on his heels.

"This is the beginning of a problem," I say to Liz.

"Only because that guy is particularly thick." Liz sighs. "Just make sure you sleep at your girlfriend's for the next few nights."

"C'mon, I just helped the old man sit down."

"But Junior there was creepy with those fat fingers and the way he slurred his words." Liz shudders.

Two days later the assistant comes to my apartment building to leave off, in my mailbox, a brown envelope on which my name has been scrawled in the shaky hand of an old man or an illiterate. Though I am relieved and happy to find a hundred thousand yen, I can't help feeling that the old man would have been an interesting fellow to know. That he could be so moved by my simple gestures hints that he may be one of those "revered" Japanese senior citizens nobody really cares for.

* * *

Liz "went out" with Miyazaki. He was from Nagasaki. Miyazaki's horrific tattoos were apparently inspired by the patterns of flash burns found on atomic bomb victims. On a closer look, the arched stripes across his chest were ridged like bamboo, and his back seemed burned with branches and the shadow of a child's hand. (Liz felt that Miyazaki's personality was as spooky as his body. Neither of us felt that he had the consciousness equal to the dark message of his tattoos.) Miyazaki admitted to Liz that as a poor but aspiring gangster he had let his body be used as a canvas by some politically active woman artist.

Like his tattoos, Miyazaki wasn't a typical yakuza either. He said he was a freelancer, a fixer, used by other yakuza for "delicate" operations. That's why he didn't live in Osaka or Tokyo: He didn't want to get too well known. He was staying in Tokyo only long enough to assist a yakuza who was having a problem with the president of a small shipping firm that was transporting used Japanese cars to Russia. (The Japanese loathe used cars and the domestic market for them is negligible. You can buy a late-model used car for less than a thousand dollars—and that often includes a year of insurance, a most expensive aspect of car ownership in Japan.)

The yakuza boss had been doing a swift business buying up used cars, fudging the paperwork, and getting them aboard ship in the port of Niigata on the Sea of Japan. Like most yakuza enterprises, this used car deal was only slightly illegal, took minimal effort, and was wildly profitable. The Russian gangsters were waiting with fat rolls of American dollars and even supplied manpower to unload the ships at Vladivostok. Mr. Y, the head of the shipping company, had been trying to cut the yakuza middleman out of the operation.

Miyazaki said he had simply gone to see Mr. Y with the gift of a thirty-thousand-dollar gold Rolex watch. "Miyazaki didn't threaten the guy," Liz said, trying to recall the outcome as Miyazaki related it. "He just listed all the advantages of doing business with his yakuza: Mr. Y has received complete protection from the many scams such as faked sales receipts, transfer papers, and insurance arrangements."

Married to the Yazuka

During the course of his presentation, Miyazaki made sure that his tattoo would be noticed below his cuffs and his open collar. Mr. Y quickly accepted the Rolex "as a token of his client's appreciation." The acceptance was the guarantee that Mr. Y would forget his dreams of becoming a used car mogul.

"Miyazaki said," Liz continued, "that it's common for a regular businessman to try to pull out of a partnership with yakuza. It makes them crazy to see how easy money can be made by going a bit outside the law."

It's also becoming common to read about citizens who have been arrested for shady deals after some kind of yakuza partnership.

Miyazaki's importance as a fixer lay in the fact that he was not truly affiliated with any gang, and, if things got ugly, he could disappear. This ability to disappear is not an option for most yakuza. "He said, 'I have no master,'" mimicked Liz in a deep, TV-samurai baritone.

Abruptly Liz's face changed from a deadpan to a mischievous smile. "How would you like to try your hand at being a pimp?" I figured she was joking, but she held up her hand and explained the situation: A Belgian real estate agent had shorted her and a friend out of sixty thousand yen after a "date" three days earlier. She was going to contact a yakuza who had helped her collect money before. But since the jerk was European, she asked me to talk with him first. At first I had reservations, but I owed Liz something after the ways she had been helping me. So, on a pay phone in front of my apartment building, I called the Belgian. At his office his Japanese wife picked up the phone, so I hung up. I reached him on his car phone. He dummied up when I growled that this would be the only time he would hear from a gaijin. From then on, I assured him, all his problems would be "Japanese." Two minutes after I hung up, he called Liz with some excuse and a promise to have the cash delivered the next day. The money was delivered that day. Liz thanked me by treating me to a pricey dinner in a nice restaurant—where the waitresses wore kimonos.

* * *

The next time I saw Liz was at the International Clinic in Roppongi. She had been beaten up by the nasty yakuza called Ito. This was the same Ito whom Miyazaki referred to with such contempt. The clinic's M.D., a retired U.S. Army doctor who had seen a lot of combat, said he'd never seen a woman pummeled like that. Neither had I. She was indeed a mess. Both of her eyes were swollen nearly shut by doughy blue-black flesh rising from her once-gaunt cheekbones. Her bottom lip had been split, and three bottom teeth moved like they were hinged. Slowly, Liz eased on the sunglasses I brought her. I helped her check out of the clinic and escorted her back to her apartment. If only her yakuza hubby were free.

Liz's answering machine held three messages of sympathy. Liz's network of longtime gaijin friends included Filipino call girls and black American musicians married to Japanese. Each caller voiced fine moral outrage against "the yakuza asshole" but offered no course of revenge. Liz, however, possessed an inner hardness, or perhaps fatalism, and accepted her temporary disfigurement as the result of bad luck—nothing more. For her, the loss of income was worse than the pain; and "Anyway, there is nothing I can do to Ito."

A few days later, I accompany Liz to the clinic where she is having her stitches removed. It's early evening, and as we're walking past the new high rise apartment building built for the policemen's families across from the stylish Temporary Personnel Building, Liz's beeper buzzes. The Tylenol with codeine Liz had ingested makes her exceptionally sanguine. She steps from a phone booth smiling and looking for a cab. That freak Miyazaki has insisted she hurry over to the Shibuya flat where he's holed up.

"He says you should come, too. It's some kind of party!" Liz says excitedly. She is happy for a few minutes, but then turns apprehensive, seems she met Miyazaki for a date just three days after her beating. And, although she had forewarned him of her condition, Miyazaki went pale at the sight of her. He made up some lame excuse, then pushed some bills into her purse and took off. I know that this sort of professional rejection, despite the extenuating circumstances, must have torn her up. In the past year or so, she has already noted the disappointment in the eyes of new customers who had been "expecting someone much younger." But those bad vibes have only come from white foreigners, never a Japanese (who still tell her she looked like Jackie Kennedy, Julia Roberts, or even Tina Turner).

It's only a short drive to the new and totally nondescript apartment on a side street above Shibuya's neon valley. Some of Tokyo's most elaborate, chrome-intensive love hotels are nearby, but the end where Miyazaki is staying is quiet and residential.

The place appears to be a "weekly mansion," a kind of efficiency hotel with little or no staff. A small office that a doorman might have once occupied is now empty and dark. The un-Japanese disorder in the lobby, with Domino's Pizza flyers and Chinese menus littering the floor beneath half-opened mailboxes, looks like a crime scene. Perhaps it is.

Miyazaki buzzes us up.

He is shirtless again, wearing only sweatpants, whose drawstring dangles over his crotch. He ushers us into his dimly lit room, actually patting me on the back as he directs Liz and me into a love seat. (This is obviously no party.) Miyazaki pours beer into some glasses as the light from a small television plays on the surreal black tattoo of his shoulder. With his difficult accent and grunted yakuza argot, I find the wound-up Miyazaki impossible to follow. Suddenly, I'm uncomfortable in that coffin-sized room with its sloppy bed and resident maniac.

Liz laughs and turns to me. "Miyazaki says you made quite an impression on that old man you helped at the casino. He's some kind of yakuza godfather. I think Miyazaki says he's retired now, but was some honcho in his time. Anyway, sounds like some people lost face when a gaijin gave help before one of the yakuza . . . "

"Shit." I sigh. "Hope I'm not in trouble."

I ask Miyazaki if everything is all right.

"Hai, hai, everything OK." He grins. Liz translates: "Actually, it looked good for Miyazaki because some men said we were Miyazaki's friends. Apparently, this old guy doesn't like Miyazaki, or maybe, his people don't like Miyazaki. So, Miyazaki says, your good manners reflected well on him . . . I think that's what he said."

Miyazaki kneels in front of us. He places a black video cassette case on the table. "The Fixer" Miyazaki is smiling like a giddy kid about to present an engagement ring to his sweetheart.

I get up and leave before the videotape is played. Somewhere deep in my soul I know that Miyazaki's video will be a snuff film. I leave, and later Liz describes the plot of the video: the bloodied face of Ito in one long close-up. Miyazaki tracked down her attacker and demolished him, then documented the result on tape. Her description makes me nauseated.

What in the world did she say to Miyazaki after the screening?

"Oh," Liz recalls with incredible equanimity. "I told him I'm sorry I missed it."

The next day I meet Liz in Ueno Station on the Hibiya line platform. She is wearing the sunglasses that cover most of her still-swollen face. We weave through the masses funneling out towards the national museum. The crush gives way a bit as we walk to the steps where the Iranians rule. It's a formidable bazaar that the big bearded men put on each weekend, rife with illicit possibilities. A small Middle Eastern man wearing a Yakult Swallows cap approaches us. He greets us in clipped Japanese before leading us up the steps, through a circle of burly men to an empty bench beneath a ginkgo tree. The Swallows fan is named Mohammed, and he speaks only Persian and Japanese—or so he says.

"What do you need?" Mohammed inquires. "Hashish or telephone card?"

"You have heroin?" Liz asks, using the drug's slang word, which sounds like "teriyaki."

"Please wait." Mohammed stands up to make eye contact with a bald man who has been intently watching us. The two men confer in the sunlight. Mohammed then strides over to where a dozen men lounge on dirty futons, watching a blurry video of some Middle Eastern musical. The bald man keeps his eyes on us. Although there have been TV reports of Iranians dating and marrying Japanese, there are absolutely no females around besides Liz. Suddenly, Mohammed reappears at our side. He sits next to Liz, whose khaki shorts reveal smooth, lightly tanned thighs. As if scandalized, Mohammed spreads out a dark blue bandana across Liz's lap. He casually drops three small foil rectangles onto the cloth, then opens a fourth, exposing the brown powder to the summer day. Liz taps the tip of her index finger lightly into the silver trough. She tastes the powder for a moment, then nods and recloses the foil.

Then Liz asks how many units are on the recycled telephone cards. Mohammed assures her that each of them has been coded with four hundred units. (Though the phone company has already rewired or replaced virtually all public phones that you can use for international calls, a few, including those in front of the Nippon Telegraph & Telephone offices, can still access the world.)

For five thousand yen Liz buys ten cards that might yield about ¥50,000 worth of long distance calls. She hands the man another twenty thousand yen for the heroin and a small cube of black opium.

Mohammed smiles and bows. On a whim I ask him if he could get any pistols. Mohammed's face tilts, as if he thought he couldn't have heard correctly.

"Gun?" Mohammed asks breathlessly. "You mean like *bang, bang*?" He pantomimes his finger pulling a trigger.

"Yeah." I shrug nonchalantly.

"Oh, no, no, no, no, no . . ." Mohammed shakes his head and slides into the milling crowd of men. Immediately, three bigger and swarthier Iranians converge on Liz, singing English pop lyrics and flashing more doctored telephone cards. I grab her arm and get us out of the park.

"All those Arab guys," Liz comments, after emerging—eyes glistening—from the subway bathroom (she has apparently sniffed the powder she has just purchased), "it's one of the weirdest things I've seen in ten years in Tokyo. They're amazing, the way they just show up here, learn the language better than any of us, and do the shit jobs that Japanese don't want. One night a couple of weeks ago, there was a construction crew outside my building. They were wearing overalls and hard hats but they looked odd to me. The men looked like giants! It took a minute before I realized they were big gaijin with mustaches. Who would have ever thought there'd come a day when gaijin would be working on city construction in Tokyo, Japan? It's strange that these guys flew, like, ten thousand miles just to bust up blacktop."

We are leaning against the end of the horseshoe-shaped bar of Roppongi's Gas Panic Club, listening to Metallica's harried thrash. Two Australian bartenders spit big fireballs that explode about a foot over the flinching customers. Most of the 150 or so undulating sweaty souls are gaijin, with, perhaps, ten Japanese among them. Some of the Brazilians display signs of Japanese heritage but their dancing is as fluid as the purebred Cariocas.

Liz, overdressed in a black Chanel suit, motions to the longhaired bartender, who blows her a kiss and promptly hands her a double bourbon. She glances down at her watch, then up to five models who are dancing on the bar. The club is crowded and becomes more claustrophobic as waves of U.S. military emerge from the elevator. The soldiers' faces instantly brighten as one of the models takes off her blouse and whips it at a tall black guy whose T-shirt says "SOMEONE WENT TO BANGKOK AND ALL I GOT WAS AIDS."

From deep within her Louis Vuitton shoulder bag, Liz's beeper plays a tinny "Camptown Races." She quickly hands me her drink, then disappears into the throbbing masses. I watch the doors of the elevator open and close.

Suddenly, two Brazilian guys near the bar begin arguing loudly in Portuguese. After some pushing and shoving, one of them pulls out a switchblade. The soldiers see the scuffle, smile, and, as if on cue, form a ring around the combatants. I hop on a stool for a better view. There's not much of a show as the unarmed Latin gracefully feigns a punch to the other's head, then executes a roundhouse kick to his opponent's gut and sends his knife crashing to the ground. A cheer goes up around the circle, but dissolves as a few other Brazilians converge to break it all up. Some of the crew-cut Americans boo.

"What happened?" Liz asks, when she reappears at my side. I try to explain as she guzzles her bourbon and slams the empty glass on the bar, but she interrupts, "A friend of mine is in trouble, please come with me . . . now!"

"What kind of trouble?" I sigh, recalling the uncomfortable encounter with the crazy Miyazaki. "Is this another yakuza problem?"

"I thought that's your thing," she teases, as she jams her cigarettes into her bag.

"Yeah, but your yakuza are weird . . ."

"Well don't worry, it's not a yakuza problem; it's a geisha problem," Liz says, as the elevator doors slide closed.

Though the trains haven't stopped running, Liz walks right up to a cab and bangs on the back window. Instead of popping the door open, the driver leans across the front seat and rolls down the window. He wants to know our destination before letting us in. Gaijin tend to live at central Tokyo addresses that can take time to locate, but the fare won't nearly add up to that of some drunk Saitama-bound salaryman. The neighborhood Liz shouts out, however, seems to impress the driver enough for him to open the door.

There are very few Tokyo sensations as pleasing as a long taxi ride that you're not paying for. Tokyo Tower disappears from the rearview mirror as we turn right on Aoyama Avenue. It seems we're taking some roundabout way to Shinjuku. We pass the guard booth at the side entrance of the Akasaka Detached Palace. The royal family is living here while the main palace in Marunouchi is being renovated. The vast Aoyama Cemetery goes by on our left as the street narrows in front of Keio University Hospital. We have been in the cab less than ten minutes, and the fare already exceeds thirty dollars.

"Is this important?" I ask Liz, who is inspecting her nose in a black compact.

"You never know." She snaps the compact closed. "But, when someone needs help, you just go."

"I didn't think your network included Japanese," I say.

"Japanese, Filipino, whatever." She shrugs. "When you've worked here for ten years, you meet a lot of women supporting themselves without men. I mean, c'mon, *you* know about the water trades, it's like Japan's biggest employer and it's women who do all the work, it's women who take all the abuse. Just like home." she adds.

"I've learned not to depend on men for anything beyond money. Other girls I've met know that too. We foreigners have no illusions, but Japanese women still hold onto romantic ideas. I don't know. But Hatsumi, who beeped me, should know better. She's a thirty-seven-year-old geisha, like a housemother for some younger geisha who work the same party circuit. Whenever this Hatsumi has a problem, she calls me . . ."

"Yeah, but how did your world overlap with a geisha's?"

"What the fuck does that mean?" Liz turns her head and gives me a hard look. "What do you think a geisha is? . . . Or what do you think I am?"

"I'm just wondering how you met Hatsumi," I say in a neutral voice.

Liz relaxes. "She wanted to study English, so a friend of a friend gave her my number."

"I didn't know you were an English teacher."

"For twenty thousand yen an hour, I became one." She smiles. At about four times the going rate, in other words. One might say that charging two hundred dollars an hour is criminal. I say something to that effect and Liz laughs.

"Well, for the money, Hatsumi got an English teacher and a best friend."

The taxi turns up a steep hill, then pulls to the side of the street as the driver announces, "Kagurazaka des."

Kagurazaka is a famous old geisha district that I had always been meaning to visit. But at first glance, God, it looks like anywhere else in Tokyo.

Liz leads me down one of the many narrow lanes off the main street. We walk past the worn wooden walls of what I recognize as *ryotei*, old and incredibly expensive geisha restaurants that serve only those elite businessmen with the heftiest expense accounts. We stop at a flight of ancient stone steps worn smooth by the feet of thousands of geisha. We pause at a landscaped, sloping piece of old Edo. With unseemly haste we proceed over the gnarled roots that grew over the steps a hundred years ago and now seem to hold the stones in place. A string of red paper lanterns wrapped in tattered plastic hangs along a path that curves through a thicket of trees.

We come up to a very traditional wooden house with windows shuttered in brown bamboo. I can almost reach the low-slung gables with my hand. "It's like being in Japan, huh?" Liz jokes, before knocking gently on the door. "Old Japan." I sigh to myself. A light shuffling sound is barely audible through the walls. An inner door slides open, then the glass paneled outside door is pushed aside by shaking fingers. The doorkeeper looks as old as the house. Though she can barely see above our waists, she greets us in an ancient dialect. Then, with painful slowness, she lays out two pairs of vinyl slippers for us and melts away.

"Thank God you are here!" booms a voice from the dark hallway. It is Hatsumi, standing beneath a single hanging bulb. With her long hair, round John Lennon glasses, and Michigan State T-shirt, the woman looks more like a grad student than a veteran of the water trade.

Hatsumi bows with precision, then unexpectedly shakes my hand, saying, "Hello, how are you?" She jabbers on in a stilted, but fairly correct English as she leads us up steep wooden steps. We enter a big tatami room that is easily twice the size of the average Tokyo flat. Though dressed in jeans, Hatsumi kneels in the formal manner to take some beer from a small refrigerator. She brings the bottles to the low table and kneels again to attend to us.

Liz and I are playing with a samisen that is propped beneath a framed poster of the prima ballerina, Sylvie Guillem. The samisen is the banjo-type instrument that makes the twangy music that foreigners associate with Japan—and the Japanese associate with geisha.

With professional élan, Hatsumi now fills our glasses with beer. My legs are falling asleep as Hatsumi and Liz trade trivialities. This goes on and on until we finish the two big bottles of Yebisu beer. Although I dig the whole tatami and bamboo ambience, my thoughts are drifting back to the party animals of Roppongi. I nudge Liz, then flatly ask Hatsumi: "Where's the fire?"

"Excuse me?" she asks earnestly.

"What's the big emergency, Hatsumi-chan?" Liz translates.

"I hate to bother you, but it's my friend Mariko-chan." Hatsumi sighs, putting down her glass. "I believe she has a drug problem this evening. If it's not too much trouble, could you look at her, please?"

"Shit, girl, that's why I came!" Liz smiles, though a bit peeved. "Where is Mariko?"

"Come." Hatsumi leads us into the hallway, then slides open another door. This room is a mess. Dozens of luxurious silk kimonos and undergarments are strewn all over the tatami. A wall of drawers has been pulled out and dumped. The elderly maid is kneeling at a futon under a half-opened window and is patting a young woman's forehead with a wet cloth. As we approach the nurse and patient, I can't help stepping on kimonos worth tens of thousands of dollars.

I lean over the quasi-conscious girl, whose sweaty round face and pouty lips are almost covered by the brocade comforter. The old maid looks at me as I touch Mariko's cool wet forehead and asks hopefully, "Are you a doctor?"

I smile and move the back of my hand against Mariko's neck. I feel like part of some nineteenth-century tableau. The girl belongs in a hospital. "Have you called a doctor?" I ask Hatsumi, whose glasses and good English, I suspect, merely give the illusion of intelligence.

"I called Liz-san," she says. Liz reaches beneath the covers and draws Mariko's arm into the light.

"Yeah, just what I thought." Liz sighs.

I shudder at the abscesses on Mariko's forearm, green with pus, and turn away from the rancid stench that seems to emanate from the unclean wounds.

"Why the fuck isn't she in a hospital?" I hiss to Liz. "She could have gangrene or hepatitis or something!"

"Shhhhh . . . ," Liz says softly. "You don't understand; these people are very ignorant. They know only their little world. They live without men, so they're used to being very self-reliant."

"That's ridiculous," I shout. "This girl's a junkie!"

"Drugs have a tradition in this world. What do you know about this anyway?" Liz scowls at me as she picks up a cordless phone and calls for an ambulance. She has to ask Hatsumi for the exact address of this geisha house. Hatsumi finds out only by asking the half-dead patient. Hatsumi writes it down on the back of a bridal magazine and hands it to Liz.

By the time Liz and Hatsumi pick up armfuls of the exquisite kimonos off the tatami to clear a path, the paramedics are here. I help them lift Mariko's emaciated body onto a stretcher. Her left shoulder bears an elaborate tattoo of burnt orange chrysanthemums. Their stems intertwine and run around her upper arm three or four times. These flowers seem much more vibrant and alive than tiny Mariko. A paramedic forces me to the side to secure the stretcher's straps.

"Are you a relative?" the paramedic asks Hatsumi, who shakes her head. "Does she have a mother?"

"Dead, I think," says Hatsumi. The question of her father's whereabouts is left unasked because a geisha's paternity is always a hazy proposition.

"Is there a boyfriend, then?" he continues.

"No."

"Well," says the exasperated paramedic, who is responsible for the paperwork. "Is there anyone connected with her?" I consider volunteering to tag along to the hospital when the bent old lady shuffles up to the paramedic.

"This is my grandchild," she whispers to the man in the white suit.

Back in 1991, Naomi Miki liked to call herself "bi" as in "a bicultural babe." High-cheekboned, buxom, and English-speaking, the eighteen-year-old Naomi was the natural leader of Tokyo's rock and roll groupies. By day she was a morose high school dropout living with her divorced father. But on certain nights she would talk her way backstage or straight into the hotel suites of visiting pop stars. For their rock-and-roll glamour Naomi traded sex along with a precocious world-weary wit. The first time I remember speaking with her was in the VIP lounge at a Roppongi nightclub. In the same room but seemingly oblivious to each other were quarterback Joe Montana, holding court with a bevy of pre-nubile Caucasian fans, and the Black Crowes, who were alone and weren't holding anything at all—and that was a problem for rock's standard-bearers of hard drug use.

Miss BiCultural didn't even recognize the blond hunk of Americana sitting on the sofa as she sidled up to the skinny Georgian rockers. Then with their half-closed eyes on her ass, Naomi walked up to me, saying that the Crowes were dying and willing to pay a hundred dollars for a Valium! None of the gaijin dealers I knew were in the place, but from my own pocket I produced not one Valium but four! That I wouldn't take any money for the worn and linty narcotics (meaning Naomi could pocket the cash) endeared me to the teenager, with whom I have since tried to maintain a big-brother relationship.

I hadn't visited Naomi since I had learned she was living with a yakuza. Hard to believe there was a time when such a development turned me off! Anyway, the boyfriend was out when I showed up at their flat in Shibuya.

Twenty-year-old Naomi sits with her back against the wall and her ass on the tatami-matted floor. She wears a sentimental ensemble: a long-sleeved surfer shirt (from the Natural Progression surf shop, Santa Monica) and men's boxers with a sewn-up fly (from Queensrÿche's bassist). Built into the wall is a wide-bodied, remote-controlled, fuzzy-logic air conditioner. It clicks loudly in showboating self-adjustment, incrementally cooling the room each time I exhale. Crumpled white sheets are bunched on her double-thick futon.

Though Naomi and her beau could afford a big-screen television and a regular VCR, she likes her micro components. Her T-shaped 8 mm video player has the sensual feel of a large smooth stone. Choosing from the cassettes scattered at her feet, she snaps in *Breakfast at Tiffany's*.

Married to the Yazuka

Naomi leans the personal video player on top of her firm stomach. To be seen clearly the tiny screen must be looked at from straight on. She likes to watch, and I'm content to watch her. As the opening credits roll and the music squeaks through tiny speakers, she pinches a few granules of shabu from a crinkled plastic bag. Holding a fresh Marlboro vertically, she pushes the ground crystals into the tobacco end. George Peppard walks down a sunny Manhattan street as Naomi lights her cigarette, then inhales, holding the fumes in her lungs.

"LIFE IS DELICIOUS!" She sings out this English translation of an old Japanese advertising slogan. From a four-month "homestay" semester in a Van Nuys high school plus a two-month experience in the L.A. porn scene, Naomi's English is nearly perfect, though laced with odd Chicano accents. Back in Tokyo, her large breasts and sexy, sleepy eyes have taken her to where she now commands five thousand dollars for an afternoon AV shoot. The career expectancy of a tuna is two or three videos, and then a producer will reel in a fresh one. Naomi's exotic voluptuousness has given her unusual staying power.

"I feel like a gaijin," she says, "because, technically, I am a gaijin." Born of a Japanese mother and a Korean father, she carries an alien registration card just like mine. Her father is now quite old. He came to Japan before the war, when Korea was part of the Japanese empire. He learned engineering, and, because big companies rarely hired Korean-Japanese, he started his own tool and die shop. Unrelated to her ethnicity, Naomi has always looked different. Her body bloomed young and full for an Asian woman. She says she would have been a victim of the viciously systematic bullying that is common in Japanese schools. Instead she became a tomboy and a ringleader of attacks against others.

"If the other kids knew I was half-Korean, I would've been slaughtered," she once told me. "I was always strong. I could beat up most of the boys in my high school. In America, I guess it's great to have big tits; you're supposed to be very popular. But Japanese boys were scared of me—and they still are!"

"When I was living in L.A., I used to dream about Tokyo," she says. "I saw myself at work, sitting at a desk, laughing on the telephone, talking to a friend or someone.

"It's not much of a dream," she admits with a sigh. "It was more like an image that would pop into my mind every time I closed my eyes. Maybe when you work in porn in a foreign place, you dream about normal, boring things. I mean, I dreamed about having a big dog and a house with a grassy yard too! But who has that in Japan?"

Aki, a friend of Naomi's who works in AV too, stops by Naomi's apartment to rest and make up for a "live show" that she does in Kabukicho. Aki has also worked the L.A. porno circuit, but she takes it more seriously than Naomi. In flip, affected English, Aki tells me of her vague "projects" in the United States and Tokyo. She evidently has delusions of being Japan's first crossover adult film superstar. I feel a real hardness in Aki's voice and manners: She trusts no one.

Aki's day sounds like a whirlwind of video cameras, slapping bodies, tissues, Listerine, and the barks of a speed-addled "director." She has allotted herself two hours in Naomi's apartment. She quickly showers, throws on a robe, and instantly falls asleep on the pile of sheets.

Naomi's boyfriend Masa is her "manager" and a yakuza to boot. Now, without exception, Naomi receives the total amount she is promised for AV shoots. Getting ripped off is commonplace. After grinding out a three-video, nine-hour shoot, many female leads are paid half, then told to call later for the rest. But Masa gets Naomi all the money, lands her roles, and hooks up the drugs. In a photo he looks like a tough guy, but not dumb. He's a kobun in a gang based right near my flat in Nishi-Azabu! She met Masa through Aki, who also had nightmares collecting her money from shadowy AV production companies. One "producer" broke her nose when she showed up at his home demanding her pay. But since Masa began managing her too, he makes sure Aki is paid in full (before he takes his 25 percent).

"If Masa wasn't yakuza," Naomi says, clicking off the video, "he wouldn't be so effective at twisting arms. I mean, he's not a tough guy at all! Masa is really very sweet and ambitious. He never complains about the weather or the economy. He's always hyper, always running around Tokyo trying to make money. He'll get involved in stupid deals—like one day last year he called me asking if I knew anyone named Tanaka. He had bought, or stolen, an unfinished tombstone with TANAKA cut down the front! OK, so it's worth like one million yen and Tanaka's the most common Japanese family name, but how the hell do you sell something like that?

"But Masa knows the Japanese mind," Naomi says, sitting up on her knees and pushing the video player onto the tatami. "He knows old farts are cheap. So he went driving out to old folks' homes in Kanagawa prefecture where he had all the Tanakas paged. Then he ushered them outside to look at the tombstone sitting in the back of his rental truck. The old people weren't offended at all. They thought it was such a nice opportunity to save money. Even folks that weren't named Tanaka were making offers for the thing!

"So, one old lady whose maiden name was Tanaka called up her brother at a hospital in Saitama—who ended up paying Masa almost three hundred thousand yen for the stone!" Naomi falls forward in a laughing fit. "Brilliant, huh?"

Naomi wakes her girlfriend at six. Aki begins her evening by pinching some shabu into two fingers of Jack Daniel's, then attempts a collect call to California. But her "boyfriend," alas, isn't home at 4 A.M., L.A. time. She slams the phone and gulps down the booze.

After composing herself, Aki pulls a lamp to her side to examine her naked complexion in a hand mirror. Her twenty-something-year-old face is ravished by reddish blotches that have spread across her cheeks and forehead. They don't seem new to her. She snaps open a bulky cosmetics case that is more of a toolbox. After fifteen minutes of concentrated work, she closes the case with a sigh, her beauty reconstituted. As she heads for the door, she hands me a comp ticket for entry into the live show she was working. "Sometimes there are yakuza there," she announces before disappearing, as if I need the additional incentive.

Masa calls to tell Naomi that he won't be home until late. She sighs, informing him that her American friend is waiting to meet the yakuza in her life. "Another time," he says to her, which she then repeats to me. My disappointment is somewhat mitigated by the thought of catching up with Aki. As it's early, I take Naomi to a bar where she relates the following story:

One evening last January, Naomi arrived home around ten after a long day. Masa was in the apartment with another young, but fat, yakuza who was crying profusely. Masa brought Naomi into the kitchen and apologized for having dumped this mess in her living room. He sheepishly explained that the bawling dude, called Kono, needed his help. Masa was trying to psych Kono into facing the yakuza rite called *yubitsume*.

Kono was obligated to chop off his fingertip because he had been late picking up his oyabun after a mah-jongg game. Kono had foolishly fallen asleep at a coffee shop and left the boss stranded way the hell out in a Tokyo hinterland called Jujo. Kono's incensed oyabun, a low-level boss in an old Tokyo gang, decided to hunt down a cab. Late at night, it can get deathly deserted in places like Jujo, and the boss was mugged by a pack of bosozoku (these minor-league gangsters evidently ignored the yakuza logo on the boss's meishi). This outrage was not reported to the Tokyo police, of course. When the humiliated boss finally reached his office, he was screaming for Kono's blood. It's rare for a boss to demand the fingertip of a neophyte, but, apparently, this wasn't Kono's first big mistake.

"I really didn't mind Masa hanging out with his friends in my apartment," Naomi says. "Especially if it was an emergency, like Kono's problem. They ended up getting Kono drunk and driving him over to the boss's office with a knife in his jacket. But the boss had left for the night, so Masa and another friend cut Kono's finger off for him! The guy fainted and spilled blood all over the office! Masa said it was nasty! They threw water on Kono's face, and he began screaming again. Then they couldn't find the finger!

Naomi laughs. "So, they dragged this big baby down to some clinic to fix him up. Then they ran back to the office, found the nub and rolled it in a napkin. They left the thing on the coffee table. So the next morning the boss shows up and freaks out over the mess, cursing about the new carpet he's going to have to buy. When he discovered it was fat Kono who left the finger, he goes crazy again, saying he didn't really mean he had to cut his finger. The boss said he would've stopped him if Kono had tried to do it in person, the proper way one's supposed to do it. Masa now knows better, he's an expert yakuza now.

"But Kono ended up getting some kind of promotion out of it." Naomi laughs. "He even helped with Masa's cocaine business."

Masa had begun using Naomi's apartment as a meeting and distribution point for his latest endeavor, selling cocaine. Though the effects of shabu, Japan's favorite drug, and cocaine are comparable, coke seemed to have huge potential in the upscale *shinjinue* market. These were the so-called new people, Japan's yuppies who came of age in the bubble Japan untouched by postwar sacrifice and striving. They needed instant gratification and preferred working in the creative new fields connected with Japan's entertainment and advertising businesses. The shinjinue were the conspicuous spenders of the go-go eighties and early nineties. Foreign luxury items from Louis Vuitton purses to Ferrari automobiles to Beaujolais Nouveau wines flown in on the Concorde were a few of the objects of shinjinue desire. Blue-collar shabu never had the necessary cachet. But cocaine, exotic and glamorous, had a natural appeal to the shijinue imagination.

Supplying shabu from nearby Taiwan and Korea, the ancestral homes of many yakuza, was one thing. It was quite another for unworldly gangsters to hook up with the Colombian cartels, no matter how much both parties long for a marriage. Rumors exist of a U.S. Mafia-brokered deal between Cali and Tokyo mobs but the coke supply side is still constricted.

"Masa used to get it through the South American Japanese working in Kanagawa prefecture," Naomi says. "But they charged around four hundred dollars a gram. The stuff was already cut so much that Masa could only resell the stuff as is. Then he had a brainstorm.

"He made me call a small-time connection I had in L.A. The guy express shipped a quarter ounce to us. We got, like, seven grams for three hundred fifty dollars. This wasn't the bullshit Masa had been getting stuck with. I showed him what I knew about how to cut and package the coke properly. Hanging around those L.A. sleazeballs taught me one thing good," she recalls, rather wistfully.

Their basic but unfounded premise was that even if the post office might check packets entering Japan via regular mail, private two-day delivery services wouldn't be checked and customs wouldn't waste time peeking into the thousands of documents flown daily into Tokyo.

Masa hooked up a British DJ, who introduced him to the manager of Club M, who, in turn, bought big then funneled it to his hundred closest friends. The mere exoticism of coke made it irresistible to the tribe with money to burn. The same people who sneered at the thought of shabu enthusiastically snorted cocaine like it was the latest food fad. "Coke was their tiramisù," says Naomi.

The affluent young thrill-seekers desired something more than the nightlife staples of pubs, hostesses, and karaoke. Entrepreneurs with sophisticated new approaches built clubs that plugged into and shaped the new Zeitgeist. Though yakuza were often the financial backers, they kept their kobun away and let slick katagi run the show. None of Masa's hip customers knew he was yakuza. For shinjinue, yakuza are like shabu: creepy and unfashionable, a part of the old order.

Masa's oyabun, Ozaki, was pleased with the threefold increase in Masa's monthly tribute and asked him no questions. Masa had remembered the perfunctory warning against messing around with "drugs," but Masa figured the boss was just talking about shabu. In the paper some Yokohama kobun had been busted in a shabu deal that was prosecuted so vigorously, it led to the arrest of his oyabun. But Masa somehow believed that cocaine wasn't a concern of the police or his oyabun.

But, still, Masa was anxious about receiving more significant amounts of coke by express delivery. With typical yakuza conservatism, he never dreamt of a cocaine empire—or even of expanding his client base beyond two clubs. Masa never gave out his phone or beeper numbers to anyone. This bothered some regular customers like the club manager, who didn't like the idea of Masa maintaining his anonymity while knowing the club users well. Under Japanese law, the drug buyer is as culpable as the dealer. This motivates arrested dealers to improve their situations by ratting on their customers. One night the manager followed Masa to his car and copied the license plate number "as insurance."

After five months of fairly lucrative coke dealing, little things began to make Masa and Naomi nervous. One time the express envelope had arrived wrapped in tape, as if the self-sealing package had been razored open, but the coke was still there. Another time, the powder was loose in the pouch and was trickling out the corners.

"One of the television networks," Naomi says, remembering the turning point of Masa's business, "either TV Asahi or TBS, did one of those overblown investigations into crazy Tokyo nightlife. They interviewed some over-sexed club girls with their faces, you know, distorted to hide their identities. They tried to sound so wild! They said guys would do anything to pick up the sexy ladies who danced up on the platforms. And then one of those airheads says some famous musician fucked her in Club M's back office. While others sniffed coke off the top of the desk, she was underneath, getting off!"

The bureaucrats like to believe that foreign plagues like AIDS and cocaine have as much of a chance in Japan as Buicks and Minute Rice. While frustration with foreign companies is a government obsession, foreign vices are downplayed as a negligible wart on the national portrait. The tabloid television reportage forced a swift response. After calling ahead to say they were coming, the police dramatically busted through Club M's unlocked back doors. A bowing older executive of the club's parent corporation was waiting for the cops with damning information already elicited from M's managers. The guy who knew Masa's license plate number knew enough to point out the yakuza.

Older yakuza are shrewder about erasing their identities before a big scam. Japan is a difficult country in which to disappear. Anonymity is acquired only gradually, over many moves and transactions, until one's personal paper trail has been thoroughly laundered. But Masa's license would reveal everything, from his address to his grammar school attendance records.

The cops busted through the door of Masa's own small flat near Ebisu Station. (He wouldn't have been there normally. Masa practically lived at Naomi's. But believing Naomi was working down in Osaka, Masa slept at home.) The detective made it clear that the arrest of his oyabun wasn't their aim. It was understood, the detective told Masa, that all "respectable" Tokyo yakuza bosses had prohibited cocaine but that sometimes they couldn't control "mafia" types like him. The theory of the new "mafia" breed of morally indifferent hustlers was in vogue. It provided cops and yakuza honchos with an easy explanation for the criminal excesses of those years.

The hyperbolic revelations of the disco girls fueled the cops' assumptions that Masa must be a link in an elaborate cocaine network. Because no coke was actually found at Masa's place, the police pressured him to give up his accomplices but not his oyabun. According to Naomi, when Masa was in custody he was about to finger some Brazilian-Japanese in Yokohama when the cops checked the records of Masa's cell phone. That led them, the same day, to Naomi's apartment, where she had just arrived from Osaka.

"It scared the shit out of me," Naomi says, shaking her head. "But I had always been strict about cleaning up after the coke. I had destroyed every envelope and receipt that had any connection with the blow. I scrubbed everything the coke ever touched. We kept the bulk of the stuff in a coin locker at the station. But there were five grams of shabu in my overnight bag. I had bought it real cheap on the set in Osaka.

"They were pissed that there was no coke," she says. "Then they found the shabu, and also my Korean passport with all these stamps from America. Well, they took their frustrations out on me. I was busted and Masa was released."

Naomi did six harrowing months in prison. "A living hell," she calls it. "But Masa visited me and was waiting for me when I was released." Naomi is no gaijin. The final footnote of taking the fall for Masa is pure *gaman*, dutiful suffering as mastered by Japanese women.

On this note, I decide to take my leave of Naomi. The free pass from Aki is burning a hole in my pocket. She did promise some possible yakuza, didn't she? It will be strictly business. . . .

In the dusk I ride out to Shinjuku, park my scooter, and walk through a pedestrian zone into Kabukicho. Modern Kabukicho's got nothing to do with Kabuki or any other traditional art. Kabukicho is glitz, the lights, outdoor speakers crying "C'mon here, Daddy . . . give it to me, Daddy . . . oh, oh give it to me, Daddy. . . oh, ohhh!" Gnarled old men traipse up and down the narrow streets wearing sandwich boards boasting "LIVE SHOW, 14-YEAR-OLDS, ONLY ¥10!" With their eyes glazed yet attentive, a white-collar crowd is prowling the sidewalks with their jackets hanging limply over their shoulders. Perhaps this uniformity is my imagination but, I'm sure, the salarymen want to get laid. A quartet of suits are accosted by a punch-permed tout who lets them examine the Polaroids of the girls "for lease" in the bar at the end of the dark descending stairway. Police in short sleeves coast right past on their bicycles, indifferent to every permutation of Kabukicho: junkie, wise guy, hustler, and mark.

I follow the tiny map on the back of Aki's comp. The side streets and alleys on the Kabukicho side of Yasakuni Avenue are twisted and dark. Twice I walk through the grimy square in front of the ratty Toho cineplex, where belated hippies are attempting Simon and Garfunkel. Sitting on a curb, two old men are washing their clothes in a battered bucket filled with water from the public toilets. They are wearing newspaper diapers.

The sex revue where Aki is performing is called something like Mirror House or Mirror Theatre. The place proves difficult to find, perhaps because I was expecting a flashing neon marquee with English subtitle. Instead I find a mere three-foot sign in Japanese over a street-level door guarded by a lone doorman dressed in a black suit with his long hair pulled back. He takes my pass while staring into my brown gaijin eyes. Finally he smiles, bows, and pulls open the door.

Another guy in a black outfit is waiting at the bottom of the carpeted stairs. He pulls open a second door, and a thousand-watt surge of thumping bass staggers me. I take three steps inside—and bang smartly into a floor-to-ceiling mirror. Now, using my hands, I feel my way sideways into a larger vestibule that is awash in intense strobe lights flickering at twice the rate of the music's hard techno beat. It's like some old hall of mirrors, but every other mirror pane frames what looks like a purplish hologram of a naked Asian girl. This life-sized oh-wouldn't-it-be-nice go-go dancer gracefully undulates back and forth ad infinitum. She smiles and blows kisses. Her reverberating giggles mesh with the harsh music that won't go away.

I keep using my hand to guide myself further into the synthetic maze. Suddenly, a distant voice becomes loud and distinct. It's a stern warning, in English: "Please follow the arrows on the floor!" Ultraviolet strips, which somehow I hadn't noticed, glow at my feet.

At long last I enter a large round atrium where the music is kinder. There's a floral fragrance sweetening the air. Before my pupils can adjust to the darkness, a short-haired waif in a clingy black dress takes me by the elbow.

"Are you the only one?" she chirps in better-than-schoolgirl

English. I admit the obvious. Then she asks if I want to sit at the bar or be "sealed" in a "private video chamber." I take a stool.

The well-attended bar surrounds a raised island populated by a half-dozen naked women. Their bodies are painted in a fluorescent range of pastel blues. Colored laser beams play about randomly. A lone prurient spotlight focuses on a particular navel or breast or face for about ten seconds before flashing off to seize on a different body feature for another ten. It's like a planetarium for perverts.

From the surface of the matte black bar in front of me, a small LCD television screen blinks to life. Now I see why the other men seem to be staring in their drinks. Still, I can't understand why my barmates seem more entranced with their own personal TVs than the actual live show of lesbian love acts from Mars. But soon the hostess reappears at my side to instruct me on how to switch channels on this erotic closed-circuit system. Surfing the channels, I discover that the programming goes beyond the dozen cameras angled at the bodies in front of me. One can also watch what is transpiring behind the closed doors of the private video chambers. Mostly it's scenes of grinning salarymen in slackened ties gawking at, but not quite touching, the tits and asses waved in their delighted faces.

Sipping my thirty-dollar draft beer (there was no cover charge, I remind myself), I'm convinced that it is indeed Aki on channel seven, smoking a cigarette with a rather hip guy. I ask if I can say "hi" to the girl on my screen.

"Fifty thousand yen for fifteen minutes," the hostess chirps.

"No," I say quickly. "She's a friend."

If I were Japanese, I probably wouldn't be indulged. But the young woman simply asks me, "What's her name, then?" I smile that I don't know her work name, but I say her name is Aki-*chan*, for familiarity. With no further ado (or solicited tip), the hostess departs. She returns in a few minutes to pick up my beer and lead me to chamber number seven.

"Hi!" Aki smiles. I try not to glance at her black bustier or think about her G-string. She introduces me to the fashionable young man, who turns out to be Naomi's boyfriend, Masa. "I was just telling Masa about you . . . "

I sit, shaking the hand of a yakuza who looks, from his narrow lapels to oval, wired-framed glasses and long, precisely cut hair, like a young advertising executive on top of the world. This guy is not underground Japan; he embodies the above-board, up-to-date Japan of television commercials and magazine covers. If this is the guy who hustled tombstones and express-shipped cocaine, he's a can't-miss for high office! I hate to judge him too quickly but I smell a future PM.

Masa smiles and, in Japanese, asks something of Aki. She responds, saying something is okay. I assume she's telling him to go ahead and speak Japanese to me. But, it seems, she is saying that it is okay for him to speak English, a daunting proposition for most Japanese, even those who teach the language. Hell, if this guy wants to practice his English with me, fine. Masa sucks a deep breath and sighs. "Another time we shall meet." He pauses. "Tomorrow."

FIXING AND BREAKING

I'm back in Shinjuku, inside the big Barneys clothing store watching Masa being measured for a dark blue Dolce & Gabbana suit worth two months of my rent. The tiny tailor works silently without asking a single question. After twenty minutes of fussing in front of the mirror (with occasional glances seeking my dubious approval and assurances), the tailor bows his leave. We take the elevator down to a basement café where pairs of women sit drinking tea, their legs hidden behind multicolored glossy shopping bags.

Our conversation continues in an awkward Japanese-English amalgam. I try to discern if he is cheating with Aki behind Naomi's back, but he just tells me that they are both "nice girls," "pretty girls." I break out the tape recorder and make some leading statements about the last gang war. I can feel that Masa is intelligent, maybe of a philosophical bent. Then, in English, I ask him directly, "Why are you a yakuza?" A question he takes (I think) to mean something closer to "What is a yakuza?"

"Besides getting in trouble . . . to me being in the yakuza is a job. That's the most important thing. You can talk about obligation or honor, but above all, it's a job. Of course, it's a big commitment, a lifetime commitment, but I don't believe it's much more extreme than the commitment a university graduate makes to the company that hires him.

"If I tell you I'm Korean, it's not going to make you get up and run away, is it? But, being Korean in Japan is treated as a shameful thing. I'm not ashamed. But I'm not proud either. Why should I be proud of a culture I don't know and a language I can't speak? In my heart, I feel closer to America than Korea!

"Maybe the situation is changing. But, when I was a kid in Koto-ward, I was taught to hide my Korean name and lie if anyone asked me. At every step you take in this country someone wants to know where you're from or wants to see your birth records.

"Anyway, I joined the bosozoku when I was still in junior high school. It was no big jump for me to become a yakuza. A friend of a friend had joined Ozaki-gumi. I went over to meet Ozaki-san. I liked him right away. The man was only a few years older than me, but he was much more focused on what he wanted from life. I had grown up in the Shitamachi seeing yakuza who were just low-class, bragging morons. But Ozaki-san was like James Bond compared to the gangsters I had known.

"Ozaki-san believes in all the traditional ideals. In his mind, the yakuza life doesn't mean a more limited existence, it means greater freedom and opportunity. But, with that freedom, you have a greater personal responsibility for your actions. A salaryman has his life taken care of from birth to death. He's told what to wear, whom to marry, and what brand of whiskey to drink. And, if he acts like an idiot by molesting some lady on the subway or falling asleep dead drunk on the sidewalk, he may feel embarrassed by his social blunder, but no natural shame.

"As a single kobun in the ancient yakuza system, I feel my basic role is not to embarrass my oyabun. I've got to act dignified at all times, which includes looking "cool," with great clothes and modern manners. Because I'm Korean, there's even more reason to act dignified and cool.

"In Japan, we don't have the civil rights movement you have in America. People of Korean or Chinese background pretty much never march in the street demanding rights. We're told to hide the fact that we might be different from the rest. So it's the yakuza who get the compensation for minorities. The big businesses and dirty

Fixing and Breaking

politicians are allowed to go on with their racism and their prejudices, but we make them pay us off!

"If they want the streets safe, fine. The yakuza will make sure the streets are safe, but you'd better pay us. You want a right-wing sound truck silenced so you can maintain your phony public image? Okay, we'll take care of it, but pay us. We're the ones who help make it seem that Japan is in harmony with itself. We keep the crime rate low; we make sure people don't sue companies; we keep scandals from becoming public. We're just the servants of rich people. But, if we get fucked, we turn some old secret into a new scandal. In many ways, we're the grease in the machine, but, of course, we're the monkey wrench as well. And, whenever they really want to, the big politicians can drive the machine over us!

"But, of all the screwed-up institutions in Japan, from the corrupt politics to the *zaibatsu*—business conglomerates—to the cruel education system, I think the yakuza is the most honorable . . .

"My boss says he wants to meet you in private before you show up at the office." Masa manages to scribble out, in Roman letters, a suburban train station where Ozaki would be waiting at noon on Saturday.

"Be on time." Masa smiles. "Or you can forget it. And don't stare at his wife, like you did with Aki. She's beautiful, and he's the jealous type!"

Green. Blue. Red. Yellow.

Squares of colored paper are being methodically folded on the kitchen table by the twenty-eight-year-old wife of Ozaki, the youngest underboss in the fifteen-thousand-member Sumiyoshi-kai organization. Her fingers are long and move nimbly. Behind round glasses her smooth, high-cheekboned face is radiant—far more stunning and womanly than any of Japan's chronically cute TV actresses. Midori Ozaki is of the chair-sitting, hamburger-eating generation of Japanese who tower over their elders. Actually, she's lean and very tall, taller than probably most of the men in the Sumiyoshi-kai, including her husband.

Striding between the kitchen and the living room, she steps gracefully beneath a long, turquoise Laura Ashley dress. Her two pigtailed daughters of three and four watch raptly as she carefully unfolds and then refolds the origami cranes back into existence. The paper cranes are a basic token of good luck whose creation every proper Japanese child should master before entering school.

Midori Ozaki is of the social class traditionally beyond romantic aspirations of gangsters. The prized daughter of a lawyer educated at Tokyo University (Japan's Harvard), she was raised in a big house in Tokyo's tony Setaguya-ward. She may occasionally long to return to the quiet affluence and social milieu from which she came, but it will never happen.

Her husband has the money and connections to move anywhere in Tokyo. But he's got other offspring whom he calls kobun and another family called Ozaki-gumi. Few of his brood would be comfortable visiting the more elegant neighborhoods Midori might prefer. So this modern Japanese woman—who has traveled in Europe, speaks French, and holds a season subscription to the Tokyo Symphony—must be content with a humble two-story house in what's called a suburb but looks just like anywhere else outside central Tokyo.

Not that Ozaki doesn't love his beautiful wife and adoring daughters. He has spent most of this Saturday driving them in their Volvo station wagon to a dog show in Chiba, to McDonald's for lunch, and back home for a game of Parcheesi.

Ozaki is momentarily slouched in a brown leather sofa, restlessly watching horse racing on a massive Toshiba Bazooka television. His neat, short hair is mussed from the girls riding on his back in a game of, yes, horsie. With the stiff strands of black hair cascading over his sharp nose and tanned forehead, Ozaki resembles a young Elvis.

Of course, Ozaki could pick up the phone and place a million-yen bet on the next race, but it wouldn't be right on the weekends, when he dedicates himself totally to his nuclear family. Anyway he is a devotee of hanafuda—Ozaki loves the clicking of the small plastic cards as they're shuffled and the wads of beige ten-thousand-yen bills piled in the middle of the floor, the whole scene. Ozaki basks in the muted grunts, silent gestures, all the controlled manners of a game far from, say, horsie. But I already know all about hanafuda. What I hadn't yet encountered was a yakuza who was a true family man. Ozaki's values seem out of whack with those of the average yakuza, as well as the notoriously absent mainstream salaryman father.

"A man can say he's been in love or loves a woman," Ozaki explains. "But until he's had children, no man can know the true power of love. But you've got to see your kids for that powerful love to kick in."

Just then the smaller girl leaps onto Ozaki's lap, letting her paper cranes flutter to the carpet. The gangster gathers the child in his lovin' tattooed arms, planting kisses on both of her plump cheeks and another on the back of her fuzzy neck.

"The love a parent gives his children is the most powerful human emotion." Ozaki smoothes down some loose black strands of his daughter's hair. "I don't care about money or, you know . . . Family is so powerful it scares some men into staying at work!"

"Don't you worry about spending too much time away from home?" I ask.

"Well, even at work, I have my kobun, my children, with me." Ozaki again kisses the child.

"No." I smile. "I mean away from here with your real family and real children?"

"They're both my real families," Ozaki states seriously. "Neither is superior to the other."

Money, it seems, doesn't mean much to Ozaki. He always loses when he gambles, but he thrives on the action. He'll fly to Vegas or Korea, blow fifty thousand dollars on baccarat before learning the rules—then lose another hunk after that. But even more than gambling, Ozaki loves the thrill of business:

"I am a businessman but not a salaryman," he says to me, after we move outside to a small picnic table, out of earshot of his wife. "I use the same principles, the same instincts, no matter what the project. If I need help with some specifics, I get help by contacting people with real expertise—and that person is rarely a yakuza. I've been successful in everything, from children's shoes to a bowling alley to a residential housing development. I'm pretty diversified." He laughs. "Maybe I'm a glamorous version of a chimpira who scalps tickets and does a little petty blackmail on the side! But the variety is what makes my work interesting. Hell, for a while even a Laundromat can be fascinating to me, if I'm the one who's putting the business together and pushing it into profitability.

"A lot of times the fact that I'm yakuza never enters into the equation. Sure, in operations like restaurants or pachinko, my position in Sumiyoshi-kai opens doors closed to citizens. But, you know, even if I'm making a loan, though it may be technically illegal, it's got nothing to do with yakuza. Many straight citizens make loans, but a yakuza has an advantage, like easy access to almost unlimited funds. Although any shark can go to yakuza for capital, he'll be hit with interest that can limit his profits. And if he has a problem with collection, a citizen can hire some yakuza muscle, but, again, it will cost him. But for a yakuza, collection isn't really a problem . . . "

Midori interrupts our conversation with a platter of thinly sliced tuna fanned perfectly around a light blue plate with a small dish of soy sauce in the center. It may be the most beautiful meal I have ever been served. Ozaki seems pleased with my appreciation of the food.

"Please try some of her homemade wasabi in the soy sauce," Ozaki suggests, with the first real acknowledgement of his wife. "It's hot but really quite exceptional."

I click off the tape recorder and pick up the chopsticks. The sashimi is exquisite.

"Tomorrow." Ozaki nods. "In Tokyo I can show you some things. Masa said you want to see, not talk; okay, then . . ."

I came away feeling that Ozaki was a wise man, way beyond his thirty-one years. Although Masa, his sophisticated assistant, was only four years younger than Ozaki, the stylish kobun didn't have the criminal charisma embodied by his

*boss. You just had to look at Ozaki's wife to presume there was more to this gang-
ster than big forearms. I am willing to bet the farm that in fifteen years Ozaki will
be one of Tokyo's paramount yakuza bosses.*

*Later that night Masa telephoned me with instructions to meet him the next
morning in front of the Imperial Hotel.*

The Imperial Hotel is a brownish metal box rising so high that its
shadow can stretch over the lovely gardens of Hibiya Park. Ozaki
steps out of his black Benz in front of the Chanel boutique at the
hotel's side entrance, where I happen to be locking my scooter.
Masa calls me over to the driver's side where he's standing, pulling
on a blazer. I bow to Ozaki, who nods before checking his reflec-
tion in the car's back window.

Masa chides me, saying that I cannot dress so casually (Levi's)
and expect to spend time with the boss. My heart sinks as Masa
says that now *he* will have to accompany Ozaki into the hotel. I'm
told to sit in the driver's seat of the illegally parked car and move
it only if the police come around.

Ozaki fastens the top button of his dark navy suit jacket and
tugs his well-starched sleeves so his diamond cuff links can radi-
ate. Ozaki's all-business demeanor tells me something's going
down, something that I am supposed to be witnessing. But because
of the endless glitches in precise communications and my natural
sloppiness, I'm left sitting in the car.

Later, back at the Ozaki-gumi Nishi-Azabu office (not two
minutes from my own apartment), Masa describes the scene in the
Imperial Office Annex:

A brass plaque in the reception area announced the name of
a senior Diet member, in both Japanese and Roman characters. A
handsome woman in her early forties greeted Ozaki (and Masa)
and laid out slippers. The woman led Ozaki into Mr. E's private
study while Masa waited in the outer office.

Riding out scandals (or nipping them in the bud) is a preoc-
cupation of Japan's dominant politicians. The seismic fall of Liberal Democratic Party power broker Shin Kanemaru (his name

actually means "money circle") and Prime Minister Kiichi Miyazawa had ended the LDP's thirty-four-year stranglehold on national politics—sort of.

In 1993, the first in a series of coalition governments was formed. Many former LDP regulars are wearing new party labels. Despite talk of reforms, some LDP big shots, like Mr. E, are still entrenched in the corrupt old ways and must deal with potentially embarrassing extortion in the traditional way: He called an old fixer in Sumiyoshi-kai. His call came through with only the barest of details, not even Mr. E's name was divulged until the job was accepted. The old fixer, a senior Sumiyoshi-kai member, tapped Ozaki for the job and phoned him at 6 A.M. Ozaki was told only the politician's name and the time and place of his appointment with Mr. E.

As Ozaki explained to Masa, Mr. E was sitting behind a big desk beneath a framed photograph of himself shaking hands with Ronald Reagan. Mr. E unfolded a single page of newspaper and slid it over to his young visitor. The paper, about twelve by twenty-four inches, looked more like a racing tip sheet, hardly worthy of its lofty title that meant something like the *All-Japan People's Journal*. In fact, it was printed on only one side.

Mr. E was direct, yet relaxed. This wasn't the first time some punk had tried to suck easy blackmail cash from him. Like most players in the government, Mr. E had set aside money for such delicate yet unavoidable situations. However, the headline across the *All-Japan People's Journal* was particularly disconcerting to the veteran politician. "MR. E SUPPORTS PM HOSOKAWA'S UNPATRIOTIC STANCE ON YASUKUNI SHRINE ISSUE."

The Yasukuni Shrine is a huge memorial to the Japanese soldiers who died in the Pacific War (as World War II is called). One of the many aspects of the Japanese constitution that right-wingers detest is the clause that prevents elected officials from participating in "war glorification." Thus, each year on Obon Yasomi (V-J Day), the media waits to see if the current PM will attend the Yasukuni ceremony for the war dead. LDP Dietmen, right of center by definition, usually go to Yasukuni as "private citizens," not "representatives of the state." This semantic duplicity infuriates liberals, scholars, and even many of the older generation who burn with memories of the nation's manic militarism.

Mr. E, like most of his peers, always avoided such touchy issues as the Pacific War and the Yasukuni Shrine. He told Ozaki that he had never taken a stance, "publicly or privately," on Yasukuni in his decades in office and he wasn't going to start now. What concerned Mr. E about the *All-Japan People's Journal* was that it might actually be backed by zealous ideologues who had become emboldened with the sudden decline of the LDP. Genuine ideologues might not simply take the money and disappear; they might continue hassling this distinguished member of the Diet.

Mr. E. was resigned to follow the standard routine. He would have one of his male "secretaries" transfer a suitable sum of money into the *All-Japan People's Journal*'s numbered bank account. Yet Mr. E was hoping Ozaki could somehow ensure that he would not be bothered again. Ozaki boldly instructed Mr. E not to pay anyone anything for twenty-four hours. He assured the nervous politician that another twenty-four hours wouldn't matter. The dubious old man agreed to put off his "gift." Ozaki folded the newspaper into a small rectangle, slid it into his jacket pocket, and took his leave.

Masa is interrupted during this update by a well-dressed woman who steps into the office. Masa greets her and serves her green tea. His hip young adman look and sophisticated demeanor makes him the perfect kobun to man this Ozaki-gumi outpost in one of Tokyo's poshest neighborhoods. The woman is here to interview for a job managing a lingerie shop Ozaki has come into.

Masa leads the woman into Ozaki's private office. The two men return together to the main office.

"Is there anything else, boss?" asks Masa.

Ozaki hands Masa the folded scandal sheet and tells him to bring it to a man in Shinjuku. He tells him to take me along. Masa bows out of the office and hustles out the steps to the street, where his black Vespa scooter gleams in the sunlight. I propose to follow him on my domestic-made version.

Wearing a trendy half helmet with leather flaps and antique goggles, Masa flies along curvy Gaien-Nishi Dori, past the vast Aoyama Cemetery up to Meiji Dori. I am right behind. We take this main artery past Studio Alta's big video screen and Barneys, his favorite store. Masa hangs a sharp right on a narrow side street, and we brake in front of a small stationery shop. An old lady in an apron is standing behind a glass case loading paper into a fax machine. She greets Masa, who nods before ducking through a curtain that hides a big step up leading to a living area.

An old man is slurping soba noodles while watching a samurai soap opera on a small black-and-white television about four inches from his face. Masa executes a deep formal bow, respectfully calling the man *"Sensai"* as if he were a teacher or doctor. The man doesn't acknowledge us until a commercial comes on. Masa declines the sensai's offer of tea and pickled radishes.

"All right, then, give it to me," the sensai says, sliding on a pair of thick, horn-rimmed glasses before handing me his noodle bowl, which I place in a metal sink. The sensai unfolds the broadsheet, spreading it out on the table before the television. He doesn't seem to actually read the bold, red headlines of the *All-Japan People's Journal*. Instead, his index finger traces the edges of the big characters on the left side of the page. Then he tells Masa to hand him a tattered stenographer's pad that's lying on top of a toaster oven. Slowly, the sensai turns the worn pages of names and addresses scrawled in such a shaky hand that Masa can't read a word.

On a pad of yellow Post-its, the sensai writes—more legibly now—the name of (what I assume to be) a right-wing faction, its Arakawa-ward address, and a telephone number. Masa is somewhat dubious because the sensai has written the phone number without the 3 that was affixed to all Tokyo exchanges back in 1991.

It's around noon when we arrive back at the Nishi-Azabu office. His door wide open, Ozaki is speaking on the phone with a boxing promoter. The promoter has called about an upcoming card at the Korakuen Hall, a small, sweaty venue attached to the modern Tokyo Dome. He wants Ozaki to buy an ad in the pro-gram. Ozaki grunts affirmatively to the promoter as he examines the address Masa has brought him.

With the sensai's information, Ozaki has all he needs to act. He orders Masa to get the car; we—all three of us—are going for a ride. I sit with Ozaki in the backseat while Masa pilots the Benz through the slow midday traffic and up on to an elevated highway where the pace is even slower. But it's not all that bad. The air conditioning is pumping while the radio entertains the hell out of the gangsters. It's an advice show where women call in to discuss personal problems. In a country where half of all marriages are arranged, there are plenty of unhappy housebound women for whom simply listening to these call-in shows is therapy—or as close as they'll ever come. Though the laughter is contagious, I find the crackling radio dialogue difficult to follow. I need Masa's rough translation to truly appreciate the woes of the young wife whose salaryman husband had come home drunk the night before and quickly fell asleep. Undressing the unconscious body, the wife was shocked to discover the husband wearing a pair of women's red panties instead of the nice white briefs she had laid out the morning before. What to do?, the young wife pleads. The stern female host instructs the wife to ignore this sole incident as likely the result of a "gag" between office colleagues. If this should ever happen again with similarly provocatively designed panties, the host muses, perhaps the wife might reassess her own choice of underwear. Your husband may be telling you to be more sexy for him. Yes, yes, the wife cries, I understand.

"I only wish I could get more salarymen to wear women's underwear." Ozaki laughs, thinking of his new lingerie concern.

The sky seems huge out here in eastern Tokyo, the so-called Low City. Most of the streets have no proper names, so it is a fine place to get lost, though I've tried to learn the area well. Out in these flatlands beyond the sleek sumo stadium and the monolithic new Edo Museum, every other building looks to be some kind of tool and die or machine shop—ready to churn out automobile ashtrays or dashboards or whatever the powers at the top of corporate food chain request.

On a hot and deserted street the Ozaki-gumi Benz is the only thing moving. Masa brakes at a cinder-block wall. We all get out of the car and, in single file, cross the scorched earth. No one speaks as Ozaki slides open a rusty steel gate in front of a wide one-story building. Its large, overlapping front doors give it the look of a small airplane hangar. A mechanical rattle and hum seeps through the walls, which appear to be made from the same corrugated metal as the roof. Inside is a grim sweatshop going full bore.

Four or five Middle Eastern men with scraggly beards and haggard eyes sit on stacks of what resemble thick comic books. Every few seconds another book rumbles down a track of steel rollers. One of the men gathers up the books and places them with their spines aligned and the titles pointed in the same direction. Some of the dark men tie up the books with rough twine while a fourth sets bound stacks on a wooden pallet in the corner.

There are short women in aprons and caps buzzing around other clacking machines that look to my eyes like printing presses, though I can't be sure. Although the Middle Eastern men are smoking and talking, the Asian ladies work silently. Though at first the whole lot stared at us, they quickly resumed their work. We wait.

"What the hell is going on!" a deep aggressive Japanese voice booms from behind the machinery. Finally a moonfaced man appears in a golf shirt, red slacks, white socks, and sandals. "Oh, hello, sir!" The overseer now smiles at Ozaki and drops his cigarette to the ground. "Can I help you?"

"Hello," says Ozaki, turning his business card so it faces the overseer. "This is who I am." Though Ozaki has a dozen different business cards connected to his various projects, the engraved card he has handed this man represents Ozaki's true essence. The top left corner displays the character for *sumi* surrounded by stylized sun rays. This is the well-known logo of the Sumiyoshi-kai organization. Ozaki's name is written in large, ostentatious characters beside his title: "PRESIDENT OF OZAKI-GUMI OF THE SUMIYOSHI ASSOCIATION."

The overseer nervously sucks air before looking up from the card. He bows and hands the card back to the young yakuza boss who slides it back into his wallet. This simple gesture of returning the card to Ozaki proves the overseer is some kind of insider. Only people who are in the rackets know that you don't keep incriminating business cards, and you insult a man by making him ask for it back.

"Is there somewhere we can talk?" Ozaki asks the man, before signaling to Masa to stay.

The man leads Ozaki across the greasy floor into a back office. Those silent ladies are the first to sense something's up. They stop working as the office door bangs shut. The men don't stop until the first horrific crash from within the office. As the rollers of the machines keep churning, all eyes are on the opaque frosted glass walls of the back room as though there's something to see. I'm sure I can hear voices yelling, but I can't tell what they're saying. Another bone-chilling cacophony of smashing metal is followed by a long silence.

Coolly oblivious, Masa is engrossed in one of the comic books. He doesn't stop reading until Ozaki, who has emerged unruffled from the office, snatches it from Masa's hands and places it on a pile. I follow the two back into the sunlight where the quiet feels sanctifying after the noise of that hellhole.

"The guy had no idea what the fuck I was doing there." Ozaki laughs in a coffee shop after the incident. "He balled himself in a corner under a water cooler." It wasn't until after Ozaki had wrecked the office that he asked the moonfaced man if he indeed was the publisher of the *All-Japan People's Journal*.

"I was relieved when he answered he was the one behind that scandal sheet. I wasn't so sure when we went in there," Ozaki admits. "But after my 'inspection' of his office, he had to tell the truth. A man in that mental state is incapable of lying. I learned that technique from the Japanese police."

When I arrive, Masa is alone manning the Ozaki-gumi Nishi-Azabu office. Ozaki himself is at a boxing gym observing the workout of a feature fighter on the upcoming card (to which I have been invited). A call comes in from an Ozaki-gumi brother in their Shibuya office. Masa interjects "hai!" five or six times as he scribbles a note. It records some bare facts: About an hour before, there had been an automobile accident in front of the Motorola Building on Meiji Dori (about five minutes from the office). A cab had run over the foot and ankle of a thirty-three-year-old woman who had been crossing the street with her small daughter. Rather than call their insurance company, the taxi company's manager contacted the office manager of Ozaki-gumi's Shibuya headquarters.

According to the National Police Agency, the yakuza intervene in over twenty thousand civil disputes each year. Japanese courts are notoriously slow and indifferent to the complaints of individuals. Essentially, the yakuza have taken on the role of lawyers-cum-negotiators.

It's a bit presumptuous for Masa to take on this problem by himself, but Ozaki isn't answering his beeper. Masa decides he's going to fake his way through. The first order of business is to get to the hospital and calm the victim. Sporting a classic seersucker suit, with his long hair conservatively plastered against his head, Masa enters the modern hospital lobby carrying an ornately packaged, hydroponically spawned muskmelon; its vivid green coloring and spherical perfection can be savored through the box's cellophane window. He's also grasping a bouquet of mixed flowers. Since the hospital is in Hiro-o, right around the corner from my own apartment, I don't feel so strange tagging behind Masa.

When Masa walks into the six-bed room, Mrs. T has already been in the hospital for over three hours. She has yet to hear from her salaryman husband, who received the news of her accident a half hour ago. Mrs. T is in the middle bed in a row of three on the shady side of the room. Her left leg is elevated beneath a blanket. Despite the recent trauma, Mrs. T looks fine and greets us with a smile. Actually, her pronounced aguiline nose, almond eyes, and straight teeth give Mrs. T an aristocratic beauty. I will try not to stare.

"Hello." Masa bows. "How are you feeling?"

Mrs. T, without knowing who exactly Masa and I are, nonetheless chirps that she's feeling well. Masa responds with the flowers and a compliment that seems half flirtatious. He places the gleaming muskmelon box on the table beside her bed. A color TV blares from the corner of the room with a samurai-era soap opera. I let my eyes wander to the screen as Masa moves closer to the woman.

"This is not a bad room." Masa looks around. "In most nice hospitals you've got to know someone to get such a nice room . . . "

"Yes," says Mrs. T, glancing in the cellophane window not two feet from her head. "The room is quite good, but the sunlight doesn't reach this side, though the ladies on the other side do get nice sun."

"Ah, yes." Masa reaches inside his jacket and produces a business card identifying himself as a "mediator." He places the card on the blanket in front of her. She picks it up and reads it.

"You have a very nice name," she says wistfully.

For the next five minutes, Masa's silly small talk makes Mrs. T nod and giggle. Several times during the conversation, Masa absent-mindedly pats the muskmelon on the table. After giving Mrs. T the name of a discount Rolex dealer in Aoyama, Masa produces an envelope containing a waiver releasing the taxi company from further responsibility beyond the flowers.

As Mrs. T takes the document and reads the fine print, Masa quietly pats the top of the muskmelon box. The TV samurai are still flashing their swords and performing multiple mid-air somersaults. Mrs. T reaches for her purse and pulls out her *hanko*, a small stamp that serves as an official signature. Masa helps Mrs. T sit up and smooths the form out on top of the muskmelon box. After she marks it, Masa slides the paper off the box, and returns it to his pocket. He looks at his watch and says that if Mr. T has any questions concerning the settlement, he should feel free to call.

Masa smiles and bows. He taps his finger on the big fruit and smiles broadly. "Please." He sighs. "It would be *so* gracious of you to accept this muskmelon on behalf of the taxi company and, of course, from me." Masa bows again.

Mrs. T's hands draw the $200 muskmelon atop her stomach, admiring its perfection behind the cellophane.

"Thank you." She almost blushes.

"It's nothing at all." Masa shrugs and nods to the older woman in the next bed who has been eyeing Masa, me, and the melon. On the way out, Masa asks the floor nurse to move Mrs. T's bed to the sunny side of the room. An hour later, the floor nurse receives a thank-you card with two ten-thousand-yen bills.

At night the line of hipsters outside of Gold is so long that it winds up a side street. Masa walks along the queue looking for a familiar face or a nice pair of unfamiliar legs. I doubt any of the girls returning Masa's glances would imagine that his black Yohji Yamamoto suit covers full-body tattoos. Does the doorman (who didn't check the guest list before waving us through) know Masa wasn't a record or advertising exec? I'd love to know, but instead I follow at Masa's heels, keeping my eyes straight ahead. I don't want to see anyone I might know in this gaijin-friendly nightclub.

Walking about six feet in front of me, as usual, Masa is comfortable with this "I" formation, which old-time Japanese husbands used to maintain out walking with their wives. Though I've grown to appreciate the superior drape and cut of Masa's well-made suits, watching the man's backside hasn't been very conducive to talking. I haven't complained, though I want more of our stilted conversation—I still want to know him better.

"Remember the lady in the hospital?" asks Masa while waiting to buy smokes.

"Of course." All of seven hours have passed.

"Was I cool?"

"Oh yeah." I laugh. "The way you fondled that melon. You were cool."

"You're laughing, but I was shitting in my pants!" Masa is serious. "I had no right to be there. It was a cowboy thing to do. It was like walking a tightrope—one slip and I'd be dead. I'm still shaking!"

This is the guy who casually read a comic book as his boss smashed some guy to pieces. Yet the bit with the melon freaks him out? I'm stunned.

Fixing and Breaking

"Listen, sensai," Masa explains. "Let's say that lady didn't like me or thought I was a hustler or thought I was threatening her. Say she called an administrator on me. He calls the cops, then what? Forcing a woman to sign a legal document right after a car accident! That's the kind of problem that snowballs and can kill you!"

"But you were cool," I remind him.

"You know what it was like?" Masa muses. "Imagine if you had to pick up a particular girl from a club and sleep with her that night or it's four years in prison! That's it!"

I suggest we catch the elevator to the dance floor where rejection is its own worst downside.

Before Masa actually enters the waiting elevator, he stops to let me catch up. Already inside are five tall Anglo-Saxon women, each of whom is smiling, including the one bending way over to push the HOLD button. If they're smiling, they must be right off the boat or high. The business of Caucasian modeling hit the skids way before the general recession. Many of the agencies that specialized in gaijin models have folded, while most have dispensed with the comfortable minivans they used to shuttle models from audition to audition. Nowadays these young women, primarily of suburban American stock, are negotiating Tokyo by rail and foot.

"C'mon, you guys!" insists one of the beauties, who are all similarly blond and pleasant. "Are you guys coming or what?"

There is a moment of silence as Masa places his hand on my chest, as if to stop me from entering what has to be the most enticing group ever to populate an elevator, which they are holding for Masa and me. Yet I can see it's true; Masa doesn't want us to take this particular trip. I can't believe it! I have to consider the possibility that Masa's just another Japanese guy who gets shaky in the presence of a gaijin woman, all right, *five* gaijin women, all gorgeous, granted. But this is Tokyo, his home court! If a handsome and tough Japanese man like Masa wimps out, I fear for Japan. We walk up the stairs to the VIP lounge, where the sweeping view of the packed dance floor both impresses and depresses Masa. It's difficult for Masa to accept that this unbelievable moneymaker is owned and run by straight businessmen.

A waitress brings over a couple of drinks, which Masa pays for with a prepaid debit card. A tall African-American floor manager enters the lounge. Then, in perfect and thoroughly masculine Japanese, he announces that a man's black leather wallet has been found beside the third-floor elevator stop. He adds that fifty thousand yen has been found in the wallet and the owner can pick it up at the bar. I'm taken aback by the nonreaction of the Japanese around us. None of the men bother checking their pockets, nor does anyone seem impressed by the well-spoken foreigner— except me.

I know there are still places in Japan where an American in the streets will be accosted and forced to sign autographs and pose for pictures. But in the cities, gaijin envy is over. Gone are the old days when Japan was a nation characterized as forever trying to catch up with American ways, selling out their culture to be like us (with many women purportedly undergoing "eye lifts" to look like white Americans). Urban Japanese have turned the tables.

Two young men approach Masa's table and bow. Masa nods and points to the empty seats. I can't imagine how these two got inside the club with their tacky threads. One of the guys is wearing a long-sleeved black silk shirt, black pants, and white shoes. The other, a stocky kid with a crew cut and tinted glasses, wears a short-sleeved shirt with leopard spots. A neutral observer would never have fingered Masa as the only real gangster among the four of us.

Masa introduces me simply as his friend. But these unfashionable guys, who may have just driven in from the countryside, are tense. Is it that they didn't expect me, or is it just being in the presence of a young yakuza like Masa, sitting there impressively in his twenty-five-hundred-dollar suit? Adding to the confusion of the moment, four fluted glasses of champagne are delivered to our small table. The waiter says they are a token from the man sitting with the blond-haired lady. Masa squints towards the twosome, who are partially blocked by another couple. But Masa recognizes the crooked nose of a well-known Inagawa-kai underboss. For Masa, the nose goes way back to his juvenile-detention days. Masa smiles, stands up, and straightens his tie before taking me over to the nose's table.

"Thank you." Masa bows to the nose and his blond escort, who mouths "hello" to me.

"You look busy," says the nose, with a nod towards our table. "You know it's almost eleven o'clock, I hope you're not doing business at this hour!" If he only knew how long this day has been!

"With the bad economy, there's not so much time for pure leisure." Masa smiles and nods shyly to the gaijin in her well-shaped sequined dress. It seems that the girl is a Brazilian who sings at a country and western club in Shimbashi. However, the club is about to close down, and the nose wants to know if Masa can think of a hostess bar where the young woman might find work.

"Maybe a nice place in Akasaka or Roppongi?" he asks Masa. "Do you know any clubs that hire gaijin?"

Masa sighs, then asks me if I can suggest names of any Roppongi clubs that may be hiring. I tell her of three off the top of my head, then I write them down.

"Thank you." The Brazilian smiles as she folds the slip of paper. The nose thanks me in English before handing Masa his meshii.

When we return, the two guys have finished their champagne, and a dirty envelope is lying there beside Masa's glass. Masa cringes at the amateurism of these boys. With a smooth, easy motion, Masa slides the money-filled envelope off the table and into his pants pocket. Then, from his jacket pocket, he produces a brown envelope containing two counterfeit Visa credit cards.

"I wouldn't use them for more than a week," Masa advises, as he slides the cards across the table. Running phony credit cards is fast becoming a dead scam. Almost every shop is double-checking the validity of any card. This might be standard practice in the West, but it is a new trend here that threatens to finish off credit card hustlers. The scams are already dead as far as Masa is concerned, but he is willing to unload a friend's stock of bogus plastic to those who don't know better.

On our way out of the club, Masa gives his debit card to an incoming girl in white pumps. She bows gratefully and gushes in honorific language. Masa just grins and steps outside. We walk across a parking lot to where a tattered red paper lantern glows above a sidewalk ramen stall. The proprietor greets Masa and me with a smile and places some chopsticks on the wooden ledge. With a skill honed by a lifetime of noodle preparation, he puts on a click-clacking performance with his ancient ladles and strainers.

"Here you are, sir," the proprietor sings out, as he places two steaming bowls of ramen in front of us. The rumble of a portable generator is masked by the music from a radio tied to a bamboo support beam. The soft vibrato of a female enka singer begins a Japanese torch song the ramen man can't help singing along with:

> I have so many memories in these tears,
> I have many wounds in my heart as well,
> Drinking alone, pouring my own,
> Listening to enka, getting sentimental with my sake. . . .

Days later, Masa calls me up. He says something big has happened. A boyhood friend of Ozaki's is in the middle of a war outside Osaka. The friend is the boss of his own independent gang and has asked Ozaki for reinforcements. At that moment, around 9 P.M. on a Tuesday in September, the entire Ozaki-gumi rank and file are in a lot behind their Shibuya office preparing to drive down to Osaka.

"We may be down there for weeks," Masa says, knowing I am leaving Tokyo in a few days. "So come over and say good-bye. I know the boss would like to see you."

I find an Ozaki-gumi kobun standing guard at the entrance to the parking lot. He is dressed in pristine gray coveralls with elaborate embroidery over the breast pocket spelling *Ozaki-gumi*. The outfit, which includes black boots, gives him a severe paramilitary look. About two dozen Ozaki-gumi kobun dressed in similar outfits are scurrying among four Mercedes-Benzes. Each of the cars has its trunk open, exposing caches of military hardware that must have "fallen off the truck" at some base. Rather than a "small turf war," this yakuza gang look like a SWAT team preparing for a coup.

"You're back?" Ozaki laughs. Dressed in a sport jacket, Ozaki looks a lot less harried than his kobun. "Maybe when you come back you can meet some of my yakuza brothers down in Shikoku. They're very traditional, you'd like them."

I thank him for everything.

"Well, good-bye." Ozaki extends a hand before heading inside.

Masa walks onto the sidewalk beside me. Behind him three kobun look to be trying on bulletproof vests.

"Will you return to Tokyo?" asks Masa.

"Maybe," I say.

"You're going to miss yakuza no michi." Masa laughs, mocking the outdated phrase I am fond of using. "Even the boss said you should become a kobun, you act just like them, standing around staring and making plans in your head about how much money you're going to make off us!"

Masa's backhanded compliment comes back to mind a few days later when I'm back in Shibuya in a dusty vacant lot. Fulfilling my promise to Takayama, I'm covering the "big" demonstration protesting the anti-gang laws. I am indeed again standing around staring at a motley assembly of protest groups running the gamut from AIDS victims to left-wing revolutionaries to radical housewives. Finally, I spot them, maybe sixty or seventy gangsters in their garish, floral-print shirts, shaking their fists and carrying signs reading, "DON'T OUTLAW PATRIOTISM!" One of the kobun recognizes me, flashes a toothless grin, and waves me into the march. I just wave back and ease myself back into the shopping masses, back into the mainstream where, after all, I belong.

ACKNOWLEDGMENTS

Nothing would have been possible without the talent, skill, and commitment of Yoshiko Tanaka, whose grace under fire was an inspiration.

I am indebted to my comrade Karl Taro Greenfeld, from whom I've learned the importance of tenacity in reporting and generosity in friendship.

To the men of the shadows in Tokyo and Kyoto: I again want to thank you for your time and patience. I owe a lot to my Tokyo friends who gave me crucial insights and assistance: especially, M. Toyama and Rie Sekiguchi (who taught me *gaman*, among other Japanese words).

I'll always remember my meetings with the journalist R. Sumiya and the lawyer M. Endo: two unconventional Japanese professionals who see the big picture yet maintain their senses of humor. To the yakuza-turned-poet Goro Fujita and yakuza-turned-painter Shu Yamamoto, thank you for your efforts on my behalf.

Thanks to the Tokyo Foreign Press Center employees who did a wonderful job in digging up the official statistics and numbers I've used throughout the book. Also, thanks to the library staffers at the *Daily Yomiuri* and the *Daily Mainichi* for their help in providing photocopies of hundreds of old crime reports.

211

ACKNOWLEDGEMENTS

At Atlantic Monthly Press, thank you to Morgan Entrekin for taking interest and Colin Dickerman for giving direction. I'm particularly grateful for the constructive criticism and patient support of editor John Newton.

Thanks to Matt Bialer, my agent, for his expertise and encouragement.

Also, I must note that my mother, Justine Seymour, helped organize my original manuscript, while my father, Edward Seymour, edited every ensuing draft.

My love of Tokyo was kindled by the works of Edward Seidensticker, and my passion for the yakuza can be traced to David E. Kaplan and Alec Dubro's *Yakuza*, a definitive work on the subject.